CATALOGUE OF EDUCATION

SARAH ETHRIDGE HUNT is an elementary school
teacher in Harrison County, Mississippi, Co-director of Camp Happy Oak at Long Beach, Mississippi, and Dean of the Children's International
Summer Village at Long Beach. She received her
master's degree from Louisiana State University,
following which she taught for fifteen years in
the department of Health, Physical Education,
and Recreation at Delta State College.

GAMES AND SPORTS
THE WORLD
AROUND

SARAH ETHRIDGE HUNT

CO-DIRECTOR, CAMP HAPPY OAK
LONG BEACH, MISSISSIPPI

Illustrated by Max Heldman

THIRD EDITION

THE RONALD PRESS COMPANY · NEW YORK

To
MEG, LAUREN, SUSAN,
ROBERT, and STEVE

Preface

This book provides teachers and recreation leaders with a comprehensive source of play activities drawn from all parts of the world. It presents play, games, and sports as pleasurable media for developing an understanding of human relationships.

Games and Sports the World Around, Third Edition, prefaces each activity with headings showing age level, number of players, playing area, necessary supplies, type, and intellectual appeal. Similarities and differences in games around the world are indicated throughout, with emphasis on the significance of folklore in the play patterns of mankind.

The material included here is offered in the hope that it will aid counselors, teachers, and parents in utilizing the atmosphere created in play to promote desirable behavior and the development of physical fitness, emotional stability, and intellectual growth in children and young people.

SARAH ETHRIDGE HUNT

Long Beach, Mississippi
April, 1964

Acknowledgments

The author is indebted to many persons and organizations for the time, information, and encouragement they have given toward making this book possible. Special thanks are given to Ernest Ogden Hunt for continual patience and understanding throughout the undertaking. Grateful appreciation is due Miss Ethel Cain for her contribution to the two previous editions of this book.

For personal conference and critical reading of the manuscript sincere thanks are given to Miss Nettie Rose, English Instructor, retired, Pass Christian, Mississippi, and to Chaplain Alvie McKnight, United States Army, retired, Long Beach, Mississippi.

For contributions of games from remote sources the author would like to express deep appreciation to these persons for games from: AFRICA. *Nigeria*, J. O. Oshin, Teacher, Baptist Boys High School; *Northern Rhodesia*, Mrs. C. T. Suckling, Secretary, The Rhodes-Livingstone Museum; *Southern Rhodesia*, Mr. and Mrs. Robert E. Beaty, Southern Baptist Missionaries; *Tanganyika*, Sister Mary Serra, Maryknoll Marian College; Thomas F. Gibbons, M. M., Maryknoll Mission.

ASIA. *Gaza*, Mrs. James M. Young, Southern Baptist Hospital; *Korea*, Mrs. Guy Henderson, Southern Baptist Missionary; *Malaya*, Dr. and Mrs. Carl Frederick Yarnell, Jr., President and Professor, Southern Baptist Theological Seminary; *Thailand*, Mr. and Mrs. J. Ralph Marshall, Jr., Southern Baptist Missionaries.

AUSTRALIA. *Western Australia*, Dr. Catherine H. Berndt, University of Western Australia; *Canberra*, S. S. Brown, News and Information Bureau; Edna Mason for her delightful portrayal of Australia and New Zealand in her books, *The First Book of Australia* and *The First Book of New Zealand;* F. D. McCarthy, Australian Museum, Sydney.

EUROPE. *France*, Mrs. Margaret Sturtevant, Pineville, Mississippi; *Portugal*, Mrs. Grayson C. Tennison, Southern Baptist Missionary; *Spain*, Mrs. Roy B. Wyatt, Southern Baptist Missionary; *Switzerland*, Dr. Vella Jane Burch, Librarian, Baptist Theological Seminary.

LATIN AMERICA. *Brazil*, Reverend Parke Renshaw, Escola De Portuguese E. Orientacal; *Colombia*, Libia Halguin and Samuel

Palacios, Cordell Hull Foundation Exchange Teachers; *Mexico,* Father Robert E. Lee, Maryknoll Mission, Yucatan.

Special indebtedness is felt to: The American Philosophical Society for permission to quote descriptions of string games and to copy designs from the original publication in the Society's *Proceedings* (D. S. Davidson, "Aboriginal Australian String Figures," Vol. 84, 1941), pp. 763–901; and Miss Maria F. Person, Carnegie Library, Gulfport, Mississippi, for assistance in securing valuable source materials.

Appreciation and thanks are due the United Nations Committee for UNICEF for permission to use information from the *Hi Neighbor Books,* No. 1, 2, and 3.

To Doris Twitchell Allen, Ph.D., Founder of Children's International Summer Villages, and Professor of Psychology, University of Cincinnati, Cincinnati, Ohio deep appreciation and love is felt by the author for encouragement in the worth of the idea that play and games are invaluable in promoting world empathy among children and youth.

The author wishes to express special thanks to Ted Morton III for assistance in planning the format of the book; to Max Heldman for his delightful illustrations; and to Nancy Dickson Crowell for her untiring effort in typing the manuscript.

Contents

GAMES AND SPORTS
THE WORLD AROUND

1

Play, Games, Sports: Gateways to Global Understanding

PLAY

Play is an age-old and universal activity of man. In its most unadorned form it is essentially the same today as it was in early civilizations. It is both a biological and a cultural phenomenon. Play is freedom. It is a stepping out of reality into a realm that has its own direction and meaning. Play is limited. It begins; it ends. It may be repeated as a pattern. It may be transmitted to other persons who repeat the pattern, whereupon play becomes tradition.

Play grows out of customs, beliefs, and man's urge for activity. It provides man with a medium of expression and communication. As man communicates with others through play, he experiences a feeling of being "apart together" with them. It is this feeling that transports the players into a realm of their own making—a realm that becomes a creative, real, and living experience.

GAMES

Games are crystallized forms of play patterns. Games are ways of behaving in play that tend to conform to patterns that are generally experienced and shared by several individuals. A game pattern is emphasized by the elements of organization that bring about a definite and often repeated climax. In a game the individual does not lose his identity, for the game itself is a situation in which the elements of success and failure are so equally balanced that only

3

the player by his own efforts, practice, and application of self can swing the balance so that he succeeds.

Folk games are today's play heritage of the past. Some changes in form, name, and the materials of folk or traditional games have evolved through the centuries. Nevertheless, an analysis of world-wide game patterns reveals *a thread of consistent similarity in play and games the world around.*

The differences in folk games are the result of differences in climate, social behavior, and even religious beliefs. These same differences are the basic causes of the differences in man's behavior in all other phases of life.

Folk games are a mosaic of man's play behavior. They tell the story that all peoples are a part of Everyman, all children are a part of Everychild, even in play. The games are real and alive. They are a kind of here-to-stay thing. They have a contribution to make to the play life of children and youth today.

GATEWAYS TO GLOBAL UNDERSTANDING AND FRIENDSHIPS

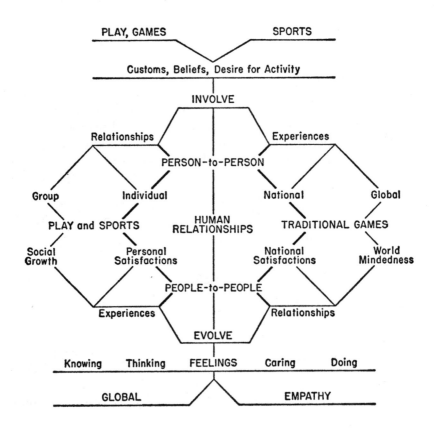

Should the players seek the origins of their patterns of play, they would find many of them buried in antiquity. On the other hand there are numerous play patterns that can be traced to their beginnings. Origins of games are important in this collection for two reasons. First, they show the deep roots of play in man's history. Second, they reflect the closeness of play, folkways, and games to fact and legend in all lands and among all peoples.

SPORTS

In reality sports or athletic games involve and demand more specialized skills of the players than do other games, contests, and relays. Sports may consume the efforts of an individual; an individual and an opponent; an individual and a partner versus two other players; or an individual as a member of a team that involves from four to twelve or more players versus another such team. Sports are more seasonal than games, climate being a determining factor of the activity and its demands of the players.

Man's sports heritage, like the beginnings of games, has deep roots in the past. Though the pattern and organization of a sport may have evolved into almost unrecognizable forms (in relationship to origins), the skills of accuracy, speed, strength, agility, and individual strategy still prevail in sports today.

Specific skills may be more closely related to one sport than to another. However, as an individual aspires to excel in any particular sport or to be a member of a specific team, he must realize that muscular coordination and emotional stability are his prerequisites and parallels for enjoyment and mastery. In light of this it is the responsibility of persons who lead and direct boys, girls, and youth in sports activities to develop progressively the skills in keeping with the individual's physical and emotional growth.

CONTRIBUTIONS OF PLAY, GAMES, AND SPORTS

Individuals *live* in a game situation. They experience living not only as individuals, but also as members of a group or team, in most instances. The processes of living within a game situation, as in most life processes, involve adjusting to other individuals and to groups. They *involve human relationships*. It is through these relationships that there is opportunity for (a) the growth and development of the individual personality, and (b) the development of harmony between the individual and a group—the individual and society.

DEVELOPMENT OF THE INDIVIDUAL PERSONALITY

Before an individual can fully or even partially sense the pulse beat of all mankind and finally feel that he is part of the whole stream of human life, he must be in harmony with himself; that is, he must be conditioned to live with himself, to be less dependent upon other resources, to make his own work or play with less supervision and regimentation.

Desirable adjustment and growth processes must be orderly, pleasurable, and progressive. In this way there is opportunity for fusion of knowledge, energy, experience, attitude, and habits. In this way the individual has opportunity to develop his own potentials and to contribute to the effectiveness of the group.

An individual's desirable adjustment to life's situations may be proportionate, directly or indirectly, to his early experiences in play, games, and sports. These activities offer opportunity for pleasurable and challenging experiences in person-to-person and people-to-people relationships. They demand that the individual make choices. Richness in life comes from varied experiences that lead to wise choices.

As an individual participates in play, games, and sports, he and his associates are "apart together" in the new relationship. This relationship may be said to be "never exactly the same"; hence it is always interesting and challenging—never dull or boresome; otherwise, play, games, and sports would soon become extinct and boys, girls, youth, men, and women would seek entirely new substitutes for play activities. (Some escape-from-reality procedures used by many persons today may be labeled as attempts to find such substitutes.)

HARMONY OF THE INDIVIDUAL AND THE GROUP— THE INDIVIDUAL AND SOCIETY

The individual's horizon must be broader than his immediate associates and his local community. It must extend to the realm of society. In its all-inclusive sense the word "society" means mankind as a whole. The individual can think of himself as an individual only against a social background. The only personality with which the home, the school, the church, and other institutions can deal is a personality with social potentialities. Therefore, the learning processes cannot escape dealing with society. *A process of learning that ignores social meanings, causes, and effects must fail, for these are the dynamics of a fruitful life.*

It is generally conceded that unless a child gradually grows and develops a social consciousness and a recognition of society from early childhood to adulthood, there is little hope for achievement of a social consciousness during later life. The reasons for excessive maladjustments in individuals and the discord between the individuals and society today are (a) inadequate training in social relationships and (b) ineffective development of social responsibility. The recognition of these facts points the way of all educational procedures in fulfilling their obligations to individuals and to society. As the individual develops the ability to adjust to varied situations and begins to show evidences of purposely directing his behavior toward ideals for the good of the group and eventually for the whole of society, he is becoming a valuable member of society and thus may be led to make his contribution to mankind.

WORLD-MINDEDNESS AND GLOBAL UNDERSTANDING

The intensity with which the peoples of the world are studying each other; the conditions of change within many societies; the relationships of these societies to the entire world; and the proximity of all nations to each other are potent factors in global awareness today. Fortunately, the technique of promoting a world-conscious individual does not depend upon overcoming some strange feature of nature. It does depend upon the process of presenting to each individual facts in regard to the traits, needs, and interests of himself and of other peoples.

Promotion of world-mindedness and global empathy does not imply impractical idealism nor does it mean docile submission. It does not suggest indifference to the interests of one's own country, nor does it mean approval of undesirable acts of nationals and their governments. World-mindedness and global empathy do mean knowing enough about peoples to know why they act as they do. They do mean accepting the peoples of other lands as flesh-and-blood individuals who have the same urgent wants as all other individuals throughout the world. These wants are freedom, security, food, shelter, worship, knowledge, dignity, and *love*. The want most lacking in fulfillment among all peoples is love—this is the want that, when fulfilled only in part, helps to sustain individuals and societies, although the fulfillment of the other wants may be tragically incomplete.

The most desirable pattern for a world order is one that evolves from mutual trust, interest, and understanding through development of cultural relationships of all peoples the world over. Desirable world citizens and leaders must have a man-to-man, people-to-people, nation-to-nation relationship that aims to help all peoples gain for themselves the best that human society can offer. This is a long-range viewpoint that must start where man is today in human relationships and develop step by step toward the ultimate goal. Communications between local, national, and international groups should be such that empathy, and not envy and hatred, prevails; that appreciation, and not apathy or prejudice, results.

TOMORROW'S SECURITY

It is encouraging that many world leaders and many of their followers realize the relative closeness of all human beings on the earth. It is reassuring that both leaders and followers recognize the fact that man's great task everywhere is to adjust to other human beings. *The frontier of human relationships at home and afar parallels that of science and technology in importance for the survival of mankind, with total maturity as the ultimate goal.*

There are many groups of people working today toward the achievement of global friendliness among children and youth. Some of these groups are the Girl and Boy Scouts with their national and international programs; the student-exchange programs of schools, colleges, and universities; the study and missionary programs of churches throughout the world; the Children's International Summer Villages; the International Junior Red Cross, and many agencies of the government.

It is urgent that the free world train its citizens in world-mindedness and global leadership. Training for world-citizenship must include the fact that Communism is not the only adversary of freedom. Another force is that of unfulfilled wants of the peoples in the world. Some of the leaders and many individuals of this third world are looking in both directions. Their acceptance of either freedom or Communism is being determined partially by the effectiveness of the fulfillment of their wants—either by the free peoples or by the Communists. It is being determined partially by the ruthlessness of Communism. Free peoples must not only extend help to the helpless but also provide effective guidance to those peoples in such a way that they may be led to help themselves.

GATEWAYS TO UNDERSTANDING AND FRIENDSHIPS

Play, games, and sports provide a person-to-person, people-to-people relationship among the players. They connect the players with the peoples from whence the activities have come. The activities provide pleasurable and quick gateways for developing and expanding attitudes and understandings.

Once the gateways are opened, a new, rich, and rewarding status of human relationships may be experienced. Learning situations must promote global awareness and not tend to focus largely on western culture as they have done in the past. Children and youth must be led to seek solutions to barriers of suspicion and mistrust that divide peoples. They must be led by adults who are concerned with circumstances that will bring a relaxation of world tensions.

Traditional games and sports reveal the culture and traits of a people. The color and quality of folklore is portrayed in play patterns just as beliefs of deep religious and social significance are portrayed through form and ceremony. Racial inheritance of energy and physical skill is expressed in the activities of the play of a nation.

The universal interest of children in play and games helps to open gateways for knowledge and understanding of other peoples. The study of English folk games brings to light the appreciation that the English have for tradition, even in play patterns. Contrary to this, there is reflected in the German games the adherence to austerity in play for promotion of physical strength. The study of Greek civilization discloses the love of the Greeks for activity—the reality of which may be made more real by the children having their own Olympic Games, in moderation. The realization that string play, a completely quiet though clever activity, is common to all civilizations—including the North American Indian, the Australian Aborigines, the early peoples of the Far East, and the colonists of early North and South America—reveals that all peoples have maintained pastime activities of relaxation and recreation.

Folk games in their many forms are concerned with human relationships. It is difficult to understand a people unless something is known about their folklore in dramatic, dance, play, and sports activities. The search for information about ideas, purposes, origins, and procedures of folk games sends roots of empathy deep into the history and philosophy of many peoples. A new light is shed on the ancient civilization of Persia (now Iran) when we learn that there was a law by which all children were to be taught three things: telling the truth, horsemanship, and shooting with the bow.

The value of folk games and play activities as tools for developing appreciation and understanding of other peoples depends upon the relationship that the activities bear to the total experiences of the participants. *Simply teaching folk games and sports to a group of boys and girls affords few possibilities of developing appreciation of life in other countries and empathy for people in other lands.*

Folk games may serve in two ways as channels for the promotion of appreciation and understanding of other peoples. One is in situations where they fill a felt need in interest centered about life in other lands. For example the teaching of "Last Couple Out" from the United States, "Gorelki" from Russia, "Two Friends" from Ghana, and "Widower's Game" from Sweden helps to show the similarities of play patterns from varied lands. The other is in situations where folk games may themselves serve as an empathic force. That is to say, when the experiences of the players are centered around incidents, characters, and customs brought to light through reading, study, and discussion, the participants will begin to live the play patterns of a people. The factual conditions under which certain folk games developed may lead to interest in the history, literature, and social customs of a country. For example, the game "Charlie Over the Water" is said to have been created in Scotland during the exile of Charles II. Thus we see that folk plays and games may function either as a part of a whole unit or as an implementing force for further study and investigation of other peoples.

Folk games and sports may serve as means of centering human interest and emotional tendencies on other peoples. A world feeling may be channeled through games of many lands, for we know that neither national patriotism nor any other group-sentiment is innate. A pattern of global empathy evolves from mental organization, from orderly participation and dynamic action, and from fusion of information with thinking, feeling, and caring.

Merely knowing about a people and its culture does not guarantee liking them; however, it is an accepted fact that ignorance nurtures many prejudices. It is important that individuals and not the diplomats alone get to know the peoples of other countries. The whole realm of human endeavor—the technical, scientific, commercial, artistic, religious, educational, tourist, and social aspects—must become a part of the great and perhaps final opportunity man will have to solve peacefully his intra- and international problems. The whole realm of human endeavor must live the peace that man talks, teaches, and preaches today.

2

Africa

The resourcefulness of the children of Africa is evident in their game patterns and in the play equipment used. The children run races, play at horses, have contests of balancing, turn "catherine-wheels," play "cat's cradle," and are fond of a game that is much like hockey.

A game of "Traders" is popular with many African children. They make clay imitations of articles used in trade by their elders and play a game of trading the articles. Stones, sticks, small twigs, hard nuts, disks of sisal, grains of corn, colored beans, birds' feathers, and brightly colored cloth often constitute their play equipment.

Athletic games are not typical of the play in Africa. Team play has not developed in this continent where the major part of life's activities for centuries has been for survival and much of this on an individual basis. It is interesting to note, however, that many of the games played throughout tribal Africa are somewhat like the games of many other lands. In recent years sports have been introduced in the schools and are being accepted with interest and growing enthusiasm.

The terms Central and Southern, Northern and Eastern, and Western are used for convenience in grouping the regions in Africa that are represented in the worldwide collection of games.

CENTRAL AND SOUTHERN AFRICA
The Congo
The Rhodesias and Nyasaland
   Northern Rhodesia
   Southern Rhodesia
South Africa
South-West Africa
Uganda

NORTHERN AND EASTERN AFRICA
Egypt
Ethiopia
Sudan
Tanganyika

WESTERN AFRICA
Ghana
Guinea
Nigeria

CENTRAL AND SOUTHERN AFRICA

THE CONGO, THE RHODESIAS, AND NYASALAND

The stone games of The Congo (formerly under Belgium) and Northern Rhodesia are typically African. The skill required for enjoying the Rhodesian version demands agility of body movements. Southern Rhodesian games are predominately of the animal-theme. Their names and characters fit into their geographic setting; otherwise the games are truly universal.

SOUTH AFRICA, SOUTH-WEST AFRICA, AND UGANDA

Singing-dancing games are everyday activities with the boys and girls of Southern Africa. The children follow their parents in their love of rhythm. The grown-ups sing as they work in the fields; they dance and sing whenever they get together for a celebration of any kind. The children's games, even the ball play, often have hand clapping and foot stamping as part of the activity.

The drama of the bridge-type game from South-West Africa is universal, although in "African London Bridge" the conversation and repetitions of the play pattern are longer and more varied than usual.

In Uganda, especially in the Northern Province, which is the area of the big hunts, the boys play at activities that help them to be good hunters when at the age of fifteen they go on an organized hunt. The boys build huts, spear the disk, and model clay figures of horses and oxen. The girls and young children play house with dolls made of clay. Uganda's "Tug-o-War" provides insight into one tribe's marriage custom.

NORTHERN AND EASTERN AFRICA

EGYPT, ETHIOPIA, AND THE SUDAN

The horse-and-rider theme is typical of Egyptian games. Marbles and other universal games such as "Leap-Frog" and "Blindman's Buff" are played by the children of Egypt. The lame-foot games of The Sudan demonstrate the dramatic element in many African games.

Boys in Ethiopia enjoy tumbling, pyramid building, and pole vaulting; however, soccer is their favorite out-of-doors sport. The girls like less strenuous activities, with rope jumping being most popular.

The game of "Gebeta" is a favorite pastime of both the children and adults in Ethiopia. The details of the game and the several lead-up games (for children) may be found in *Hi Neighbor* (Book 3, UNICEF, United Nations, New York City). This fascinating and quiet pastime is so popular in Ethiopia that the curbstones in some of the streets of the capital city, Addis Ababa, are carved with holes so that the children can play leisurely there, and hand carved wooden gebeta boards are often given as a wedding gift from father to son.

TANGANYIKA

A popular pastime is hunting birds, especially the small, brightly colored finches. The accuracy of the young hunters, small boys with slingshots, as they run through the corn fields is amazing. Small boys improvise toys such as soccer balls of sisal or cloth, and tops carved out of wood; and hoop games by rolling old bicycle rims down narrow paths. At times they make wheels of wood and play at keeping them in motion for long periods of time. The girls improvise most of their games, though they find it more difficult to keep active. Sisal provides their rope for the popular rope jumping at which they are quite skilled.

Both boys and girls enjoy trips and picnics to their favorite lake as well as excursions into shaded coves and hidden glens. Lake Victoria has the added attraction of hippopotamuses bathing in the mud and crocodiles crawling along the shore.

Track meets provide great pleasure to the school children, who prepare the field themselves the morning of the events. Jumping hurdles is the big event of the meets.

Soccer is popular with older boys. The fields are easily built by cutting tall grass in an area and putting up goal posts of sisal.

Other sports have been introduced to the boys in most of the schools. Football has been tried but cannot compete with their interest in soccer. Volley ball is enjoyed by both boys and girls. Basketball is becoming popular but suffers because of little team work among the participants.

WESTERN AFRICA

GHANA, GUINEA, AND NIGERIA

Stones, sticks, palm nuts, pebbles, and twigs are often used as game equipment by the children of Ghana and Guinea. Rhythm is also a part of several of their game patterns. Hand clapping, jumping, and stamping add variety and excitement to the play.

The "Blindfold Horse Race" and the "Boat Race" from Nigeria are unique and have great appeal to boys. The game "Teaching Attention of the Mind" is suggestive of "Birds Fly" and the "Simon Says" type games played by children in the United States of North America. The details carried out to entrap the participants in the Nigerian game are more challenging than those in the American versions. A consistent element of fun in several games from Nigeria is that the player caught in a chasing game is expected to and does accept a playful beating from the one who catches him.

GAMES AND SPORTS—CENTRAL AND SOUTHERN AFRICA

THE CONGO

Bokwele (Bok-WEH-le)

Ages: teen
Players: 20 or more; two-group; informal
Place: gymnasium; out-of-doors
Supplies: beans, corn, or stones
Activity—hunting: chasing, running
Appeal: competition, problem solving

Players are divided into two or more teams. Each team draws a large circle in which it places colored beans, stones, grains of corn, or any other objects different from those used by another team. The players run from their own circles and cry "Bokwele, Bokwele" as they try to steal the object from their opponents and at the same time try to avoid being caught by the opponents. The team that steals all the beans, stones, or corn wins the game.

Bokwele

Ages: teen
Players: 10 or more; two-group; informal
Place: gymnasium; out-of-doors
Supplies: two long poles
Activity—pastime: breath-holding
Appeal: skill

Bokwele is also the name of another game that may be enjoyed for its element of skill in breath-holding. It may be used as counting-out game.

The players are divided into two teams. Each team has a long pole marked with alternate black and white or light and dark rings. Each ring is wide enough to be encircled by a player's fingers. The African children peel the bark from the pole to make rings.

Each team chooses a player to start the game. The player tries to climb his pole with his hands (fingers encircling the white rings) while he says, "Bokwele, Bokwele, Bokwele," as long as he has breath. The player whose hands reach the top of his pole first wins for his team.

NORTHERN RHODESIA

Stone Game

Ages: 9–12
Players: 4–8; single-group; circle
Place: out-of-doors
Supplies: small pebbles

Activity—pastime game: running, throwing
Appeal: skill

The players sit in a circle, the center of which is designated by a hole containing about 15 small stones. One player starts the game by taking one of the stones and throwing it high into the air. While the stone is in the air, the player quickly grabs the pebbles in the hole and then gets in position to catch the *falling stone*. If he is successful, he then throws the stone up a second time. While it is in the air, he replaces all stones except one in the hole and then gets ready to catch the *falling stone*. Should he succeed, he places the one stone that he has earned to one side.

The whole procedure is repeated with the remaining stones. If the player is successful during the second inning, his score increases to two as he places to one side the second stone that he has earned. He continues the play as long as he catches the *falling stone* and at the same time successfully scoops out all stones and then replaces all except one. When he loses his turn, another player tries his luck with the remaining stones and thus the game continues. Should the game progress to the point where only three stones remain in the hole, the player throws one of the stones into the air and quickly tries to place one of the two remaining stones on the near, and one on the far, side of the hole. He then tries to catch the *falling stone*. The player who earns the greatest number of stones wins the game. The stones are often waterworn. Hard nuts are also used.

SOUTHERN RHODESIA

Hawk and Hens

Ages: 5–8
Players: 20 or more; group-and-one; informal
Place: gymnasium; out-of-doors
Supplies: not any

Activity—hunting: chasing, dodging, running
Appeal: dramatization, problem solving

One player is chosen to be the *hawk*, the others are the *hens*. The *hawk* tries to catch the *hens* as they fly (run) from one safety zone to another. The last one to be caught designates the *hawk* for the next game. This game is from the Baratosi tribe in Southern Rhodesia.

Hen and Wild Cat

Ages: 5–8

Players: 20 or more; group-and-one; circle

Place: gymnasium; out-of-doors

Supplies: not any

Activity—hunting: chasing, dodging, running

Appeal: dramatization, problem solving

One player is the *hen* and leads her *brood*, the other children, around the *cat*, a chosen player. The *hen* warns her *brood* of the danger and the *cat* tries to catch any foolish chicken who fails to heed the warning of the mother hen.

Xoxo

Ages: 5–8

Players: 10–20; single- or two-group

Place: gymnasium; out-of-doors

Supplies: not any

Activity—contest, relay, stunt: hopping

Appeal: competition, skill

Xoxo, meaning *frog*, is pronounced "xo" as the clicking of the tongue in saying "giddap" to a horse and with an "o." The children of the Matebele tribe play Xoxo in several forms.

The players squat on the ground with the hands flat on the ground and between their knees, thus forming four *legs*. Then, by hopping on all fours, they race to a point; they often have a relay, or play follow the leader.

SOUTH AFRICA

Handball

Ages: 9–12

Players: 10 to 20; two-group; informal

Place: gymnasium; out-of-doors

Supplies: playground ball

Activity—athletic game: catching, clapping, stamping, throwing

Appeal: competition, skill

The players are divided into two sides. The ball is given to one player and he throws it to another player on his side. Each teammate who has the ball wishes to keep it passing from one of his side to another while the other side tries to gain possession by intercepting the ball. Each of the players with the exception of the one who holds the ball claps his hands together once, and sometimes stamps his feet, every time the ball is caught. Children in the United States play this game, calling it "Keep Away," without the rhythmic hand clapping and foot stamping.

Melon Dance

Ages: teen
Players: 10 to 20; group-and-one; circle
Place: gymnasium; out-of-doors

Supplies: playground ball
Activity—athletic game: catching, leaping, passing, running
Appeal: problem solving, skill

This activity is described as a dance but since it has active game skills as well as rhythmical steps it may well be called an athletic game. It was especially popular among the Hottentot girls and will be written for girls, although boys could enjoy the activity today.

The players encircle a *center* player who has a small round melon in her hands. The *center* girl runs about the circle, waving her arms, throwing, and catching the melon while the circle players imitate her movements. Suddenly she stoops, then leaps into the air and throws the melon under her feet toward the player who is behind her. The second girl must catch the melon without moving from her place. If she fails, the *center* player remains the leader; otherwise, the second player becomes the leader. The *center* girl may try to catch the others off guard and even pretend to throw the melon several times before actually doing it. A playground ball may be used instead of a melon.

SOUTH-WEST AFRICA

African London Bridge

Ages: 5–8
Players: 20 or more; transition
Place: gymnasium; playground
Supplies: not any

Activity—hunting game: chasing, running
Appeal: dramatization, repetition, rhythm

One player is the *mother* and all the others are her *children* except two who form an arch. One by one a child is caught between the arch and asked the choice between a cake of gourd seed or a peanut porridge, a necklace of beads or a bow and arrow. As the *children* are caught they go to the side of their choice. Finally only the *mother* is left and she is now called the *only child*. The once numerous family goes to the bush, but from time to time the *mother* goes forth to throw a handful of grass toward the others who ask in chorus:

"How is the only child today?"
"She creeps about now," says the mother.
"He-e-e!" the others exclaim.
"What age is the only child today?"
"She walks about now."
"He-e-e!"

This is continued until the *only child* has grown up, married, and had a child of her own. The same questions continue to be asked the *child* of the *only child*.

The *grandmother* may respond, "She walks, she sets traps, and she catches fishes. One day she killed a little bear, another day she killed a big bear, and today she killed a tiger." "He-e-e!" At the climax one *child* after another goes from the bush to beg a piece of tiger. When the *mother* finds a *child* who pleases her, she gives him a piece of meat. Then the *mother* and *child* run away with all others following.

UGANDA

Bow and Arrow

Ages: teen
Players: 5; individual
Place: out-of-doors
Supplies: arrows, bow, target

Activity—pastime: aiming, shooting
Appeal: competition, skill

Players agree upon the distance they will stand from the target. If the first player to shoot hits the target, he challenges each of the others by saying, "Come and shoot from my eye."

If the *challenged player* hits the target, he gets his arrow, and the next player shoots. If the *challenged player* misses, the *challenger* collects the arrow and the player tries again. The *challenger* must also shoot again. If both miss, the *challenger* says, "You collect my arrow and I will collect yours." If the *challenged player* misses again, the *challenger* picks up the arrow. The winner of the match is the player who has the most arrows after each player has accepted the challenge.

Inzema

Ages: teen
Players: 10 or more; two-group
Place: out-of-doors
Supplies: gourd, spears

Activity—pastime: bowling, throwing
Appeal: competition, skill

One player takes a gourd and bowls it down a level field. The other players form two lines facing each other and try to spear the gourd as it passes. The player who first spears the gourd is allowed to bowl the next time.

This and other "spearing" games can be considered as target practice for the young boys.

Uganda Tug-of-War

Ages: 9–12
Players: 20 or more; two-group
Place: gymnasium; out-of-doors
Supplies: long rope

Activity—hunting: chasing, pulling, running
Appeal: dramatization, strength

The players are divided into two teams: One is the *bride's family*, the other is the *groom's family*. Each team stands in file formation behind a chosen *leader*. A dividing line is marked on the group between the two *leaders*. The *leaders* of the teams and all players on each team grasp a long rope and get ready for action. Meanwhile one player who has been selected to be the *bride* stands by "ready for action."

When the signal to start is given, a tug-of-war between the two *families* takes place. The *bride* immediately begins weeping, pretending that she is reluctant to leave her family. The secret of the game is that the *groom's family* is always allowed to win! When this action does take place, the winners quickly grab the *bride* and carry her to the home of the *groom*. The *bride's family* chases them, pretending to want her back. To provide the fun of winning to both groups, the *families* may change names after several plays.

The game has developed from the traditional premarital custom of the Banyankole (ban-yun-KO-le) tribe of Uganda. It is the custom among this tribe for families to pre-arrange the marriage. The bride and her family are supposed to pretend that they do not want to carry it out. The two families actually have a tug-of-war before the ceremony and the bride pretends to weep; the groom's family always wins the mock war; and the bride's family always gives them a faked chase to recover the bride.

GAMES AND SPORTS—NORTHERN AND EASTERN AFRICA

EGYPT

Fox

Ages: 5–8
Players: 20 or more; group-and-one; circle
Place: gymnasium; out-of-doors
Supplies: handkerchief

Activity—hunting: chasing, dodging
Appeal: dramatization, problem solving

One player, the *fox*, walks around the outside of a circle formed by the other players. As the *fox* walks, he starts and continues a conversation with the circle players in an effort to distract the attention of the players from him. Finally the *fox* drops a handkerchief behind a circle player and immediately tries to stand beside the player before being tagged. If he is successful, the circle player takes the handkerchief and becomes the next *fox*. If the *fox* is tagged, he must try again. Each player should be given a chance to be the *fox*.

Horse

Ages: teen
Players: any number; groups of 3; informal
Place: gymnasium; out-of-doors

Supplies: not any
Activity—stunt: balance, coordination
Appeal: dramatization, strength

Two players form the *horse* by one of them facing the back of the other and placing his hands on the shoulders of the boy in front. The third and smallest player is the *rider* and he mounts the *horse* and rides astride the arms of the player in the back. This activity may be used in relay formation.

ETHIOPIA

Spearing the Disk

Ages: 9–12
Players: 3 to 10; single-group; line
Place: out-of-doors

Supplies: disk, pointed sticks
Activity—pastime game: throwing
Appeal: competition, skill

Each player needs a spear or a pointed stick. A disk made of soft wood is also needed. The players line up, spears in hand. The *leader*, 30 or 40 feet away, starts the disk rolling across the playing area. Each player throws his spear, trying to pierce the disk and score one point. The player with the most points at the close of the play wins. A variation of the game is to throw at a hoop that is rolled down the field.

THE SUDAN

Getting the Bride Home

Ages: 9–12
Players: 10 or more; group-and-one; informal
Place: gymnasium; out-of-doors
Supplies: not any

Activity—hunting: chasing, hopping, running
Appeal: dramatization, problem solving

One player is the *bride*. The other players are in two teams, one is assigned to protect the *bride* as she tries to return home. The other team attacks the *bride*. Each player must hop on his left foot as he grasps his right foot with his left hand.

Ethiopia—Spearing the Disk or Hoop.

It is interesting to know that the children of Syria and Lebanon play a similar game of "Hop Tag" but without the drama of the bride-theme.

Sheep and Hyena

Ages: 5–8
Players: 20–30; group-and-two; circle
Place: gymnasium; out-of-doors
Supplies: not any

Activity—hunting: chasing, dodging, running
Appeal: dramatization, problem solving

Players form a circle. One player, the *hyena*, is on the outside, another player, the *sheep*, is on the inside of the circle. The circle players move around as they try to keep the *hyena* from breaking through to catch the *sheep*. The chase ends when the *hyena* catches the *sheep*. Two other players start the game anew. The same game is called "Cat and Rat" in the United States.

Taia-ya-taia (TI-ah-yah-tí-AH)

Ages: 9–12
Players: 10 to 20; group-and-one; line
Place: gymnasium; out-of-doors

Supplies: not any
Activity—hunting game: chasing, dodging, hopping
Appeal: competition, skill

One player is chosen to be *It*. He takes his place in front of the others who stand in a line. *It* shouts "taia-ya-taia," then hops off on one foot as if lame. He then tries to tag one of the players without putting his lame foot down. If he catches a player, the one caught must be *It*.

TANGANYIKA (tan-gan-YEE-kah)

How Many?

Ages: 9–12
Players: 3 or more; individual; informal
Place: home; schoolroom

Supplies: beads, corn, or pebbles
Activity—pastime: guessing
Appeal: chance, suspense

Any small object can be used as *counters,* such as pebbles or beads, but African children prefer to use something profitable, for example, roasted grains of maize. Each player has the same number of *counters,* from 15 to 20, which he holds in one hand. With the free hand he secretively takes any number of objects from none to four and extends the closed fist with the question "How many?" If the one guessing gets the number correctly, he gets all the grains. If he guesses wrong, he must pay according to the table below:

	Guesser	
If Holding	Gets If He Is Right	Gives If He Is Wrong
4	4	1
3	3	1
2	2	1
1	1	1
0	2	2

The players take turns guessing. The game is won when one player has all the grains; the loser is named *PA-ka* (cat) or perhaps *Ki-BO-ko M-JIN-ga* (silly hippo).

Kando

Ages: 5–8
Players: 10 or more; group-and-one; line
Place: gymnasium; out-of-doors
Supplies: not any

Activity—hunting: chasing, running, tagging
Appeal: dramatization, problem solving

The players form a line, each player holding on to the waist of the one in front. The player at the head of the line is the *mother* who tries to protect her *children* from the *old woman* who is looking for a child to help her with her work. The *old woman* tries to tag the last player in line, with the line weaving back and forth to avoid her. When a player is tagged he must help the *old woman* catch the player now last in line. *Kando* (KAN-do) means "side," presumably as the line goes from side to side like a writhing snake to avoid the *old woman.*

Moto

Ages: 5–8	Supplies: not any
Players: 20 or more; two-group-and-one; circle	Activity—hunting: running, stooping
Place: gymnasium; out-of-doors	Appeal: dramatization

One player, the *leader,* stands inside a double circle formed by the other players who are in pairs and face the center of the circle. The inside circle players are the *children* and squat; the outside circle players are the *mothers* and place their hands on the head of their *child.* The leader calls out "Moto," which means "fire," and keeps repeating the word. The mothers run around the circle shouting, "Kilimani" (Ki-li-MA-ni), "on the mountain top." As long as the leader says, "Moto, Moto, Moto," the *mothers* keep running; when he says, "Moto Kabisa" (Ka-BI-sa), "extremely hot fire," he then runs quickly and stands behind one of the *children;* all *mothers* stand still behind a *child.* The player left childless is the next leader. When the *mothers* are running about, the *children* pretend to be afraid of the fire.

My Children, Come to Me

Ages: 5–8	Supplies: not any
Players: 20 or more; two-group-and-one; line	Activity—hunting: chasing, running
Place: gymnasium; out-of-doors	Appeal: dramatization, problem solving

One player is chosen to be the *mother hen;* another is the *hawk.* All other players are the brood of *chicks.* Two lines are marked about 60 feet apart. The *mother* stands behind one line, the *chicks* behind the other. The *hawk* stands anywhere between the two lines. The play starts with a dialogue that is said twice:

The hen (calling to her chicks): "My children, come to me."
The chicks: "We can't."
Hen: "Why not?"
Chicks: "Because the hawk is near."

When the *hen* calls for the third time "My children, come to me," the *chicks* try to run across the play area and safely to the *mother hen* without being caught by the *hawk*. Those tagged by the *hawk* become *little hawks* during the next round of play. (The student in Tanganyika who contributed this game wrote, "The game is played to show how the hawk preys on chickens and how the mother hen fights for them.")

My Little Bird

Ages: 9–12
Players: 20 or more; group-and-one; line
Place: home; schoolroom

Supplies: not any
Activity—pastime: listening
Appeal: alertness, coordination

One player stands before the group and says, "My little bird is lively, is lively." Then he quickly calls out the name of anything he wishes, "Goats . . . fly!" If the thing named can fly, the players must raise their arms in a flying motion. If the thing named cannot fly, the players should remain still. Should a player move his arms at the wrong call, he is out of the game. A game known as "Birds Fly" is played in the same manner by children of North America.

GAMES AND SPORTS—WESTERN AFRICA

GHANA

Ampe

Ages: 9–12
Players: 10 or more; group-and-one; semicircle
Place: gymnasium; out-of-doors

Supplies: not any
Activity—pastime: clapping, jumping
Appeal: chance, rhythm

Players stand in a semicircle with one player, the *leader*, facing the first person at the head of the line. The play is done to rhythmic chant or to a three-beat clap, which may be carried out by all players. The *leader* and the *player* he faces both clap hands, *beat one*; both jump in place, *beat two*; each jumps, placing a foot forward, *beat three*. If the *player* places forward a foot opposite to the *leader's*—that is, if the *leader* has his right foot forward and the *player* his left foot forward—the *leader* must repeat the procedure with the same player. After a third try the leader is out and the *player* takes his place. If a *player* puts forward the same foot as the *leader*, he takes the *leader's* place and the leader goes to the foot of the line.

If the *leader* reaches the end of the line without being put out, he scores one point and starts again. The *player* who scores ten points first is the winner of the game.

Big Snake

Ages: 9–12
Players: 20 or more; group-and-one; informal
Place: out-of-doors

Supplies: not any
Activity—hunting: chasing, running
Appeal: dramatization, problem solving

One player is chosen to be the *snake* and goes to its *home*, which is a space about ten feet square. The object of the game is for the *snake* to catch the other players. When one is caught he must join hands with the snake and the two continue the chase. As players are caught the *snake* gradually grows longer. Only the players on either end of the *snake* may tag a runner. The player first chosen to be the *snake* makes decisions as to which players should be at the end and who should be chased next.

Should the *snake* break because the players let go their hands, the runners may tag the *snake* and thus force it to return to the *home*. The runners may spank the *snake* lightly as it runs for home. Once back home the *snake* rejoins and begins the chase anew. The game is over when all players are caught.

When the *snake* becomes long enough it may add excitement to the game by trying to encircle the players. However, the runners who are encircled may break the *snake*, thus causing it to return home and consequently give the runners a chance to scatter.

Grab It

Ages: 9–12
Players: 8 or more; two-group; line
Place: out-of-doors
Supplies: small twig, handkerchief

Activity—athletic: alertness, dodging
Appeal: problem solving

Players are divided into two equal teams who face each other several feet apart. An object, such as a handkerchief or a small twig, is placed exactly halfway between the teams. At a given signal two players from each team run toward the object. Each player tries to pick up the object without being tagged by his opponents. If a player succeeds in doing this, one point is scored for his team. If a player is tagged as he picks up the object, a point is scored for the opposing team. A score of ten or more may be set as a game. The game "Steal the Bacon," especially popular with boys of the United States, is played in the same manner.

Pebble Counting

Ages: 9–12
Players: 10 or more; individual; line
Place: home; schoolroom

Supplies: pebbles
Activity—contest: breath-holding
Appeal: competition

The players are seated in a line facing a long line of pebbles. The first player in the line stands, takes a deep breath, and walks down the line of pebbles, touching each pebble consecutively and saying "La loo lu loo la loo lu loo" until he gives out of breath. If he can go the whole line in one breath, he may claim one of the pebbles and remove it from the line.

Each player in turn goes down the line. The play continues until all pebbles are claimed. The player having the most pebbles at the close of the game wins.

Two Friends

Ages: 9–12
Players: 15 or more; couples-and-one; lines
Place: gymnasium; out-of-doors

Supplies: not any
Activity—hunting: chasing, running
Appeal: dramatization, problem solving

A player is chosen to be It and stands at the head of the other players who line up in pairs. It calls, "I'm looking for a friend," and raises his clasped hands. At this signal the last couple starts to run forward, one on either side of the double line and past It. As the players run by It, he runs after them, trying to tag one before the two join hands. Should It succeed in tagging one of the players, that player becomes the friend of It and they become the head couple. The other player becomes It. If It does not tag one of the couple before they meet, he continues as It until he does catch a friend.

The same game by the same name is played by the children of Togo just east of Ghana. In the United States the game is called "Last Couple Out." The Swedish children call it "Widower's Game" and play it with a slight variation.

GUINEA

Ball Toss

Ages: 9–12
Players: 6 or more; individual; informal
Place: out-of-doors

Supplies: small balls or nuts
Activity—pastime: aiming, tossing
Appeal: competition, skill

This game is popular with both girls and boys and is played the year round in Guinea. A hole is dug in the ground; players stand on a line ten or more feet from the hole. Each player tries to toss a palm nut or a small ball into the hole. The player who gets his ball in or nearest the hole is the starter of the play. He tosses again. If the ball goes into the hole, the player scores a goal and takes his place near the hole. As the other players take turn at throwing for the hole, he tries to hit their ball with his ball as they throw, thus keeping them from scoring. When every player has scored, the game ends.

Bathing Game

Ages: 9–12
Players: 10 or more; single group; circle
Place: seashore

Supplies: not any
Activity—contest: leaping
Appeal: competition, skill

This game is a form of leapfrog that is played on the seashore. Each player builds a mound of sand about two feet high upon which he sits. The mounds are about two feet apart in circle formation. At a signal every player raises himself on his arms and swings his feet forward, the object being to come down sitting on the mound in front of him. If a player's feet touch the sand he is disqualified. The winner of the game is the last player left.

NIGERIA

Abumbutan (AH-boom-BOO-tahn)

Ages: 9–12
Players: 6 to 8; single group; informal
Place: out-of-doors

Supplies: sand heaps
Activity—pastime: chasing, running
Appeal: problem solving, skill

A piece of stick about eight inches long is stuck into a heap of sand. All players sit around the heap talking and removing the sand little by little with both hands. When the sand is almost scattered, the players carefully use a finger to remove the sand because whoever makes the stick fall is in danger of being chased and beaten. The chase lasts until the player is caught and beaten in a joking manner. The players then begin the game anew.

Aiming at a Target

Ages: 9–12
Players: 4 or more; individual; informal
Place: out-of-doors

Supplies: sisal or hemp, large nail
Activity—pastime: aiming, throwing
Appeal: competition, skill

This game is played by a team of four, six, or eight. Sisal hemp or any other soft stem is cut out into pieces at which each player aims and throws a six-inch nail. In turns, players try to spear and remove the pieces one by one. A player continues using the nail as many times as he spears at least one piece. If he fails to catch one of the pieces at any time, he passes the nail to the next player. Should both teams agree to leave one piece in the center, the *best shooter* is determined by the ability to get the only piece with the nail. The *best shooter* orders other players to return any number of pieces to the center to have the game continued. Many best players request six pieces or eight or ten pieces. Should some players fail to get as many to submit, they borrow from their neighbors with the hope of gaining next time to return them. Should their debt increase unwieldily, they are turned out. The game is won either by the team having the most pieces when play is over or by the *best shooter* spearing the last piece with the nail.

Attention of the Mind

Ages: teen

Players: 20 or more; group-and-one; informal

Place: gymnasium; out-of-doors

Supplies: not any

Activity—pastime: alertness, chasing

Appeal: dramatization, rhythm

One player, the *leader,* faces the others who stand in lines or informally in a group. Play begins and continues with much rhythmic conversation.

Leader: "Which things have blood?"
Group: "Many things have blood."
Leader: "A goat has blood."
Group: "Oh! yes, has blood."
Leader: "A sheep has blood."
Group: "Oh! yes, has blood."
Leader: "A man has blood."
Group: "Oh! yes, has blood."
Leader: "A stone has blood."
Group: (No answer)

The *leader* should be clever and fast in choosing things with blood and those without blood in attempt to trap the players.

If a player should say "Oh! yes, has blood," for any object without blood, he is chased and beaten, when caught. Play then continues with the following rhythmic conversation:

Leader: "Answer-not "Yes" three times."
Group: "Yes."
Leader: "Answer-not 'Yes' three times."
Group: "Yes."
Leader: "Answer-not 'Yes' three times."
Group: (No answer)

If a player says "Yes" the third time he will be chased and beaten.

Blindfold Horse Race

Ages: junior and teen
Players: 12 or more; couples; line
Place: out-of-doors
Supplies: blindfold

Activity—relay: balance, running
Appeal: competition, dramatization

One player of each couple is the *horse*, and is blindfolded and supports his *rider*, piggyback fashion. The race track is laid out with sticks, tin cans, or boxes, with gates designated through which the horses must run. The rider must guide his horse through the gates and around the course without speaking to him. He may use only one hand in giving signals such as tapping him, pulling his ear, or any other pre-arranged signal. The couple reaching the finish line first wins. A relay, with several couples on a team, may be played.

Nigeria—Blindfold Horse Race.

Boat Race

Ages: intermediate
Players: 18 or more; two-group; file
Place: gymnasium; out-of-doors

Supplies: long poles
Activity—relay: balance, running
Appeal: competition, dramatization, skill

The players are divided into teams of nine players each. The playing area, the *river*, is the space between the starting and the finish line. The course of the river is winding and is marked by rocks, or sticks in the ground. Eight members of each *crew* stand, single file all facing backward, at the starting line, and holding a pole between their legs. The ninth player of each group is the *cox*, or *steersman*, who faces forward.

Upon signal, all crews run backward down the river, guided by the *steersmen*, who control the *crews* by means of their poles. The object of the game is to see which *crew* reaches the finish line first. Nigerian players use bamboo poles about 12 feet long. A broomstick may be substituted.

Catch Your Tail

Ages: intermediate
Players: 12 or more; two-group; line
Place: gymnasium; out-of-doors

Supplies: handkerchiefs
Activity—hunting: chasing, dodging, running
Appeal: problem solving, skill

Players are divided into two equal teams. Members of each team grasp each other around the waist. The last player of each team has a handkerchief, his *tail*, tucked lightly into his belt at the back. The head player, the *captain*, of each team leads his team in a chase, trying to capture the *tail* of its opponent. Players must hold to the one in front. Three teams may add to the fun of the game.

Hide and Seek

Ages: 5–8
Players: 10 or more; group-and-one; informal
Place: out-of-doors

Supplies: not any
Activity—hunting: chasing, dodging, running
Appeal: problem solving

A home base is established by marking a circle about ten feet in diameter. One player, the *leader*, and another, the *seeker*, stand in the circle. The *leader* covers the eyes of the *seeker* while all other players hide. When all are hidden, the *leader* releases the *seeker* who tries to catch at least one player as all try to get to the home base safely. If the *seeker* catches a player, that player becomes the next *seeker*. If he fails to catch a player, he is given two more trials. Should he fail after the third trial, another player takes his place.

Jumping the Beanbag

Ages: teen
Players: 20 or more; group-and-one;
  circle
Place: gymnasium; out-of-doors

Supplies: beanbag, long rope
Activity—pastime: jumping
Appeal: skill

One player, chosen to be *It*, stands in the center of a circle formed by the other players. *It* holds a beanbag that is tied to a rope that he gradually slings and lets out until the players have to jump to avoid being hit by the bag. When a player fails to jump and is hit by the bag, he is out of the game. As the players decrease in number, the speed of the bag increases. The last player in the circle is the winner.

3

Asia

The games of the children of Asia are as varied, as numerous, and as interesting as are the peoples, their customs, their religions, and the physical features of their vast continent. In order to group the games into a pattern consistent with global thinking, the continent will be considered as three regions, namely, the Far East, the Middle East, and Southern Asia. An overview of the regions will give a word picture of the total countries represented in the collection of games from Asia.

FAR EAST
Eastern and Southeastern Area   Southwestern Area

China	Korea	Burma	Malaya
Japan	The Philippines	Indonesia	Thailand

MIDDLE EAST   SOUTHERN ASIA

Gaza	Lebanon	India
Iran	Syria	
Israel	Turkey, including Armenia	

Although there are similarities within the game patterns of the various cultures and societies of Asia, as there are similarities in all play of all children throughout the entire world, there are unique play characteristics within each society.

FAR EAST

The play patterns of the Far East present an overall picture of individual competition in athletic games and sports. This is unlike the team effort of competition in the western world. There is also less strenuous activity in the majority of games from the Far East. This may be due in part to the influence of climate and in part to the oriental philosophy of leisurely living.

Dramatic play is found in many of the games. Rhymes, conversation, and questioning, as in guessing games, provide opportunity for clever usage of language and ideas. The procedure of breath-holding as part of the competitive element is a distinct characteristic of many Far East games. The *It* in the games loses his place if he loses his breath before a specified time expires or a certain activity is achieved.

Eastern and Southeastern Area

The game contributions of this area of the Far East reach from antiquity into the space era of today. The overall similarities of play and games from the Orient, along with the noticeable contrasts of intra- as well as intersocietal units, are interesting.

The games provide a peek into the democratic past of old China; a glimpse of the gracious individuality expressed in the play and games of the once subservient peoples of Japan; a display of the clever and daring ingenuity of the Korean children and youth; and a conviction that play in the Philippines has not always been the calm and pleasant activity that it is there today.

CHINA

The country of China, the China of the pre-Communist era, is rich in games. These games appeal not only to the Chinese boy and girl and to children around the world but also to the student of play and games as they provide insight into the friendly and genuinely democratic attitude of the Chinese people before their domination and indoctrination by the Communists.

The delightful and varied play patterns of China warrant the place given them in the mosaic of games. It is through the games that the play leaders and participants around the world can have knowledge, understanding, and empathy for the children of this once-great land. In their play the Chinese are dramatic, clever in character portrayal, warm in protective concern for the hunted, and show an attitude of readiness to follow the leader who knows what he is doing and where he is going. It is interesting to note, however, that none of the games of the Chinese children are in relay form.

JAPAN

Through the centuries play has been traditionally popular in Japan. Drama often enters into the game patterns. The element of guessing plays a part in many games of the Japanese boy and girl. Although the Japanese folk games have the competitive element present, the competition is more often individual than big team effort. Relays, as competitive activities, are popular.

Today the children and youth of Japan are learning games and sports of the United States. Baseball is the most popular sport in Japan. Soccer, rugby, and swimming are a part of many city school programs. *Judo* is an accepted activity among the Japanese youth especially as a method of self-defense. A type of wrestling, *Sumo*, is enjoyed by the boys and men. Educators in Japan are accepting play today as a desirable channel for helping children to understand themselves and other peoples.

KOREA

This country is often called "The Land of the Morning Calm," because the winds and sea are so quiet early in the morning. It is a land of many delightful games played by its children. Generally speaking the games indicate the serious attitude of the Koreans toward their play. There is the attitude that the participants must gravely accept the challenge to win over their opponents. The intricate patterns of play in several Korean games demand the concentration of the players.

It has been an age-old custom in Korea to have wrestling matches in the early part of June. Prizes of oxen are given to the winner of the men's matches and bolts of cloth to the winner of the boys' contests. The girls and women call the day "Swing Day." Swings are hung in the beautiful wooded areas: low swings for the children; high swings for the older girls and women; even grandmothers seem surprisingly young on that day as many of them swing, too.

THE PHILIPPINES

Another land of the Far East that commands attention is that of the Philippine Islands. The quantity of games from this small yet scattered group of islands bears evidence that play is a big factor in the lives of the children and youth.

The once-popular field sport of head-hunting among the Filipinos has given over to the more civilized sports of boxing, tennis, volleyball, golf, and baseball. Basketball is the national game of the Islanders. They celebrate holidays with religious processions, feasts, plays, fireworks, and games.

Southwestern Area

The lack of printed material on play and games from this part of the world is a handicap. Nevertheless the quest for games common to the area has been rewarding. It has brought to light interesting facts about the peoples of this part of Asia, especially in regard to their attitude toward play. It has enriched the collection of games, since many of the games have come first hand from persons living and working among the everyday people. It has also stimulated the hope that the thousands and thousands of children in these lands will in time be provided more opportunity to play; more opportunity not only to develop more play patterns of their own but also to experience through play an awareness and understanding of children of other lands.

BURMA AND INDONESIA

The most typical pastimes of the children of Burma are the universal games of marbles, peg tops, and leapfrog. Kite flying is another activity that, along with that of sailing toy boats in miniature regattas, is enjoyed by the Burmese children.

The republic of Indonesia fills in the mosaic of play in the Far East by way of the contributions from Borneo, Celebes, and Java, which the Indonesians prefer to call Kalimantin, Sulawesi, and Djawa, respectively. The games played by the children of these islands reflect frugal use of natural materials as play equipment.

MALAYA AND THAILAND

A first reaction from one working with the children of Malaya was, "But the children here do not play!" And to amplify this statement there was the continuation of the thought in these words, "I have seen only one little Malayan girl playing with a doll. Most of the little girls 'play' with real dolls. This is due to the fact that from the time the children are big enough [and before, according to our North American standards] they are required to help in the home, particularly with the care of smaller children." Despite these observations and those of nationals who were consulted, there are four games that are reported to be unique within this society. Other games that were reported, such as "Do This, Do That," "Hide and Seek," "Cat and Rat," "Dodge Ball," and various forms of relays, indicate that they are local versions of the same games played in the United States and doubtlessly in many other countries.

The games from Thailand, the country formerly known as Siam, appear to have come through the influences of forces outside the Buddhist culture. Buddhism, the religion of the country, is not noted for any contribution toward living the everyday life; therefore, play is completely ignored. It is known, however, that kite flying was traditionally a sport of the noblemen who, for centuries, even employed professional kite men to make and fly the kites. Today, during the summer season, March, April, and May, the City Committee of Kite Flying in Bangkok sponsors contests near the palace grounds each Sunday. Prizes are given to winners.

It is a common procedure in Thai games to exact a penalty of a loser and sometimes to inflict mild physical punishment on the loser.

MIDDLE EAST

When the size of this area is compared with that of the Far East and India, the variety of the games is most pleasing. The age-old civilizations in the Middle East, the climatic conditions, and the close association of the area with the western world, which promotes play as a way of life among its children, may account in part for the supply of games available. With the exception of the games from Gaza, the written accounts of such games have been in play and games literature for many years, scattered as they may have been.

One noticeable characteristic in many active games of the Middle East is the "horse and rider" pattern that calls for one player to mount and sit on the hips of his partner. Variations of "Bat and Ball" (long and short sticks) games are popular. The children of these lands are ingenious in their play-ideas and in use of simple play equipment.

The contribution of the Middle East to the worldwide collection of games is second to none. This part of the world is timeless in cultural overlays, is important in intersocietal significance, and is a potent factor in global considerations today.

GAZA, IRAN, AND ISRAEL

The games from Gaza have come first hand from a source close to the children in the country. Nevertheless, the patterns of play closely resemble games played in other countries to the extent that they may be said to have been influenced by the Far East, the English, and even the North American versions of play.

Iran, formerly known as Persia, has considered chess, even for young children, a favorite game for centuries. Other games enjoyed by the Iranian children through the years consist of large group activity that provides for development of skill in fundamental body movements. Again sticks, pebbles, and rocks provide play equipment. The youth of Iran are showing increasing interest in basketball, soccer, tennis, wrestling, and skiing as part of their sports program.

The play patterns of Israel, the country called Palestine until the twentieth century, show interesting similarities to the games of the younger areas of the world. The games, "One Old Cat," "Hide and Seek," "Cat and Rat," and surprising variations of "Blind Man's Buff" are found among the games from this age-old country. Clever applications of old "characters" in new relay forms make up much of the play of the children of Israel today.

LEBANON, SYRIA, AND TURKEY

The children of Lebanon employ the simple and available sticks for athletic playing materials; participate in guessing games; and have a ball-bouncing game that demands more than the average skill in ball handling. The bride-theme games of Lebanon and Gaza reach back into ancient marriage customs that no doubt caused many a groom-to-be to ask, "What Is My Bride Like?"

The young girls of Syria have few games. They spend their time about the house, helping their mothers bake, clean and grind corn, gather wood, and care for the smaller children. The boys participate in games of tag and shinny. A favorite activity with them is to display their skill in throwing with slings. The slings, made of goat hair, are part of a shepherd boy's equipment in guarding his flock.

Wrestling and dancing contests are considered the two national sports of Turkey. Before entering the ring the wrestlers often cover their bodies with olive oil. Of course this prevents the use of any particular technique but provides much amusement to the spectators, who witness the "catch-as-catch-can" method of wrestling.

Many traditional games that are universally popular with children are known to the Turkish boy and girl. "Follow the Leader," "Hot Hand" or "Tag," "Prisoners' Base," "Leapfrog," "Swat Tag," and "Blind Man's Buff" are among the active games enjoyed by the children.

SOUTHERN ASIA

INDIA

Games from India are rich in opportunity for development of skill in chasing, running, dodging, catching, striking, and throwing. An outstanding characteristic of the games besides the athletic skills is that they call for the holding of the breath as a game skill. A few games of this type are included in the collection, although many similar ones are popular in India.

The children of India decide who will start a game, or be *It* by reciting a rhyme something like the English "Eeny, meeny, miny, mo." Their words, when translated in English, read, "One, two, three and a half, what do I care for horses' eggs?"

The universally popular game of badminton was originated in India by Englishmen who were serving military duty there.

GAMES AND SPORTS—FAR EAST

Eastern and Southeastern Area

CHINA

Buying a Lock

Ages: 5–8

Players: 6–12; single group; line

Place: gymnasium; out-of-doors

Supplies: not any

Activity—(stunt): grasping, stooping

Appeal: repetition

The players stand in a long line side by side, holding hands. Each player claps his neighbor's hand so that the palm of his own right hand faces backward and the palm of his own left hand faces forward. The players repeat a verse, while one end of the line starts to pass under the raised arms of the two players at the opposite end. Instead of passing entirely under the arch the next to the last player makes a three-quarter turn so that his own left arm is across his chest and is joined with his neighbor's right that rests on his right shoulder. When all players have thus turned, they should be in a single file one behind the other. The players unwind in reverse order, still repeating the verse that is similar to this one:

Away we go to buy a lock;
What kind of a lock shall we choose?
Let's try a broom handle, and if that does not work,
Then a poker we'll buy and use.
Should neither the broom nor the poker work
We'll break it then with a stone.

Call the Chickens Home

Ages: 5–8

Players: 10 to 20; group-and-one; informal

Place: gymnasium; out-of-doors

Supplies: handkerchief

Activity—hunting: chasing, dodging, running

Appeal: competition, dramatization

One player is blindfolded and stands apart from the others who are the *chickens*. The *chickens* run by and touch the *blind one* after he says, "Tsoo, Tsoo—come and find your mother." If a *chicken* is caught by the *blind one*, the two exchange characters in the game.

Cat and Mouse

Ages: 5–8
Players: 20 or more; group-and-two; circle
Place: gymnasium; out-of-doors
Supplies: not any

Activity—hunting: chasing, dodging, running, stooping
Appeal: dramatization, problem solving, repetition

One player is selected to be the *cat*, another is the *mouse*, and the others form a circle around the *mouse* while the *cat* is outside. The circle revolves as the *cat* asks, "What time is it?" The players reply, "Oh, it's about nine." The *cat* then says, "What's the mouse doing?" The players answer, "Getting ready to dine." Suddenly the circle stops revolving and the chase begins. The *cat* rushes in the circle while the *mouse* runs out under the joined hands of the players. The *cat* must follow exactly the path chosen by the *mouse*. The players favor the *mouse* by raising their hands, but they try to hinder the *cat* by lowering or raising their hands. When the *mouse* is caught the *cat* eats his victim; the *cat* becomes the *mouse* and a new *cat* is chosen. The eating process affords much amusement, and as every *cat* uses his own imagination during the procedure, it is not practical to describe it. One of the characteristics of a good *cat* is to be a good eater.

When the Chinese childen play this game, the two runners often wear masks, such as tigers, mice, cats, bears, dogs, or other animals. The same game is played in many countries. It is especially popular with children in North America where the drama of the game is less evident.

Catching Fishes in the Dark

Ages: 5–8
Players: 8 to 20; group-and-one; informal
Place: gymnasium; out-of-doors
Supplies: handkerchief

Activity—hunting: chasing, dodging, guessing, running
Appeal: dramatization, problem solving

One player is blindfolded. The other players secretly name themselves some *fish*. The *fishes* run past the *blindman*, trying to tag him without being caught. If one is caught, the *blindman* guesses the player's name. If he guesses correctly, the *fish* becomes the *blindman;* otherwise the *fish* is free.

Chinese Chicken

Ages: 9–12
Players: 10 to 20; two-group; line
Place: gymnasium; out-of-doors
Supplies: shoes, wooden blocks, or
   beanbags

Activity—pastime: balancing,
   hopping, kicking, stooping
Appeal: competition, skill

Shoes are placed in straight rows of five to fifteen each with a space of 10 inches between. The players may divide into groups of four to ten as for a relay, each group facing a row of shoes.

The game may be competitive between groups but was originally for one large group. The first player is a *lame chicken* and hops over each shoe until the end of the row of shoes is reached. He takes his *lame* (lifted) foot and kicks the last shoe away, then picks it up and carries it back over the same route. The play continues, the *lame chicken* hopping on the opposite foot, until he fails. If he touches any shoe except the last one, he must give his place to another. The player with the most shoes at the close of the game is the winner.

Small blocks of wood, sticks, or beanbags are often used instead of shoes. The boys and girls of the United States would make a competitive activity of this game, most likely playing it as an organized relay.

Chinese Wall

Ages: 9–11
Players: 20 or more; transition
Place: gymnasium; playground
Supplies: not any

Activity—hunting: chasing, dodging, running
Appeal: competition, problem
   solving, skill

The *wall* is marked off by two lines 10 feet apart and across the center of the playing area. Parallel to the *wall* are drawn two goal lines 15 to 20 feet from the wall. One player is chosen to be the *guard* and he stands on the wall. The other players stand behind a chosen goal line. When the *guard* calls "Start!" the players must run to the opposite goal. The *guard* may not step over the wall line, but any players caught on the 10-foot wall become *guards* and help catch when the next call is given. The last player caught is the *guard* for the next game.

Cow's Eye

Ages: 9–12
Players: 10 or more; group-and-one;
   circle
Place: gymnasium; out-of-doors

Supplies: not any
Activity—hunting: a counting-out
   game
Appeal: dramatization, rhythm

This is a popular game with young Chinese girls. The players sit in a circle with their feet to the center. One player counts out the rhyme and the one whose feet are touched on the word "out" gets out of the circle. The rhyme is repeated until all except one are eliminated. This player then removes her shoes and receives a slap on the bottom of her feet from the other players.

The rhyme is:

> One, two, three, and an old cow's eye,
> When a cow's eye's blind she'll surely die.
> A piece of skin and a melon too,
> If you have money I'll sell to you,
> But if you're without,
> I'll put you out.

Dove and Hawk

Ages: 5–8
Players: any number; groups of three; informal
Place: gymnasium; out-of-doors
Supplies: not any

Activity—hunting: chasing, dodging, running
Appeal: competition, dramatization, skill

The children are arranged in groups of three. The center person represents a Chinese child playing with her pet dove. The child on the left represents a *hawk* and the child on the right a *dove*. The center player makes a motion as if to pitch the *dove* into the air. The *dove* flies away and then the *hawk* is released to try to catch the *dove*.

The center player claps her hands, which is a signal to call her *dove* home. If the *dove* has not been caught by this time she returns home safely, but if the *hawk* catches her, neither of them returns and another *dove* and *hawk* are chosen. The game is also called "Let Out the Doves."

Eating the Fish's Tail

Ages: 5–8
Players: 8–12; single-group; line
Place: gymnasium; out-of-doors
Supplies: not any

Activity—hunting: dodging, grasping, running
Appeal: dramatization, problem solving

The *fish* is formed by the children joining hands one behind the other. The front players represent the *head* and the last ones, the *tail* of the *fish*. The *head* tries to catch and eat the *tail* while the *tail* tries to escape. The longer the *fish*, the greater the excitement. If a player breaks his hold he must drop out of line.

Fishing by Hand

Ages: 9–12
Players: 20 or more; group-and-one;
  informal
Place: gymnasium; out-of-doors
Supplies: handkerchief

Activity—hunting: clapping, dodging, grasping, running
Appeal: dramatization, problem
  solving

Boundary lines are established. One player, the *fisherman* is blind-folded and extends his right arm forward with the palm upward. The other players, the *fish*, tease him and try to tag his palm with their index finger. Should the *fisherman* close his hand upon the finger of a *fish*, that *fish* is caught. The two players exchange places provided the *fisherman* guesses the name of the *fish* before remov-ing the blindfold.

During the game, the *fisherman* may say, "The tide is high," whereupon the *fish* move as if playing in deep water. Should the call, "The tide is low," be given, the *fish* move about carefully as if playing in shallow water.

Flower Pot

Ages: 9–12
Players: 3; single-group
Place: gymnasium; out-of-doors;
  schoolroom

Supplies: not any
Activity—stunt: grasping, high
  stepping
Appeal: problem solving, skill

The players are numbered 1, 2, and 3. All stand in a triangle formation, each with his left hand joining the right hand of another and crossed in the center. Then, by putting arms of Nos. 1 and 2 back of No. 3, No. 3 may step into the center and by stepping over two arms he is on the opposite side. The players again cross hands in the center and the other players go through in the same way. By repeating the rhyme below the players add merriment to the stunt:

> You first cross over, and then cross back,
> And step in the well as you cross the track,
> And then there is something else you do,
> Oh, yes, you make a flower pot too.

Forcing the City Gates

Ages: 9–12
Players: 20 or more; two-group; line
Place: gymnasium; out-of-doors
Supplies: not any

Activity—hunting: grasping, pulling, pushing
Appeal: competition, problem solving

The players form two lines facing each other. The members of each line hold hands very tightly. A player from one line runs out and tries to press through the opponents' line. If he succeeds the two whose hands he parted join his side. If he fails then he must join the opposing team. The lines alternate turns until all the players are on one side. The game is called "Red Rover" in England and in the United States of America.

Fox and Geese

Ages: 9–12
Players: 10 to 20; group-and-one; line
Place: gymnasium; out-of-doors
Supplies: not any

Activity—hunting: chasing, dodging, grasping
Appeal: dramatization, problem solving, repetition

The following dialogue is sometimes used to open a game:

The Fox taunts the geese by saying, "Geese, geese, gannio."
To which the Geese scornfully reply, "Fox, fox, fannio."
The Fox asks, "How many geese have you today?"
The Gander replies, "More than you can catch and carry away!"

One player is chosen to be the *fox* and stands in front of all other players. The other players stand one behind the other with their hands on the shoulders of the one next in front. All are in single file behind the *gander*. The *fox* may tag only the last *goose* in the line or the last five or ten if the line is very long. The *gander* can dodge or spread his arms or use any means he wishes to keep the *fox* from the last *goose*. All the line should cooperate with the *gander* to protect the last one. If the *fox* tags the last *goose* (or the last five or ten), that *goose* takes the place of the *fox*, the *fox* becomes the *gander*, and the game continues.

The game is played in almost all lands, under names of various animals. In England it is known as "Fox Tail." North American boys and girls play "Fox and Geese" and similar games called "Hill Dill" and "Tom Tiddler's Ground." Tom Tiddler was originally Tom t'Idler and is mentioned in one of Dickens's Christmas stories.

Foxes and Cabbages

Ages: 9–12
Players: 20 to 30; three-group; informal
Place: out-of-doors
Supplies: sticks

Activity—hunting: chasing, dodging, hiding, running
Appeal: dramatization, problem solving

A home base is established. The players are divided into three groups, *foxes, gardeners,* and *cabbages.* The *cabbages* are planted in rows by the *gardeners* who then hide for about ten minutes. While the *gardeners* are hiding, the *foxes* enter the garden, each *fox* carrying a pole across his shoulder. He seizes a *cabbage* and forces him to grasp the pole, then the two hurry out of sight and hide from the *gardeners*. When the ten minutes have passed the *gardeners* seek the *foxes* and *cabbages*. Should a *gardener* find a *fox* and *cabbage*, he chases them back to the home base, trying to catch a *cabbage*. If he succeeds before the *fox* and *cabbage* return to the base, the *fox* must pay a forfeit to the *gardener;* otherwise the *fox* receives a forfeit from the *gardener*.

Fruit Sale

Ages: 5–8	Supplies: not any
Players: 20 or more; group-and-two; line	Activity—hunting: grasping, stooping, swinging
Place: gymnasium; out-of-doors	Appeal: dramatization, repetition

One player is the *market man* and another the *buyer*. The rest of the players are *fruit*. They clasp their hands under their knees. The *buyer* asks, "Have you any fruit for sale?" The *market man* replies, "Plenty, today. Would you like some?" The *buyer* places his clasped hands on their hands. Some he says are too hard, too soft, too sour, etc., until at last he finds one to suit him. (If any *fruit* has laughed he must pay a forfeit to be redeemed at the close of the game.) The *market man* and *buyer* then take the selected fruit by the arms. If he does not release the grasp after swinging forward and backward three times, he is bought. The game is continued until all *fruit* are bought.

This is an old game that is popular in many countries. In Italy it is called "Chicken Market," while in England it is known as "Sale of Honey Pots."

Going to Town

Ages: 9–12	Supplies: not any
Players: any number; couples	Activity—stunt: lifting, pulling, pushing
Place: gymnasium; out-of-doors; schoolroom	Appeal: skill

Two girls stand back to back with arms locked and lift each other upon their backs as they repeat the following verse:

> Up you go, down you see,
> Here's a turnip for you and me;
> Here's a pitcher, we'll go to town;
> Oh, what a pity, we've fallen down.

The two then sit down and engage in this dialogue:

> 'What do you see in the heavens bright?'
> 'I see the moon and the stars at night.'
> 'What do you see in the earth, pray, tell?'
> 'I see in the earth a deep, deep well.'

'What do you see in the well, my dear?'
'I see a frog and his voice I hear.'
'What is he saying there on the rock?'
'Get up, get up, ke'rh Kua, ke'rh Kua.'

Then they try to get up without touching their hands to the ground. The boys play a similar game called "Pounding Rice."

Hawk Catching Young Chicks

Ages: 9–12
Players: 20 or more; group-and-one; file
Place: gymnasium; out-of-doors
Supplies: not any

Activity—hunting: chasing, dodging, grasping
Appeal: dramatization, problem solving

The player is the *hawk* and stands in front of a larger player, the *hen*. Behind the *hen* are all the *chicks* who grasp each other around the waist and seek protection from the *hawk*. The *chicks* dodge from one side to the other. When the *hawk* has caught all the *chicks*, the game is ended.

The same game is played by English children under the name "Hen and Chickens." It is known to the children of the Philippine Islands by the name *Lawin at Sisim* or "Hawk and Chicken."

Jumping Fox

Ages: 9–12
Players: 6–12; single-group; informal
Place: out-of-doors

Supplies: one long stick for each player; one short stick
Activity—athletic: striking
Appeal: competition, problem solving, skill

A small stick, called the *fox,* is sharpened at each end. A longer stick is necessary for each player. A two-foot square is drawn to represent a *city*. The *fox* is placed about three yards from the *city*. The object of the game is to make the *fox* jump into the *city* by striking it with the long stick. The number of strikes allowed each player varies with the distance from the *city* at which the *fox* is placed. The player who gets the *fox* in the *city* with the smallest number of strokes wins.

Kick the Marbles

Ages: 9–12
Players: two; informal
Place: out-of-doors
Supplies: two marbles

Activity—pastime: kicking
Appeal: competition, problem solving

This game is most successfully played when there are only two participants. Each player has two large marbles about one and

China—Jumping Fox.

one-half inch in diameter. One of the players places both his marbles on the ground, points to one of them, and tells the other player to "kick this marble north." He may say "kick this marble east, or west, or south." The player must do as he is told, and he has but one chance. If he is successful in kicking the marble in the proper direction, he has won, and because he has won, he has another chance. This time he tries to kick so that the first marble will touch the other. If he does this, he scores two points. Each boy tries to leave the marbles in as difficult a position as possible for the next player. However, if the marbles are left in too difficult a position for the opponent to kick, he may refuse to play and the first player is forced by a rule of the game to kick from his own difficult position. Herein lies a peculiarity that we do not find among the other games of the world. It pays tribute to the Chinese golden rule of "Do not unto others what you would not have them do unto you."

Kick the Shoes

Ages: 9–12
Supplies: shoes
Players: 10 or more; single-group; informal
Activity—pastime: kicking, running
Place: gymnasium; playground
Appeal: competition

The players take off their shoes and place them in a pile and then kick them. Each player grabs all the shoes he can. Sometimes the winner is the one with his own shoes, the greatest number of shoes, or a pair that fits him. This is a good test of the players' alertness.

Knocking the Stick

Ages: 9–12
Supplies: sticks 10–15 inches long
Players: 10 or more; single-group; line
Activity—pastime: throwing
Place: out-of-doors
Appeal: competition, problem solving

Two lines eight feet apart are drawn on the ground. A stick 10 to 15 inches long is placed upon one line. The object of the game is to throw another stick at the one placed on the line and knock it over the opposite line. The player knocking the stick over first wins.

Man Wheel

Ages: teen
Supplies: not any
Players: 5; single-group
Activity—stunt: grasping, turning
Place: gymnasium; playground
Appeal: rhythm, skill

One large player stands in the middle, two middle-sized players stand to each side of him, one facing north and one facing south. Two smaller players stand beside them. Each of the two outer players clutch the others' girdles and the center player grasps the free hand of the outside players. In this way all are bound together. As the wheel begins to turn the smaller players are gradually lifted from the ground; as the wheel turns faster, the smaller players are swung out to a somewhat horizontal plane. A similar stunt, using four players, and called "Windmill," is popular in the United States.

Meat or Vegetables

Ages: 9–12
Supplies: shoes
Players: 10 or more; single-group; informal
Activity—pastime: hopping, throwing
Place: gymnasium; out-of-doors
Appeal: competition, skill

The players hold their two shoes in front of them and drop them. The way they fall determines what meat or vegetable they are.

If the shoes fall upright and at right angles, the toe of one shoe resting on the toe of the other, they form a *dark alley*. A *big black tiger* is formed if the shoes fall upside down. If both shoes fall on the side, they form *double beans*. *Honest officials* result if both shoes fall in the upright position. *Dog's legs* are formed if one shoe falls bottom up and the other in upright position. The player whose shoes first form a *dark alley* throws a pebble through the *alley* (under the toe of the top shoe) three times. If he succeeds, he picks up the shoes and throws them back of him and then hops to each shoe and kicks it over a drawn line. After kicking the shoes over the line, the player hops over the line himself. If he fails in any step, he must give another player a chance.

Pitch Brickbats

Ages: 9–12
Players: 6 or 8; single-group; line
Place: out-of-doors

Supplies: brickbats
Activity—pastime: pitching
Appeal: competition

Two lines, fifteen feet apart, are drawn. One is the *goal line*, the other the *starting line*. The players stand on the *starting line* and throw a brickbat to the *goal line*. After the throwing the action centers around two players. The player whose brick falls farthest from the *goal line* places his brick on that line. The player whose brick falls nearest the *goal line* stands on the *starting line* and throws at his opponent's brick, the object being to knock the brick from the line. If he fails, the opponent in turn tries to displace his brick. If he succeeds, he pitches his brick near that of his opponent. He hops over and kicks his brick so as to knock over his opponent's brick.

He then carries his own brick in different positions as follows:

Walking—with brick on head, each shoulder, back, and chest
Hopping—brick in the groin and in the bend of the knee
Shuffling—brick between his legs

Each time he must drop his brick on that of his opponent and knock it over. At last he marks a square 18 inches around the brick, then hops back and forth over it and the square ten times. Thus he becomes the winner.

Protecting Eggs

Ages: 9–12
Players: 10 or more; group-and-one; informal
Place: gymnasium; out-of-doors

Supplies: stones
Activity—hunting: dodging, reaching
Appeal: problem solving, skill

One player is chosen to be the *protector,* and the others are *robbers.* Near the feet of the *protector* there lie stones or *eggs* for each *robber.* The *robbers* try to steal the *eggs.* If the *protector* tags a *robber* with hands or feet, the two exchange places. If the *robbers* get away untouched with all the *eggs,* the *protector* must serve again.

Riding the Bicycle

Ages: 9–12
Players: any number; groups of three; line
Place: gymnasium; out-of-doors

Supplies: not any
Activity—stunt: walking
Appeal: competition, skill

Two players stand side by side, joining the inside hands, while the third player stands astride the joined hands of the first two. The groups form in a line. At signal, all groups start walking toward a designated goal line. The group that crosses the line first is the winner.

NOTE: A first attempt at this stunt might be tried with the third player sitting on the joined hands of the first two. Confidence grows as coordination and balance progress.

Seek for Gold

Ages: 9–12
Players: 10 or more; single-group; informal
Place: gymnasium; schoolroom; out-of-doors

Supplies: pebbles
Activity—pastime: stooping
Appeal: competition, skill

Pebbles are scattered on the ground. The players squat around them and one player draws her finger between two of the pebbles, trying to snap one against the other. If he fails, another player takes his turn. In the end the winner is the player with the most pebbles.

This game is sometimes called "Bandit's Gold."

Select Fruit

Ages: 9–12
Players: 20 or more; two-group; line
Place: gymnasium; out-of-doors

Supplies: not any
Activity—hunting: stooping
Appeal: problem solving

Two *captains* are selected and the players are divided into two equal teams. Each team stoops in a line 20 feet apart. Each player chooses the name of some kind of fruit. One from a line is blindfolded by his *captain* and a boy from the opposite side steals quietly over and touches the blindfolded one and then returns to his place.

The blindfolded one is allowed to see and is told to go over and select the *fruit* (boy) that touched him. He may identify the guilty one by noting a change in position, by trying to get him to smile, or by any means he sees fit to bring about a confession. If he guesses correctly he wins the guilty one on his side; otherwise, the blindfolded one must remain with his opponents. Play is continued until all players are on one side.

Shuttlecock

Ages: teen
Players: 2 or more; single-group; circle
Place: gymnasium; out-of-doors

Supplies: shuttlecocks
Activity—pastime: kicking, striking
Appeal: competition, problem solving

Two or more players form a ring. One player tosses or kicks the shuttlecock up into the air so that it will fall near another player. If it is impossible for the player receiving the shuttlecock to kick it, he may hit it with his hand and in this way send it to another player or he may strike it so that it may be easily hit by the foot. The foot strokes consist of hitting the shuttlecock with the flat soles of the shoes. The most common stroke is made with the inner side of the sole of the right shoe.

The object of the game is to keep the shuttlecock in the air as long as possible. The shuttlecock is made of several layers of skin instead of cork as we usually see it. The layers are of paper or shark's skin. Three duck's feathers are used.

Skin the Snake

Ages: 9–12
Players: 4–20; single-group; file
Place: gymnasium; out-of-doors
Supplies: not any

Activity—stunt: grasping, turning, walking
Appeal: repetition, rhythm, skill

The boys stand in a file one behind the other and bend forward, each putting his right hand between his legs and grasping the left hand of the boy behind him. All start walking backward. The one in the rear lies down and the others begin to stride over, each lying down as he backs over with his neighbor's head between his legs and so on. The last one down gets up first and walks forward astride the line and raises each one up after him until all are in their original position.

Striking the Stick

Ages: teen
Players: 4–8; single-group; informal
Place: out-of-doors
Supplies: wooden blocks, sticks 10–15 inches long

Activity—athletic: striking, throwing
Appeal: competition, problem solving, skill

A square of 5 or 6 feet is drawn on the ground. One player stands in the center with a stick 10 to 15 inches long in his hand. Another places a block on the square in a place that he thinks will be hardest to hit by the *striker* in the center. The latter may turn on one foot and place the other outside the square in order to secure an advantageous position. He then aims and throws his stick at the block to knock it out of the square. If he fails, the player who placed the block becomes the *striker* and another places the block for him. If he succeeds, he is allowed three trials at striking the block in the following manner: He first strikes the block perpendicularly, trying to cause it to bounce two or three feet in the air, and then drives it as far as possible, as one would hit a baseball. If he drives it the distance agreed upon, which may be anywhere from 20 to 500 feet, he has won the game.

Throw Cash

Ages: 9–12
Players: 4 or more; single-group; informal
Place: playground
Supplies: cash pieces
Activity—pastime: throwing
Appeal: competition, skill

Each player takes a coin from his pocket and presses it against a wall. He releases the coin and lets it roll down the side of a wall and as far away as possible. The player whose coin is farthest away picks it up and throws it at the wall with force to make it bound back a great distance. Each player does this in turn. The one whose coin bounds farthest back places his foot on the spot where his coin was and pitches it at the coins of the other players. He keeps all the cash that he hits. If he misses, all who have cash begin the game anew. The winner is the player who takes up the most cash.

Tiger Trap

Ages: 9–12
Players: 20 to 30; group-and-two; line
Place: gymnasium; out-of-doors
Supplies: not any
Activity—hunting: chasing, dodging, running
Appeal: competition, problem solving

One player is chosen to be the *tiger*, another is the *kid*. The others stand in two lines facing each other at about 12 feet apart. The *kid* stands at one end of the lines and bleats. The *tiger* goes in between the lines at the other end and the two lines rush toward each other to form a circle and close the trap. The *tiger* tries hard to break out while the *kid* runs about outside bleating very loudly. If he fails to break out another player becomes the *tiger*. If the *tiger* breaks out and catches the *kid* then he becomes the *kid* and another *tiger* **is** chosen.

Turning the Mill

Ages: 9–12
Players: any number; couples
Place: schoolroom; gymnasium;
   out-of-doors

Supplies: not any
Activity—stunt: grasping, turning
Appeal: dramatization, rhythm,
   repetition

Two players take hold of each other's hands and turn halfway around by putting one arm up over their heads and bringing their left or right sides together, facing in opposite directions. The players then stand still and engage in the following conversation:

> Where has the big dog gone?
> Gone to the city.
> Where has the little dog gone?
> Run away.

Then, as they begin to turn, they repeat:

> The big dog's gone to the city;
> The little dog's run away;
> The egg has fallen and broken,
> And the oil's leaked out, they say.
> But you be a roller
> And hull with power,
> And I'll be a millstone
> And grind the flour.

The same activity is played by children of the United States under the name "Wring Out the Dish Rag."

Water Sprite

Ages: 9–12
Players: 20 or more; two-group-
   and-one; line
Place: gymnasium; out-of-doors
Supplies: not any

Activity—hunting: chasing, dodg-
   ing, running
Appeal: competition, problem solv-
   ing, skill

The players stand facing each other in two lines 20 to 30 feet apart. The space between them is the river. The *Water Sprite* stands in the middle of the river. A player on one side signals to a player on the other side to change places with him. As they run across the river the *Water Sprite* tries to catch one of them. If a player is caught he must be the *Water Sprite*.

This game is sometimes played under the name "Hill Dill." It also resembles "Pom Pom Pullaway."

Wolf

Ages: 9–12
Players: 20 or more; group-and-
  one; informal
Place: out-of-doors
Supplies: not any

Activity—hunting: chasing, dodging, jumping, running
Appeal: dramatization, problem
  solving, skill

The *sheep* choose a pen and blind their eyes. The *wolf*, a chosen player, hides while the leader of the *sheep* counts to 100. When the *sheep* look for the *wolf* they must stay behind their leader who says, as soon as she sees the *wolf:*

> All my sheep
> Gather in a heap;
> For I spy the woolly, woolly wolf!

The *wolf* must make a jump at the *sheep* before he chases them to their pen. The *wolf* may not jump or chase them before he hears the word *wolf*. They may tantalize the *wolf* by saying, "Woolly, woolly—cat!" or any other animal and at last say *wolf*. If the *wolf* tags a *sheep* before it reaches the pen, that *sheep* joins the *wolf*. If there are several *wolves* the leader of the *sheep* may stop as soon as she sees any one of them. When one *wolf* runs, all the *wolves* may run. If the *wolf* spies the *sheep* before they spy him, he may call, "Stand your ground, three feet!" The *sheep* must then take three steps toward him before he jumps and chases them to the pen. If the *wolf* can reach the pen before any *sheep*, he may do so and catch the *sheep* as they enter. One *sheep* may try to gain the attention of the *wolf* while all the other *sheep* run in. When all *sheep* have been caught, the game is over.

This game is also played by Japanese children.

JAPAN

A Counting-Out Game

Ages: 9–12
Players: any number; couples; in-
  formal
Place: home; schoolroom

Supplies: not any
Activity—pastime: counting-out
Appeal: dramatization

This game consists of a series of rapid arm movements by two players. The movements are interpreted as follows: The hand doubled into a fist represents stone, with two fingers extended it is scissors, and outstretched it represents paper. The two players start the game simultaneously as each doubles her right fist and moves the arm rhythmically from the elbow three times saying *"jan-kem-po."* At the end of the third move the hands are lowered and brought forward in the position each player has chosen; the hand doubled into a fist, the hand with two fingers outstretched, or the hand outstretched. Each position is interpreted in the following manner: Stone breaks scissors, and therefore stone conquers scissors; scissors cut paper and therefore conquer paper; paper wraps (and so conquers) stone. The outcome is pure chance. The winner is determined by the conquering player of two out of three rounds. In cases of a tie, another round is played.

Bamboo Pole Race

Ages: teen
Players: 12–24; two-group; line
Place: gymnasium; out-of-doors

Supplies: bamboo poles
Activity—relay: running
Appeal: competition, skill

The teams are in threes along parallel lines 40 feet apart. Midway between these lines two flags or standards are placed about 50 feet long. At a given signal one team goes to the right around one pole, then around the opposite pole and back to the next group, which goes through the same route and so on until all have gone. The opposing team starts at the same time and continues in like manner except they first circle the flag to the left, then the one to the right. The team whose groups complete the race first is the winner.

Big Lantern Game

Ages: 9–12
Players: 20 or more; single-group; circle
Place: home; schoolroom

Supplies: not any
Activity—pastime: moving arms quickly
Appeal: rhythm, skill

The players sit on the floor in circle formation. The game is started by one player putting her hands close together and saying, "Big lantern." The next player says, "Little lantern," and puts her hands far apart, and so on the game continues. It is very amusing when quickly played. Interest in the game may be increased by having players drop out of the game when they fail to follow the leader, the winner being the last player to move her hands incorrectly.

Bounce the Ball

Ages: 9–12
Players: 3–6; single-group; informal
Place: gymnasium; out-of-doors

Supplies: playground ball
Activity—stunt: bouncing a ball; striking, turning
Appeal: rhythm, skill

The player bounces a ball upon the ground with considerable force and immediately turns around to face the ball in time to slap it on each rebound for five consecutive times.

Crab Race

Ages: 9–12

Players: 10–30; single-group or file; 4–6 in a file

Place: gymnasium; out-of-doors

Supplies: not any

Activity—relay: walking on hands and feet

Appeal: competition, skill

If there are many players the race may be run in relays. If not, the winner will be the individual first reaching a marked goal or the individual who laughs least. The players race by propping themselves upon their feet and hands with their backs to the ground and walking in the position backward like crabs.

Cup Game

Ages: teen

Players: 12 or more; group-and-two; line

Place: home; schoolroom

Supplies: ten cups

Activity—pastime: guessing

Appeal: problem solving

This game is suited to an indoor party. Ten teacups are placed upside down in a row upon the floor. Each cup is numbered, though the numbering is known only to the *leader* and *It*. The group is seated on the floor and faces the cups. *It* leaves the room and the group is asked by the leader to choose the number of any one of the cups. The *leader* assures the group that *It* is so intelligent that he can readily tell the number of the cup chosen by the group when the *leader* points to it with a stick.

After the group has chosen the number of a cup, *It* returns to the room. The *leader* then points to several of the cups. If the cup selected is numbered eight, the *leader* points to that cup the eighth time. The secret of the game is that the number of the cup and the number of the pointing must be the same. The lower the number chosen by the group the easier it is for *leader* to keep it in mind. *It* may impress the group by saying "no" very emphatically until the chosen cup is touched. The group may be led to confusion by the *leader* if he skips about in pointing to the cups and by modifying or increasing the tone of his voice. He must be careful, however, not to let numbers match until the correct cup is touched.

Hana, Hana, Hana, Kuchi

Ages: 9–12

Players: 10–20; group-and-one; circle

Place: home; schoolroom

Supplies: not any

Activity—pastime: follow the leader

Appeal: repetition, rhythm, skill

The players sit in a circle and imitate the *leader*, who taps her nose and says, "*hana, hana, hana, kuchi*," meaning, "nose, nose, nose, mouth." The *leader* continues to repeat the words but quickly taps some other feature, as for example her eye. The players must do what the *leader* says and not what she does. If a player fails to do this, she must be the *leader* or allow her cheek to be daubed with flour and water. The names of the features are: *me*—eye; *mimi*—ear; *hana*—nose; *kuchi*—mouth.

Harbors of Truth

Ages: 5–8
Players: 20 or more; group-and-one; informal
Place: gymnasium

Supplies: not any
Activity—hunting: chasing, dodging, running
Appeal: dramatization, skill

The children of Japan play that the corners of a room or space are *harbors* of truth. The runner is a *demon*. The *demon* taunts the players and tries to catch them as they exchange harbors. In the United States a game much the same is known as "Puss Wants a Corner," which is also similar to "Oh! Neighbor! Have You Fire?," a Lebanese game.

House Cleaning Relay

Ages: teen
Players: 12–32; 6–8 in a heat; line
Place: out-of-doors

Supplies: smock, broom, dust cloth, towel, large pail, small pail
Activity—relay: running
Appeal: competition, skill

A smock, a towel, a large pail, a broom, a small pail, and a dust cloth are needed for this relay. The articles are placed about 15 yards apart. At a given signal the first heat runs to the smock and puts it on, to the towel and wraps it around her head, to the large pail and carries it in her hand, to the broom, to the small pail, to the dust cloth, and on to the finish line. The winner of first place gets a white flag with one red stripe, the second a flag with two stripes, and the third a flag with three stripes. Each winner receives the same award, but the judges keep a record of the winner of each heat. Before the second heat is run the articles are replaced.

Japanese Tag

Ages: 9–12
Players: 10 to 30; group-and-one; informal
Place: gymnasium; out-of-doors

Supplies: not any
Activity—hunting: chasing, dodging, running
Appeal: competition, skill

It, a chosen player, calls out a position, such as "Touch left hand," "Put right elbow on left knee," or "Touch both hands to ground," then quickly calls "Halt!" Each player must stay in the position he was in at the time of the command. Only the players who hold the position required in the first command are privileged to chase *It*. The player who catches him becomes *It*. The game is also called "Statue."

Konkonchiki

Ages: 9–12
Players: 3; single-group; circle
Place: home; schoolroom
Supplies: bowl, cloth

Activity—pastime: quick arm
  movements
Appeal: problem solving, skill

This is a popular game with Japanese girls. Three players sit on the floor. Two of them grasp the ends of a piece of ribbon or cloth in which a loose knot has been tied while the third girl tries to move a small bowl filled with water through the knot. At the same time the others draw the knot and try to catch her hand.

Japan—Konkonchiki.

Kumi

Ages: teen	Supplies: cards
Players: 4–8; four-group; informal	Activity—pastime: memory
Place: home; schoolroom	Appeal: competition, problem

The players are divided into four groups. Each group takes a place at a square table and receives 25 cards, which are placed on the table, face up. The last line of a familiar song or poem is written on the face of each card. A *leader* reads the first line of one of the songs. If a group having the card with the last line finds it first, the card is placed in the center of the table and it is no longer in play. If any player in the other group sees the card first, his group gives two cards to the slow group for failure to recognize its *last lines.* The group that is out of cards first wins. The losing players, if boys, are painted with black or white rings on their foreheads; if girls, a wisp of straw is put in the hair.

It is easy to read Japanese scrip upside down and the players may remain in their seats to read their opponents' lines. The game is sometimes called "Alphabet" because each proverb begins with a letter of the Japanese alphabet. This is an old game of Japan and may have been the source of a number of card games today.

One-Legged Race

Ages: 9–12	Supplies: rope
Players: 10 to 30; 4–6 in a file; file	Activity—relay: jumping, running
Place: gymnasium; out-of-doors	Appeal: competition, skill

The first player of each team is given a colored band. At a signal this player carries the band to a flag set about 45 feet directly in front of him. When he reaches the flag he ties both his ankles with the band and returns by hopping to the starting line. The winner is the team finishing first, all players having run in relay formation.

Otadama

Ages: teen	Supplies: bags of rice two inches square
Players: any number; individual; informal	Activity—pastime: juggling
Place: gymnasium; home; out-of-doors	Appeal: skill

This activity is a favorite with young Japanese girls. The game is started by the players first juggling two bags in the air. After each one has played with two bags for some time, then three bags are kept going. Later four bags are used and sometimes the players are so skilled that they can keep five or six bags going at the same time.

The bags are about two inches square and are made of bits of bright colored silk half filled with rice. A small bell is sewed to the bag and the tinkling of the bells adds to the game.

Piggyback Race

Ages: junior and teen (boys)
Players: 12 or more; couples; files
Place: gymnasium; out-of-doors

Supplies: not any
Activity—relay: balance, strength
Appeal: competition, skill

Partners stand in a double line behind the starting line. On a given signal one player jumps on the back of his partner and is carried to a goal line 20 feet away. When they reach the goal line, they exchange positions and return. The first pair returning to the starting line is the winner. This may be used in relay formation with several couples in each file or in circle formations.

Satsuma Ken

Ages: 5–8
Players: 6 or more; group-and-one; informal
Place: home; schoolroom

Supplies: not any
Activity—pastime: guessing
Appeal: problem solving

The players stretch out the fingers of one or both hands simultaneously. The one who is *It* is blindfolded and tries to guess the total number of extended fingers, calling the number aloud.

Shadow Tag

Ages: 5–8
Players: any number; couples; informal
Place: out-of-doors

Supplies: not any
Activity—hunting: chasing, dodging, running
Appeal: problem solving, skill

At a given signal each couple starts its individual chase. Each partner tries to step on his partner's shadow and at the same time tries to keep the partner from stepping on his shadow.

Spoon Ball Carry Relay

Ages: teen
Players: 8–24; 4–6 in a file
Place: gymnasium; out-of-doors

Supplies: tennis ball, wooden spoons
Activity—relay: balance, running
Appeal: competition; skill

A large wooden spoon containing an old tennis ball is given to the first member of each team. At a given signal they run with the spoon and ball to a certain point and back and hand the spoon and ball to the next player. The team finishing first wins. If the ball drops from the spoon, it must be scooped up with the spoon and otherwise never touched. This type of relay is often played in the United States, the contestants carrying an egg or a potato in the spoon.

Warship Race

Ages: 9–12
Players: unlimited; 2–3 warships in
    a file; file
Place: gymnasium; playground

Supplies: one 6-foot rope per three
    people
Activity—relay: running
Appeal: competition, skill

A *warship* consists of three players whose left ankles are tied to-gether so that they are an arm's length apart. The *leader* carries the flag. The *warships* stand in single-file relay formation. At a given signal the first warship of each fleet runs to a mark and back to touch the next *warship*, who have already tied their feet. The win-ner is the fleet that finishes first.

Weaving Relay

Ages: teen
Players: 20 or more: 4–6 on each
    file; file
Place: gymnasium; out-of-doors

Supplies: cloth for each file
Activity—relay: passing, running
Appeal: competition, skill

The players form two lines 10 feet apart, facing each other and with players in each line an arm's distance apart. At the signal the first player with a cloth in hand turns to face his team. He then weaves in and out to the end of the line and runs straight back to his place. He passes the cloth to the second player in line who be-gins weaving in and out to the end of the line and runs back to face the first player in line and then weaves around him and back to place. The cloth is passed to the next player who weaves to the end of the line. He runs straight to first player, and weaves around him and the second player back to his place. The cloth is passed from one to another until all have woven in and out and back to position. The team finishing first wins.

KOREA

Chase and Catch

Ages: teen
Players: 20 or more; two-group; file
Place: gymnasium; out-of-doors

Supplies: not any
Activity—relay: chasing, running
Appeal: competition, skill

The players are divided into two teams numbered *A-1, A-2, A-3* and *B-1, B-2,* and *B-3* and so on according to the number of par-ticipants on each team. Team members line up behind each other, several feet apart and parallel to the members of the opposing team. It is important that each player know the corresponding number on the opposite team; also the member ahead of him on his own team.

A-1 starts to run to his right and toward the end of his line. After a count of three, *B-1* chases him. After a count of three, *A-2* chases

B-1; B-2 chases *A-2; A-3* chases *B-2; B-3* chases *A-3;* and accordingly until all players have had their turn. The object is for each player to run around to the end of his own line to safety. If a player is caught he is "put in jail." Play continues until all of one team are captured or have returned to their line safely. A catch is good only upon the person numerically ahead of the runner. This is a favorite game of Korean girls.

Clamshell Combat

Ages: 9–12   Supplies: shells
Players: any number; couples;   Activity—pastime: throwing
  informal   Appeal: competition, skill
Place: out-of-doors

The players pair off for a combat, each player having an equal number of clamshells. To decide which of each pair shall have first play both players drop a shell from a height of three feet. The one whose shell falls with the hollow down shall have first play. If they tie at first they shall continue to drop shells until one wins. The unsuccessful player puts a shell on the ground and the other tries to break it by throwing his shells at it. If he succeeds another shell must be put down by the opposing player. If the thrower fails to hit the shell or breaks his own, the opposite player takes his turn at his opponent's shell. The winner is the player who has an unbroken shell the longest. When there are many players there may be opposing teams and players throw as their captains call for them.

Coin Game

Ages: 9–12   Supplies: coins
Players: 2 or more; individual; in-   Activity—pastime: pitching
  formal   Appeal: competition, skill
Place: out-of-doors

A circle about two feet in diameter is drawn on the ground. Several coins of equal value are placed in the circle. Each player takes turns at tossing a stone into the circle, trying to hit a coin. The player who hits the most coins is the winner, though the players do not keep the money.

Ha-Taik-Kyen-Ha-Ki

Ages: teen (boys)   Supplies: not any
Players: couples; informal   Activity—pastime: balance
Place: gymnasium; playground   Appeal: competition, skill

This is a form of wrestling enjoyed by young boys and men. The players stand facing each other with their feet apart. The object of the game is to kick the opponent's feet from under him. Each player may move backward one step.

Hunting the Ring

Ages: 9–12
Players: 4–6; single-group; informal
Place: out-of-doors

Supplies: large ring, sand heap, sticks
Activity—pastime: no skill
Appeal: chance

The game consists of probing a heap of sand with long slender sticks in search of a hidden ring. The winner is the player who successfully gets the ring on his stick and lifts it out of the sand.

Mek-Kong

Ages: 9–12
Players: 2 or more; individual; informal
Place: home; schoolroom

Supplies: small nuts or stones
Activity—pastime: guessing
Appeal: chance

One player takes several small nuts or stones in one hand and then extends forward both hands closed. The other players guess which hand holds the nuts. If one guesses the correct number, the nuts are given to him; if he fails, he must give to the other player the number of nuts that he (the other player) had in his hand. Each player must have a supply of nuts. The game is similar to "Hull Gull" and "Old Gray Horse."

Nobleman's Play

Ages: teen (boys)
Players: four; single-group; line
Place: gymnasium; playground

Supplies: not any
Activity—stunts: balance
Appeal: dramatization, skill

One player bends forward and a second player mounts and rides on his back. Two other players each take one hand of the first player and lead him forward.

Peggity

Ages: 9–12
Players: 4 or more; group-and-one; informal
Place: out-of-doors

Supplies: sticks
Activity—pastime: alertness, catching
Appeal: problem solving, skill

A peg or small stick is placed on the ground. Another stick that is longer and curved at one end is grasped by a player who slips the curved end of the stick under the peg. With a quick upward jerk he tosses the peg into the air. The other players try to catch the peg before it falls to the ground. The players take turns in tossing the peg. The player who catches the peg the greatest number of times wins.

Pickle Jar

Ages: 5–8
Players: 8 or more; group-and-one; rows
Place: gymnasium; out-of-doors

Supplies: not any
Activity—hunting: chasing, holding
Appeal: dramatization, strength

The players are divided into groups of four or more. Each group chooses one of its players to be its *leader*. The other players squat on the ground in a row, each holding the shoulders or around the waist of the player in front. These players are the pickle jars. The *leader* stands in front of a jar and calls, "Ready," and then runs around to the last player or jar and tries to steal her. The others shout, "Hold on tight, don't let her steal you!" When the *leader* succeeds in stealing the jar that player becomes the *leader* and the original *leader* becomes the first jar in his group.

Kimchi, pronounced KIM-chee, is a favorite pickle of all Koreans. It is made of so many different food combinations that it actually seems to be many different kinds of food. It is stored in large earthen jars. Often when the jars are washed and set in the sun to make them fresh and clean for the new *kimchi,* the young children spend much of their time playing hide-and-seek around the long rows of jars.

Pomul Pa-at-ki (POH-mul PAH-at-kee)

Ages: teen
Players: 20 or more; two-group; see diagram
Place: out-of-doors
Supplies: boxes, treasure

Activity—hunting: chasing, running
Appeal: competition, problem solving, skill

Pomul Pa-at-ki means Treasure Steal. It is an active out-of-doors game and a great favorite of Korean school children.

A large court is marked on the ground as in the diagram. Players are divided into two teams. Each team is then divided equally; one half, *guards,* the other half, *runners,* who try to steal the treasure from the opposing team's court.

Team "A's" *runners* leave by "A's" door and run around the court and outside to try to enter "B's" door. At the same time the "B" *runners* leave at "B's" door and on to the outside to try to enter "A's" door. The *guards,* who must remain inside the court, try to prevent their opponents from entering. If anyone is pushed over a line, he is *dead* and must leave the game. The object is for each

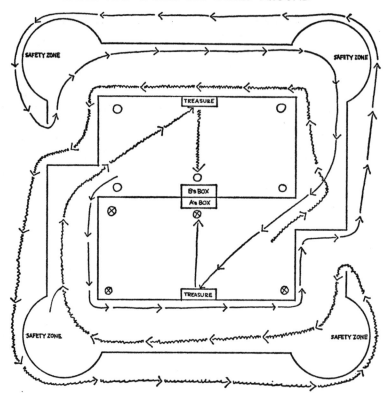

Korea—Diagram of Court for Pomul Pa-at-ki.

team to steal the opponents' treasure and get it to its own box in the center before the opposing team accomplishes the same for its side.

Shuttlecock

Ages: teen

Players: 10 or more; two group; informal

Place: out-of-doors

Supplies: cork, feathers

Activity—pastime: picking, running

Appeal: competition, skill

Korean boys are especially fond of this game. They use a round piece of cork in which a crown of feathers is stuck. The players are divided into two teams trying to score by kicking the cork over a designated goal line of its opponents. The play starts from the center of the playing area. The size of the area and the length of the playing time or set score depends on the number and age of the players. One point is scored with each kick of the cork over the goal line.

Teeter Totter

Ages: 9–12
Players: 2 or 3; single group; on board
Place: out-of-doors

Supplies: wide board, 6 feet long
Activity—pastime: balance, jumping
Appeal: skill

This unusual game, sometimes called "Jumping Board" and again known as "Nul," is played in Korea only by girls. It is said to have developed from the custom of the young betrothed never being allowed to see each other before the wedding. The girls designed a pattern of play that often gave them a chance to peek over the garden wall. As they were tossed high into the air, sometimes as high as six feet, they hoped to catch a glimpse of their husbands-to-be. Doubtless the boy, by way of previous arrangement, eagerly awaited a glimpse of his future wife. The activity of the game will appeal to and challenge boys in the western world since the mores are different from those of many areas of the east.

Today the game of "Teeter Totter" is still popular although the custom that prompted its origin is not as prevalent as it was in the past. A wide board about six feet long is placed over a sandbag, a low mound of dirt, or a bundle of rice sacks. One girl stands on each end of the board. Upon agreement one of the girls begins the play by jumping high into the air and coming down on the board thus causing the other girl to bounce in the air and make a high jump. This continues until one player is bounced off the board or calls for time-out. For safety of young girls, who follow their sisters in play sometimes, a rope is stretched and tied across the courtyard so that the players may grasp the rope as they jump high into the air. At times a third player sits on the center of the board.

Tok-Ki-Chi-Ki (TOK-ke-CHI-ke)

Ages: 9–12
Players: 4–10; two-group; informal
Place: out-of-doors
Supplies: sticks

Activity—athletic: batting, catching
Appeal: competition, skill

A stick about 5 inches long, rounded with ends tapering into dull points, called a "Tok-ki," is needed. Another stick about 18 inches long (no special shape) is the bat.

A circle approximately 6 feet in diameter is drawn on the ground. (The Koreans make a "human compass" by having one child as the center and by holding hands with enough children to make the correct size circle, they go around and the outside child draws the circle with a stick.)

Inside the large circle a small circle about 2 feet in diameter is drawn. One hundred points are allotted the inside circle, and 50 points for the outside.

"A" player stands behind a line about 5 feet from the circle and faces away from the circle toward "B" player, who is about 10 to 12 feet away. "A" tosses the Tok-ki into the air and hits it as far as possible with the longer stick. If "B" catches the Tok-ki, he gets 100 points. Play then starts over with "B" hitting the stick. If he cannot catch it, "B" picks it up and tosses it toward the circle. If it lands in the circle, he gets the number of points allotted.

If the Tok-ki lands outside the circle, "A" then takes his long stick and, without picking up the Tok-ki, hits it on its pointed end and knocks it as far as possible. He does this three times. "A" and "B" then guess how many feet from the circle. The one guessing the nearest figure gets that many points. If the Tok-ki lands 50 feet from the circle, and 49 feet was guessed, he does not get the points. If it lands at 51 feet, he does get the points.

Teams then exchange sides and "B" hits the Tok-ki. This continues until one side has 1,000 points or any number of points decided on before the start of the game.

Yoot

Ages: all
Players: 2 to 6; individual; informal
Place: home; schoolroom

Supplies: playing board, beans
Activity—pastime; no skill
Appeal: chance

This game of chance is probably one of the most popular games in Korea. It is played by both young and old with equal enthusiasm.

A playing board of wood or heavy paper is needed and must be marked as shown in the diagram. The circle should be large enough for players to move their men freely on the surface.

The Korean players use a specially made set of four sticks with one flat and one rounded side. These are gaily painted in interesting designs. Four large beans may be used. They must be split in half and have a rounded side and a flat one. Other beans (whole) may be used as *men* by the players.

The first player tosses the four beans near the board and the progress of play is as follows:

1. All beans landing flat side up, the player moves *five spaces*.
2. All beans round side up, player moves *four spaces* and takes another turn.

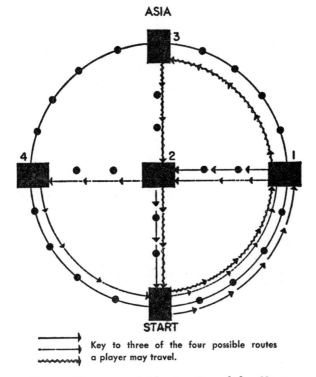

Key to three of the four possible routes
a player may travel.

Korea—Diagram of Playing Board for Yoot.

3. Three beans round side up, player moves *three spaces.*
4. Two beans round side up, player moves *two spaces.*
5. One bean round side up, player moves *one space.*

The play is counterclockwise. The first player puts his *man* on *Start.* If a player lands on *Station One,* he is allowed to take the short route back to *Start* by making a left turn. If on the next play he lands on *Station Two,* he again may turn left and proceed toward *Start.* If from *Station One* he has more than enough moves to reach *Station Two,* he may not turn, but must proceed in a straight line across the circle. If the player passes *Station One,* he proceeds to *Station Three.* If he lands on *Station Three,* he can go directly toward *Start* by way of *Station Two.* If he passes *Station Three,* he goes on toward *Station Four* and thence to *Start.* The first player to return to *Start* wins.

If a player lands on a space already occupied by another player, the first player must return to *Start* and begin anew, regardless of where he is at the time he is overtaken. This makes the game most interesting.

THE PHILIPPINES

Cat and Dog

Ages: 9–12

Players: 20 or more; group-and-one; circle

Place: gymnasium; out-of-doors

Supplies: shoes, sticks, or stones

Activity—hunting: chasing, dodging, running

Appeal: skill

The players are called *cats* and stand outside a large circle line that is drawn on the ground. In the center of the circle there are several shoes, sticks, or stones that represent *bones*. One player is chosen to be the *dog* and sits near the *bones* in order to guard them. The *cats* tantalize the *dog* and try to steal the *bones* without being caught. The *dog* must remain seated; otherwise, he may touch the *cats* with his hands or his feet. If the *dog* touches a *cat* the two players exchange places. If the *cats* successfully take all the *bones* without being caught, the same *dog* starts the new game.

Coconut Shell Hitting

Ages: teen

Players: 4–10; two-group; lines

Place: gymnasium; out-of-doors

Supplies: coconut shells

Activity—pastime: bending, hopping, kicking, throwing

Appeal: competition, skill

The players are in two equal groups. The groups stand on lines that are parallel and about 12 yards apart. Each player holds a coconut shell. The toss of a coconut shell decides which group is to have the first round.

The game consists of six rounds that are played as follows:

Round I. Rolling. The players of *Group A*—that is, the group losing the toss—arrange their shells on one line. The other players, *Group B*, stand on the opposite line with their shells between their feet and with their backs to their opponents. At a given signal, each member of *Group B*, moving backward, kicks and rolls his shell toward the shells belonging to *Group A*. The group wins the round and proceeds with Round II even though only one player makes a successful kick. If no one succeeds in hitting the shells of *Group A*, *Group B* places its shells on their line, and *Group A* plays the first round. Two trials are allowed each player.

Round II. Kicking. The players hold their shells between their legs and stand on the line. At a signal, they hop forward, drop the shell to the ground, and kick it toward the shells of *Group A*. The second trial calls for half of the players to hold the shells between their ankles while the other members of the group kick them to hit *Group A's* shells. Again the group wins if only one player successfully hits an opponent's shell. Should the group lose the round, *Group A* has its turn at kicking. Each group is allowed two trials.

Round III. Hopping. This time the players throw their shells to hit the shells belonging to *Group A.* They quickly follow the throw by hopping forward to recover the shells that fall upside-down. They may ask *Group A* to space their shells about 1 yard apart. Then the members of *Group B* hop back to their line and have a second trial. One player may win the round for his group if he makes a successful throw. Two trials are allowed.

Round IV. Bending. The players of *Group B* stand on the line with their backs to the shells of *Group A. Group B* players bend their bodies backward and throw their shells to hit the opponents' shells. In this round each player, being allowed two trials, must make a successful throw. Should a player fail to hit a shell, he may ask a member of his group to throw for him.

Round V. Throwing. The members of *Group B* face the shells belonging to *Group A.* The skill for this round consists in throwing to hit the shells of *Group A* in one trial only. If a player fails, a member of his group must try for him, since every shell belonging to *Group B* must hit an opponent's shell.

Round VI. Heads-Up. Each player throws his head well back, runs a certain distance, and throws at the shells of *Group A.* Again only one trial is allowed.

Each group continues the game from the point where it failed since it is not allowed to begin a new round until this one is completed. The losing group must pay a forfeit by dancing to the music made by the winning group striking their coconut shells together.

Coin Game

Ages: 9–12
Players: 4–10; single-group; informal
Place: home; schoolroom

Supplies: basin, coins, flour
Activity—pastime: bobbing
Appeal: competition, skill

A basin is filled with flour into which are dropped several coins. The players, usually very young boys, try to find and pick up the coins with their mouths. This is a popular game at Hallowe'en parties in the United States.

Digging Peanuts

Ages: 5–8
Players: 20 or more; group-and-two; informal
Place: gymnasium; out-of-doors

Supplies: not any
Activity—hunting: dodging, running
Appeal: dramatization, skill

A player, usually a girl, is chosen to be *leader*. She sits off in one corner holding up her extended right hand. The other players quickly touch her palm and withdraw fingers immediately as they call out "Piko, piko, piko" (PE-co), which means "peck." The *leader*, pretending not to notice them, suddenly snatches the hand of one of the players. The child whose hand is caught becomes the *dog*.

The other players run away from the *leader* and *dog* and sit down on the ground. As they scratch into the ground as if digging for peanuts they call out, "Mani, mani" (ma-NE), which is a small bean. The *leader* calls back:

"How do you sell your peanuts?"
One of the players answers: "Twenty centavos for one ganta."
The *leader* replies: "Too dear; will you sell it for fifteen centavos?"
The player answers: "No."
Leader says: "If you do not let me have one ganta for fifteen centavos, I will send my dog to chase and bite you." [*Ganta* is a special measure.]

The *dog* then chases the players. The player caught by the *dog* is taken to the *leader* and becomes the *dog* in the new game. If the *dog* fails to catch anyone he remains the *dog* and a new game is started. The Filipino children call the game "Piko-piko." The Chinese game "Cow's Tail" is similar.

Football

Ages: teen (boys)
Players: 10–20; two-group; informal
Place: out-of-doors
Supplies: rattan ball, 4 inches in diameter or football

Activity—athletic: batting, jumping, running, tossing
Appeal: competition, skill

This is a very old form of football and quite unlike the American sport by the same name. The players are divided into two teams who group themselves informally within a playing area about 50 × 75 feet. The game is started by tossing the ball between two opposing players who bat the ball high into the air. The object of the game is to keep the ball in the air by batting or hitting it with any part of the body.

It is suggested for inexperienced players that one point be counted against the team that allows the ball to touch the ground. A time limit may be agreed upon before play begins. The team having the fewest marks against it at the close of the game wins.

Get a Corner

Ages: 9–12
Players: 5, 7, or 9; group-and-one; rectangle
Place: gymnasium, out-of-doors

Supplies: not any
Activity—hunting: running
Appeal: problem solving, skill

A rectangle is drawn on the ground or floor. For five players a small base is marked in each corner; for seven players an additional base may be added to the center of each side line; or for nine players an additional base may be added to the center of the two side and end lines.

The *tagger* stands in the center of the rectangle. All other players stay on bases drawn on the boundaries and corners of the rectangle. As the players try to exchange places by running across from base to base the *tagger* tries to rush to a vacant base. If the *tagger* is successful in securing a base, the odd player now becomes the *tagger* for the new game. Players may try to confuse the *tagger* by rushing from their bases and turning back immediately.

The game is also called "*Vende, Vende Candela*," which is translated "Sell, Sell a Light." The implication of this name is that it may have its origin in the early custom of candle-merchants selling their wares throughout the villages.

Grab the Husk

Ages: 9–12
Players: 1–20; two-group; lines
Place: gymnasium; out-of-doors
Supplies: coconut husk

Activity—hunting: dodging, running
Appeal: competition, skill

The players are divided into two equal groups. The groups stand on *goal lines* that are parallel and about 15 feet apart. Midway between and parallel with the *goal lines* there is a *neutral line*. In the center of the *neutral line* there is a hole in which a coconut *husk* is placed. The object of the game is for the players to capture the *husk* and carry it across their *goal line*.

At a given signal, the players of both lines rush to the hole and try to grab the *husk*. As soon as a player succeeds in getting the *husk*, he runs toward his *goal*. His opponents chase him and try to capture the *husk*; at the same time his own men try to protect him. The group that carries the *husk* over the *goal line* wins the game.

A variation of this game is to have the players in circle formation. The husk is placed in a hole in the center of the circle. The effort is individual; each player tries to capture the husk and carry it outside the circle. The first player to do so wins the game.

Greased-Pole Contest

Ages: teen (boys)
Players: any number; individual; informal
Place: out-of-doors

Supplies: bag coins, pole
Activity—contest: climbing
Appeal: skill

The Palo (PA-lo) or pole is a bamboo, placed firmly in the ground and held there with a guy rope of rattan. A bag of coin hangs from the top of the pole, being attached there by means of a stick thrust through the top of the bamboo. The smooth pole is greased and offers great difficulties for the contestants who take turns in trying to climb to the top. One person is allowed only one trial at climbing. If he loses his grip and slides down, he must give way to another.

Jump over Thorns

Ages: 9–12
Players: 6–8; two-group; informal
Place: gymnasium; out-of-doors
Supplies: not any

Activity—pastime: jumping, running
Appeal: competition, skill

The players are called *children* and are divided into two equal groups. Each group chooses a *mother,* supposedly the best high jumper among them. By tossing a shoe or slipper it is decided by the *mothers* which group will be on base, the other group will have the first jump. The object of the stunt is for the players to make a clear jump over a span of hands placed upright.

Two members of the group on base sit facing each other and place the soles of the right feet together. One by one the members of the opposing group jump over the feet. After the last player jumps, one of the seated players places one hand above the toes of the two extended right feet. The hand is spread into a wide span. All opposing players jump over the hand. After the last player jumps another hand is added and so on until a span consists of all hands of the groups on base. If the jumpers make a clear jump over the extended span of hands, the same group must remain on base. If a *child* touches the hands while jumping, he is at fault and the *mother* will jump for him. Should the *mother* fail, the two groups exchange places, and the game starts again.

Laughing Game

Ages: 9–12
Players: group-and-one; informal
Place: gymnasium; home; out-of-doors; schoolroom

Supplies: any object with two distinct sides, such as a coin, post card, or slipper
Activity—pastime: laughing
Appeal: merriment

The players sit informally about the room after having selected a two-sided object to use in the game. They come to an agreement as to which side of the object will serve to start or stop them from laughing. One player flips the coin and calls *heads.* If *heads* falls uppermost and if that is the signal to laugh, all players laugh as heartily as possible. The coin is flipped again. If it falls *tails*, the players must suddenly stop laughing, otherwise they continue to laugh.

The requirements for laughing may be varied by the players having agreed that the laughter will last as long as the object is in the air. As soon as it falls the laughter must stop.

Pase En Orden!

Ages: 5–8
Players: 10–30; transition; informal
Place: playground

Supplies: not any
Activity—pastime: running
Appeal: dramatization, repetition

One player is selected to be the *mother*. The rest of the players group around her and listen for her command, "Pass in order." Instead of obeying the *mother*, the players reply, "Steep convent." The *mother* answers this by saying, "All of you rush and bring me leaves from the banana tree!" Whereupon the players run to seek the leaves or whatever object the *mother* desires.

The player who returns first with the leaf presents it to the *mother* and remains with her. The game continues until all players have presented a gift to the *mother* and remain with her.

Prisoner

Ages: 9–12
Players: 5–12; group-and-one; line
Place: gymnasium; out-of-doors
Supplies: can, stones

Activity—hunting: dodging, running, throwing
Appeal: skill

This game is similar to the Greek game, "Duck on the Rock," from which many games originated.

Each player is given a large *stone*. One player, the *prisoner*, guards an empty can that is placed seven or nine yards from a *throwing line*. All other players line up on the *throwing line* and take turns throwing at the empty can. If one succeeds in knocking the can down, the *prisoner* replaces the can and tries to tag the player who must recover his stone and get back over the *throwing line*.

Each player is required to recover his own stone after each throw. When a player is tagged by the *prisoner* while recovering his *stone* within the *throwing line*, he becomes the *prisoner* for the new game.

Tag Game

Ages: 9–12
Players: 20 or more; group-and-one; circle
Place: gymnasium; out-of-doors

Supplies: not any
Activity—hunting: chasing, dodging, running
Appeal: problem solving, skill

Several circles of varying size are drawn on the floor. The circles may touch each other or they may be scattered far apart. One circle is larger than the others and serves as the resting place for the runners.

One player is selected to be the *chaser* and remains outside the circles; the other players are *runners* and must stay within the circles. The *runners* may go as a large group from one circle to another or they may separate and run in small units, occupying all circles. As the *runners* go from one circle to another, the *chaser* tries to tag them. He must not run across or step inside any circle. When a *runner* is caught he and the *chaser* exchange places.

Throw the Handkerchief

Ages: 9–12

Players: any number; groups of three; informal

Place: gymnasium; home; out-of-doors

Supplies: handkerchief

Activity—hunting: balance, catching, throwing

Appeal: skill

The players are in groups of three, scattered informally about the playing area. Two players in each group are the *carriers*. They form a saddle with their hands and the third player sits upon their hands and arms. A *seated player* starts the game by throwing a handkerchief to another *seated player*. Should a player fail to catch the handkerchief, he and one of his carriers exchange places.

Whisper to the Priest

Ages: 9–12

Players: 20 or more; two-group-one; lines

Place: gymnasium; out-of-doors

Supplies: not any

Activity—hunting: balancing, mounting, running

Appeal: competition, problem solving

The players are divided into two equal groups. They stand in parallel lines about ten feet apart, facing each other. Each group selects a *captain* who stands at the head of his line. About 15 feet from the *captains*, another player, the *priest*, takes his position. The *captain* of Group I runs to the *priest* and whispers the name of one of the players of Group II and goes back to his place in the line. Then the *priest* commands, "Approach!" Any one of the players of Group II goes to him. If this player happens to be the same one whose name was whispered by the *captain* of Group I, the *priest* calls out, "Bung!" whereupon the player falls to the ground and remains near the *priest* as a prisoner.

If the player is not the one whose name was given, he is privileged to advance and in turn whispers to the *priest* the name of one of the players of Group I. The game continues until one group loses by all of its players becoming *prisoners*. Each member of the losing group fulfills an agreement to carry an opponent upon his back for a short ride.

Wrestling Match

Ages: teen (boys)   Supplies: not any
Players: couple; informal   Activity—contest: wrestling
Place: gymnasium; out-of-doors   Appeal: competition, skill

Each wrestler gets a firm grip on the other by grasping the waistband of his opponent. After an instant of pause each contestant pulls and tugs at the other, trying to lift him from his feet and throw him to the ground. Tripping is not allowed. A bout may be decided by a single fall or by the best two out of three.

GAMES AND SPORTS—FAR EAST

Southwestern Area

BURMA

Frog Dance

Ages: 9–12   Activity—contest: kicking, clap-
Players: 20 or more; single-group;   ping, stooping
    circle   Appeal: competition, repetition,
Place: gymnasium; out-of-doors   skill
Supplies: not any

The players squat on their haunches in a circle. They hop rhythmically, throwing out first one foot and then the other. As each player hops, he claps his hands in front of his knees, then behind his back, trying to make the other players fall over. When a player falls he is eliminated. The one who dances longest without falling is the winner.

Loo K'Bah Zee

Ages: 9–12   Activity—hunting: dodging, reach-
Players: group-and-two; line   ing, running
Place: gymnasium; out-of-doors   Appeal: problem solving, skill
Supplies: small ball or stone

All the players stand in a line with their hands behind them. A player is chosen to be *It*. He passes a ball or similar object down behind the line, pretending to place it in the hands of one after another. As soon as the object is left in the hands of a player this player must run out of the line. Those on either side must then try to catch him without leaving their places. If the runner escapes he takes *It's* place and *It* joins the line. If the runner is caught, *It* must pass the stone again, and so on.

Straddle the Pole Catch

Ages: 9–12
Players: 10 to 30; group-and-one; line
Place: gymnasium; playground
Supplies: pole

Activity—hunting: dodging, jumping, reaching, running
Appeal: competition, problem solving, skill

All the players but one stand astride a pole that is laid on the ground. The odd player is called the *catcher* and he stands in front of the group. He may never cross the pole but always must go around it. To escape the *catcher* the other players may cross the pole any time and even run away. The *catcher* may not tag a player unless they are on the same side of the pole. When a player is caught, the *catcher* may lead him by the ear to the pole or ride his back to the pole. The one caught then becomes the *catcher* and the game continues.

Zum Zum

Ages: 9–12
Players: 4; couple; line
Place: gymnasium; out-of-doors
Supplies: not any

Activity—hunting: chasing, dodging, holding breath, running
Appeal: competition, repetition, rhythm, skill

The players are arranged so that there are two on each side of a drawn line. One player advances across the line saying zee-e-e-e-e, etc., or dee-e-e-e, etc. He continues as long as he can on one breath and at the same time tries to tag an opponent. When he gets out of breath his opponents may tag him before he crosses the line. The winning side is determined by whichever succeeds in tagging. If both fail to tag, then the opponent crosses the line with the same sound. The sides alternate until someone is tagged. The two winners mount the opponents' backs like men on horses. The *riders* roll a handkerchief into a ball and throw to one another. If the handkerchief should fall to the ground, the *rider* or *horse* who first picks it up starts the new game. The Thai game, "Theeeeeeeeeeee," is similar to this one.

INDONESIA

Fiber Game

Ages: 9–12
Players: any number; couples; informal
Place: gymnasium; home; out-of-doors

Supplies: fibers from banana leaf
Activity—pastime: striking
Appeal: competition, skill, problem solving

The players make a toy from a banana leaf by pulling long fibers from the midrib of the leaf. Enough of the rib is left attached to provide a handle to the strand. Each player selects what he judges to be the strongest fiber. He then inserts the unattached end into a small piece of bamboo in which there is a slight split. The closing of the cleft in the bamboo insures its firm attachment to the fiber. The object of the game is to cut the opponent's strand by wrapping one's own around it or, by quick jerking movements, to snatch the handle from the opponent's grasp.

Foot Game

Ages: intermediate
Players: 2 or more; individual; informal
Place: out-of-doors

Supplies: stones
Activity—contest: balance, strength
Appeal: competition, skill

Each player selects a smooth stone, one around which he can curl his toes. A starting line is drawn and one by one the players throw the stones from between the toes, as far as possible. The losing player has to carry the winning player piggyback from the starting line to the winning stone.

Jumping Bars

Ages: teen
Players: groups of three; informal
Place: gymnasium; out-of-doors

Supplies: 2 wooden bars or wands
Activity—stunt: jumping
Appeal: problem solving, skill

Played in the manner of the Dyaks, a tribe of central Kalimantan, this is a somewhat dangerous pastime. Two ironwood poles about eight feet long are placed parallel on the ground and about five feet apart. Facing one another and each standing behind the center of one of the poles, two players grasp opposite ends of two forty-pound ironwood bars. These bars are about six feet long and are resting on the eight-foot poles. The men crouch on the ground and rap the bars together quickly while a third player dances up and down, placing one or both feet between the bars. The object of the game is to catch the player between the bars. It may readily be seen that the weight of the bars is so heavy that serious injury may result if an ankle is caught with force between the pieces of wood. Children may adapt the game to more civil usage by substituting canes or ropes for the bars.

Ring and Loose Rope Game

Ages: 9–12
Players: 10–30; group-and-one; circle
Place: gymnasium; out-of-doors

Supplies: ring, string
Activity—hunting: alertness, strength
Appeal: competition, skill

The players sit in a circle, each holding a string with both hands. The string must be a little longer than needed to go around the inside of the circle. A finger-ring is placed on the string that is tied with a small knot, allowing the ring to pass over the knot. *It* stands in the center as the players pass the ring from one person to another and chant "Wora-wora tjintjin" (pronounced war-ra and chin-chin) going faster and faster. *It* may call "Stop" only after the chant has been said four times, then he gets one guess as to the whereabouts of the ring. If he is correct, he changes places with the player caught with the ring. If he is incorrect, he has to give the player he "misjudged" a piggyback ride around the circle and then be *It* again. This is a common penalty with the children of Indonesia. This game is popular in East Java.

Three Sticks

Ages: 9–12
Players: 3 or more; individual; informal
Place: out-of-doors

Supplies: bamboo or light wood
Activity—athletic: striking
Appeal: competition, skill

The children of East Java enjoy this game and use bamboo. Two pieces are about 8 inches long, the third is 6 inches long. Sticks of light wood may be used.

One of the long sticks is placed on the ground on the starting line. The shorter stick is balanced on the long one, making a cross. The player chosen to start the game takes the remaining long stick and hits one end of the short stick. As soon as the short stick flies into the air, the player hits it away and as many times as possible before it lands.

Score is counted in this manner as measured from the starting line to the short stick and counting the number of hits:

1 hit: measure distance from starting line to short stick, counting each length of long stick as a score of one.

Indonesia—Three Sticks.

2 hits: measure distance from starting line to short stick, using each
length of short stick as a score of one.

3 hits: same as 2.

4 hits: use short stick as a measure and double the score.

A player is out and goes to the field if he fails to hit the short
stick while it is in the air.

MALAYA

Finding the Leader

Ages: 9–12

Players: 10 or more; group-and-
one; informal

Place: gymnasium; out-of-doors

Supplies: not any

Activity—pastime; alertness,
observation

Appeal: problem solution

A player chosen to be *It* is sent away from the group. Another
player is selected to be the *leader*. *It* is recalled and finds the group
doing some action such as clapping, stamping, or waving the hands.

The group follows the *leader* who may change the action at any time. *It* tries to find the *leader*. If he fails after three guesses he must pay a forfeit and another player becomes *It*. If he guesses the right player the latter becomes *It*.

A variation of the game is to have the group clap softly when *It* is near the *leader* and loudly when he is far away.

Kick Basket

Ages: junior and teen

Players: 6; two-group; informal

Place: gymnasium; out-of-doors

Supplies: badminton net, soccer ball

Activity—athletic: kicking, throwing

Appeal: competition, skill

The playing court is 22 by 44 feet. A badminton net and a soccer ball are needed. Malayan children use an open work cane ball or basket about 6 inches in diameter. The height of the net is 2 inches higher than the height of the tallest player.

Players in teams of three take their places on opposite sides of the net. Two *A* and *B* players from each team take their positions close to the net. The third player, *C*, on each team stands about a third of the way down the court in the center.

Player *A* throws the ball to *C* who kicks it over the net. The opposing team is allowed three kicks on its own side as it tries to return the ball. If the team fails in its attempt, a point is given the other team which again starts the play. If the serving team fails to get the ball over the net, service goes to the opponents. The game consists of 15 points.

Main Bailing Tin

Ages: 9–12

Players: 10 or more; group-and-two; informal

Place: out-of-doors

Supplies: pebbles, tin can

Activity—hunting: chasing, hiding, running

Appeal: problem solving, skill

One player, chosen to be *It*, stands in a circle with another, the *leader*, who holds a tin can in his hands. The can contains a few pebbles that are securely enclosed. Play starts as the *leader* throws the can as far as possible. *It* has to retrieve the can and replace it in the circle; meanwhile all other players hide. After the can has been replaced, the hiding players try to get back to the circle and kick the can out before being caught by *It*. If a player is caught he is placed in the circle; if he is successful, he may rescue any player who has been caught. The game continues until all hidden players have been caught. The same pattern of play is popular in the United States of America under the names "Kick the Can" or "Tin Can."

Toi

Ages: teen
Players: 12 or more; group-and-3; diagram
Place: out-of-doors

Supplies: not any
Activity—hunting: chasing, dodging, running
Appeal: problem solving, skill

Diagram I shows the position of the guards and the players at the start of the game. Diagram II shows how it is possible for guards to cover players when they are caught between the lines.

The *guards*, A and B, take their positions on their lines, which are about 40 feet long and 30 feet apart. Each *guard* is responsible for

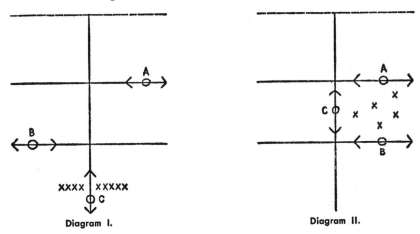

Diagram I.   Diagram II.

Malaya—Toi.

his line. He may move along the line in either direction but never away from it. *Guard* C stands at one end of his line, which intersects *lines* A and B. The players who stand in a line near *guard* C start the game by touching C's hand and then running forward. They try to cross *lines* A and B, to go to the area where *line* C ends, and to return to their starting place without being caught by any of the *guards*. If a player succeeds, he shouts, "Toi!" The game starts anew with the players starting from where they are when "Toi" is called. If the players are bunched together between lines it is possible for the *guards* to corner them when play does start anew.

THAILAND

Circle Tackraw

Ages: teen
Players: 10 or more; group-and-one; circle
Place: gymnasium; out-of-doors

Supplies: badminton net, soccer ball
Activity—athletic: kicking, passing
Appeal: competition, skill

The Thai boys use a ball woven of wicker. A soccer ball may be substituted. The players, in circle formation, start the game by tossing the ball to one player who either heads or kicks it to another player. The ball is kept in play as long as possible by using any part of the body except the hands. This is an excellent game for practicing soccer skills of short passes.

A variation of the game is to play it by badminton rules, using a badminton net, soccer ball, and limiting the players to two or three on a team. This variation suggests "Kick Basket" that is popular with the children of Malaya.

Master and Slaves

Ages: teen
Players: 10–20; two-group; informal
Place: out-of-doors

Supplies: soccer ball
Activity—athletic: dodging, pitching, throwing
Appeal: competition, skill

Players are divided into equal teams and group themselves informally as they face each other. One player is chosen to start the play by tossing a ball in an underhand pitch to any member of the opposite team. If the player catches the ball he must try with an overhand throw to hit a member of the opposing team. If he succeeds in hitting the opponent, who tries to dodge the ball, the opponent becomes a *slave* and must drop out of the game. When one team has lost all members, the winning team becomes *masters* and calls on the *slaves* to dance one by one.

The Snake Eats His Tail

Ages: 5–8
Players: 10 or more; single-group line
Place: gymnasium; out-of-doors

Supplies: not any
Activity—hunting: holding, reaching, running
Appeal: dramatization, skill

The players are arranged in a row from the tallest first to the shortest last. Each player holds the waist of one in front. The first player is the *head* of the *snake* and tries to catch the last player or the *tail*. The players hold fast and turn, trying to save the *tail* from being caught. When the *tail* is caught, he then becomes the *head* and play continues until all have been caught.

This game is somewhat the same as the Chinese game "Eating the Fish's Tail" that is sometimes called "Catching the Snake's Tail."

Te-Toom (Te-TOOM)

Ages: 5–8
Players: 20 or more; group-and-one; circle
Place: gymnasium; out-of-doors

Supplies: whip
Activity—hunting: chasing, running
Appeal: problem solving

One player, *It*, walks around a circle formed by the other players who are seated. *It* drops a whip or similar object behind a player and then continues around the circle. If *It* completes the circle before the player discovers the whip behind him, *It* picks up the whip and spanks the player. Should the player discover the whip, he chases *It*, trying to spank him. *It* may try to escape being caught by finding an empty space in the circle. The other players may shift to fill up the spaces. If *It* sits down before he is caught, the chaser becomes *It*. If *It* is caught, he continues to be *It*.

The Thai children play another game called "Hiding the Cloth," which is quite similar to "Te-Toom" except for the use of a handkerchief instead of the whip.

Theeeeeeeeeeee

Ages: 9–12
Players: 10 or more; two-group; informal
Place: gymnasium; out-of-doors
Supplies: not any
Activity—hunting: chasing, holding breath
Appeal: competition, skill

The name of the game is a sound more than a word. The sound is made by exhaling the "th" more than just pronouncing Thee.

Teams of equal number are separated by a line drawn on the ground. *Team A* sends a player into the territory of *Team B*. *Team A* player must yell "Theeeeeeeeeeeeeeeeee" in one continuous yell as long as he stays in enemy territory. While in the territory he tries to touch as many of the *Team B* players as he can. If he manages to escape their hold and return to his own territory, all *Team B* players tagged by him are *dead* and out of the game. If he is captured and does not escape, he is *dead*. *Team B* then sends a player into *Team A's* territory. The team wins that has the most men at the end of playing time. The breath-holding procedure used here also is found in many games from India.

The Tiger Eats the Ox

Ages: 5–8
Players: 10–30; group-and-two; circle
Place: gymnasium; out-of-doors
Supplies: not any
Activity—hunting: chasing, listening
Appeal: dramatization, problem solving

One player is chosen to be the *tiger* and another to be the *ox*. Both players are blindfolded and stand within a circle formed by the rest of the players. The *ox* beats two sticks together to call the *tiger* who tries to catch the *ox*. After the catch is made, two other players are chosen to continue in like manner.

The Thai language for "The Tiger Eats the Ox" is *Sya-gin-wua*, pronounced SUE-a gin-WOO-a, in saying "gin," actually say "kin" but use a "g" instead of the "k."

GAMES AND SPORTS—MIDDLE EAST

GAZA

Al Mazh-Hul (Al Mazh-HOOL)

Ages: teen	Supplies: not any
Players: 10 or more; group-and-one; informal	Activity—pastime: guessing, listening
Place: home; schoolroom	Appeal: problem solving

One player, the *guesser,* leaves the room and while he is out the others decide on an object in the room. Each letter in the name of the object is assigned to one or more players. The *guesser* returns to the group to solve *Al Mazh-Hul* (The Unknown). Each player begins to chant the letter assigned to him. The guesser tries to guess name of object chosen by listening to the various letters being called and putting them together.

Baa't Ruzzak (BA-at ROOZ-zah)

Ages: 9–12	Supplies: not any
Players: 10 or more; group-and-one; circle	Activity—pastime: alertness, listening
Place: home; schoolroom	Appeal: dramatization

One player is chosen to be the *buyer,* the others sit in a circle and are numbered consecutively. The *buyer* stands before a player and asks, "BA-at ROOZ-zah?" "Have you sold your rice?" The player replies, "Not yet, I'm waiting." The buyer then asks, "What price do you ask?" The answer may be, "Seven piasters," or any number up to the number of the seated players. The player who has the number called immediately answers, "Here I am." The procedure is repeated by the *buyer,* who asks the same question of other players. Should the player whose number is called fail to answer within one or two seconds, he is punished by having his hands slapped.

Hanna Ala Nahar (HAN-nah EYE-lan NAR-har)

Ages: 5–8	Supplies: not any
Players: 20 or more; group-and-one; circle	Activity—hunting: dodging, stooping
Place: gymnasium; out-of-doors	Appeal: dramatization

The players are in a circle with the *leader,* John, in the center. The circle players join hands and walk around saying, "John is on

the river, John is in the tree, John can catch everyone, but can't
catch me." As the last word, "me," is said the players all stoop and
John tries to catch a player before he stoops. The one caught
becomes the next John, otherwise the first player in the center continues the game. The words may be sung to the tune of "Baa, Baa,
Blacksheep."

Tara Al Hamam (TAH-rahl Ha-MAM)

Ages: 9–12   Supplies: not any
Players: 20 or more; group-and-   Activity—pastime: alertness, mov-
  one; circle   ing hands
Place: home; schoolroom   Appeal: dramatization

Players are seated around a table or at their desks with both
hands on the table, palms down. One player acts as *leader* and
spokesman. When he says, "The pigeon flew up," the players raise
their hands quickly; when he says, "The pigeon flew down," the
hands are placed on the table. The *leader* may call out the same
command twice in succession in an effort to catch some players off
guard. Anyone who moves either up or down on the wrong command is out of the game. The winner is the last one at the table. He
may have the privilege of being the next *leader*. Translated *Tara Al
Haman* is The Pigeon Flew.

Tock, Tock, Tockeeya (Tok, tok, to-KEE-ya)

Ages: 9–12   Supplies: cap
Players: 20 or more; group-and-   Activity—hunting: chasing, dodg-
  one; circle   ing, running
Place: gymnasium; out-of-doors   Appeal: problem solving, skill

The word "tockeeya" means cap and the "tock" is simply the first
syllable of the word "cap" repeated.

All players except one sit in a circle. The one is *It* and is outside
the circle with a cap in his hand. As he walks around the circle he
chants, "Tock, tock, tockeeya," and is answered by the circle players
with, "Rin, rin, ya jaras (rin, rin, ya JA-ras) which means "Ring,
ring, oh, bell." The chants continue alternately until *It* drops the
cap behind a seated player. He then runs, trying to make it around
the circle without the cap being discovered by the player behind
whom it is dropped. If *It* succeeds he gets to hit the player on the
head with the cap and to continue as *It*. If the player behind whom
the cap is dropped discovers it, he chases *It* around the circle and
hits him with the cap when he catches him. *It*, when caught, joins
the circle players, and the player who caught him is the next *It*.

What Is My Bride Like?

Ages: 9–12

Players: 10–30; group-and-one; informal

Place: home; schoolroom

Supplies: objects in room

Activity—pastime: alertness, observation

Appeal: problem solving

One player, the *groom,* is asked to leave the room. The other players then choose an object in the room. The *groom* returns and asks one player, "What is my bride like?" The player answers by giving one characteristic of the object chosen, for example, if the object is a vase, the answer may be, "Your bride is tall" or "Your bride sits on a table" and so on. The *groom* goes from one player to another repeating the questioning until he successfully guesses the object that was chosen.

This game is similar to the bride-theme pattern of play from Lebanon. The game there is "My Bride Is Lost, What Is She?"

IRAN

Borkem Topa

Ages: 9–12

Players: 10 or more; group-and-one; informal

Place: gymnasium; out-of-doors

Supplies: hat

Activity—hunting: kicking, striking

Appeal: competition, skill

A circle about three feet in diameter is marked on the ground. The player who is *It* places his hat in the ring, and stands on guard with one foot on the ring mark. The others try to knock the hat out of the ring by striking with hands or feet. *It* attempts to tag them. If he is successful, the player thus tagged becomes *It.* If a player succeeds in knocking the hat out without being caught, *It* must run away from the ring and try to tag the players. The one tagged is *It* and starts a new game.

Chinnabeer

Ages: 9–12

Players: 20 or more; two-group; circle

Place: gymnasium; out-of-doors

Supplies: stick

Activity—hunting: guarding, reaching

Appeal: competition, problem solving

The players form a double circle around a stick that has been placed on the ground. The *inner circle* is to guard the stick. If an *outer circle* player encircles one of the inner circle players this player is *dead,* and is out of the game. If an *inner* player hits an *outer* with the palm of his hand, the *outer* player is *dead* and cannot continue. One player of the *inner circle* remains by the stick constantly to guard it. If the *inner circle* is broken up first and the stick is captured the *inner circle* becomes the *outer*. If the *outer* is broken up first the *inner circle* holds the defense for another game.

Dima

Ages: teen (boys)
Players: 6–12; group-and-one; file
Place: gymnasium; out-of-doors

Supplies: not any
Activity—athletic: leaping
Appeal: competition, skill

The players stand in file ready to leap over *It*, who is crouched in front of the file. The first time each player leaps he shouts, "Dima!" (Do not Hit!) and is allowed to touch *It* with his hands. In the second round they must not touch him at all and the cry is "Ochma." The third time over they shout, "The third is little," meaning they can touch him lightly. The fourth cry is "Give way," and is the signal for everyone to leap as he pleases. "On the fifth, pinch," is the next call, and as each player leaps he tries to pinch the victim. The next round is again an easy leap. The climax comes on the seventh round, when all shout, "On the seventh, we ride the palanquin" and as he leaps each player tries to secure his seat on the back of *It*. If anyone fails, he in turn has to be *It* and the game starts anew.

Glass Blower

Ages: 9–12
Players: 2 or more; individual; informal
Place: gymnasium; home; out-of-doors

Supplies: hat, stick
Activity—stunt: twirling
Appeal: dramatization, rhythm, skill

The players take a cap and twirl it as fast as they can on the end of a stick while saying a rhyme which has the following meaning,

> Be careful! please, glass blower!
> Or the bowl you will break.

Excellent opportunity for practice of concentrated rhythmic control.

Hide and Seek

Ages: 5–8
Players: 20 or more; group-and-two; informal
Place: out-of-doors

Supplies: not any
Activity—hunting: chasing, dodging, hiding, running, seeking
Appeal: problem solving, skill

Two players are selected to remain at *home* and shut their eyes while the others hide. As soon as the *hidden ones* are discovered they give chase and try to catch the *seekers* before they can get back *home*. If the ones who are *seekers* are caught they must try again, but if they reach *home* without being tagged, two of the *hidden ones* become the *seekers*.

Kuku Kuku

Ages: 9–12
Players: 20 or more; group; circle
Place: gymnasium; out-of-doors
Supplies: pebbles or sticks

Activity—pastime: hopping, throwing
Appeal: skill

One player is chosen to be the *orphan*. The others pair off and form a circle. Number One of each pair stands, while Number Two crouches at his feet. Numbers Two lay pebbles or sticks on the ground and say, "*Kuku, Kuku!*" The *orphan* hops around the circle without falling and picks up the sticks or pebbles. He then tosses them all into the air. If most of them fall in the circle, the boys cry out "Plenty" and begin a new game. If most of them fall outside, the players cry, "Famine." At this they all jump and run away to try to find a new companion. The one left is the *orphan* and the game begins with the *orphan* as the odd player.

Marbles

Ages: 9–12
Players: 2 or more; individual; informal
Place: out-of-doors

Supplies: marbles
Activity—pastime: pitching
Appeal: competition, skill

Each player should have three or more *ashog* or marbles. Often the children use the round knuckle bones of sheep or goats. Pebbles and small stones may be used. Each player digs a hole in the ground and stands about eight feet away from the line of holes or cups. He then tries to pitch or roll his marbles into his own cup. His score corresponds to the number of marbles in his cup. If a player rolls a marble into another's cup, that marble is counted for the latter. The game may consist of several trials for each player or a certain score may be set before the game begins.

Mounting Mollaks

Ages: teen (boys)
Players: 20 or more; two-group-and-one; circle
Place: gymnasium; out-of-doors

Supplies: not any
Activity—hunting: reaching, running, mounting
Appeal: skill

The players form a double circle. All in the *inner circle* join hands except one player, the *guard*, who goes around the *outer circle*. The object is for the *outer circle* player to jump on the back of the *inner* player before being tagged by the guard. The *guard* may only tag the *outer* player when in the act of jumping. When a player is once on the back of the *inner* player, he may sit there as long as he wishes. When the guard tags one, the sides change position.

Nose and Ear

Ages: 9–12   Supplies: not any
Players: 10–20; single-group; circle   Activity—pastime: self-control
Place: home; schoolroom   Appeal: competition

The players are seated in circle formation. One, the *chief*, starts the play by lightly pulling the nose, ear, or hair of the player on his right. The player then repeats the action on his neighbor on the right. The action continues until it returns to the *chief* who may start another action around the circle. The action may be a funny face or a light poke in the ribs. Players who laugh, giggle, or make a noise of any kind during the play are put out of the game. The winner is the one who shows most control.

Slaves

Ages: teen   Supplies: not any
Players: 20 or more; two-group;   Activity—hunting: chasing, dodg-
  line   ing, running
Place: gymnasium; out-of-doors   Appeal: competition, skill

The players are divided into two equal sides and stand on lines 30 feet apart. A line is drawn midway between the two teams. One player advances and tries to tag one of the other team and runs back before being tagged himself. If he is tagged before crossing the midway line, he is taken as a *slave*. If he succeeds in crossing the midway line without being tagged one of his men may chase the pursuer and try to tag him before he can return to his base line. Each team keeps its *slaves* in prison. As soon as one side wins, the *slaves* ride their *masters* on their backs across the playing area as many times as was agreed upon before the game began.

ISRAEL

Alam

Ages: teen   Activity—athletic: catching, run-
Players: 4–10; two-group; informal   ning, throwing
Place: out-of-doors   Appeal: competition, skill
Supplies: ball

This game is something like "One Old Cat." The *alam*, a stone, is placed upright at one end of the field. The players divide into two teams and decide which team is in bat first. The play begins as the first *batter* calls "Radoor," which means "ready." The *batter* then throws a ball in a series of different ways: first overhand and then underhand. He may face his opponents or quickly turn his back to them, each time recovering the ball. The final play for him is to drop the ball and kick it. The *fielders* try to catch the ball on the fly. If a fielder succeeds, the *batter* is out; otherwise the first fielder to recover the ball throws at the *alam*, trying to upset it as he calls, "Dustur," which means "by your leave." If the *alam* is upset, the *batter* is out, and his team goes to the field. The game continues with each team being allowed one out in each inning.

Ben Hur

Ages: teen
Players: 16 or more; two or more files; file
Place: out-of-doors

Supplies: brooms
Activity—relay: holding, running, sitting
Appeal: dramatization, skill

Two old brooms are needed. Players are divided into two equal groups and line up in couples in relay fashion. An *arena* is established with a goal designated. Two couples, one in each couple as *Ben Hur,* the other as his *horse,* enter the *arena.* The *horse* supports the *carriage* (the broom) and *Ben Hur* sits on the bristles. At a signal each carriage starts for the goal and returns to the starting line. The winning pair earns one point for its team. The team with the most points wins the game.

Blind Cow

Ages: 9–12
Players: 12 or more; 4-and-one; line
Place: gymnasium; out-of-doors
Supplies: blindfolds

Activity—hunting: alertness, marching
Appeal: competition

One player is chosen to be the *instructor.* The others are blindfolded and stand as organized groups in a line in front of the *instructor.* Play starts by the *instructor* calling out drill commands or marching instructions that must be executed immediately and until the *instructor* blows a whistle or gives the command, "Halt!" The players must stop where they are and the group judged to have the best formation is the winner. Points for each win may be given and the team that accumulates the greatest number of points at the end of play is the winner.

Deeb

Ages: 9–12
Players: 20 or more; group-and-one; circle
Place: gymnasium; out-of-doors

Supplies: not any
Activity—hunting: dodging, leaping, reaching, running
Appeal: competition, skill

One player is chosen to be the *deeb* or wolf. He stands outside the circle formed by the other players who are called *sheep*. As the *sheep* skip around and around the *wolf* tries to grab one of them. When a *sheep* is caught he must stand in the center of the ring. The last *sheep* to be caught becomes the *wolf* and the game begins anew. A *sheep* may try to prevent capture by letting his heels fly, as a lamb would in leaping.

Dress Up Relay

Ages: teen
Players: 12 or more; two or more files; file
Place: gymnasium; out-of-doors

Supplies: miscellaneous articles
Activity—relay: agility, running
Appeal: competition, dramatization

Players are in two or more teams that stand in file formation behind a starting line. Three circles are drawn several feet apart and in front of the files. At a given signal, the first player from each team runs forward to his team's first circle and removes an article of clothing and places it in the circle. He runs to the second circle, removes another article of clothing, and places it in the circle; then to the third circle and places an article of clothing in it. After this the player runs around a turning point, which has been established several feet ahead, and returns to his line, putting on each article of clothing as he reaches each circle on the return trip. The players of each team follow the procedure in relay fashion. The team that finishes the race first wins. The clothing may be a cap, a belt, a pair of shoes, a pair of socks, or a handkerchief.

Hail, O King

Ages: 9–12
Players: 20 or more; group-and-one; informal
Place: gymnasium; out-of-doors

Supplies: not any
Activity—pastime: guessing, pantomime
Appeal: dramatization

One player, chosen to be the *king*, sits on his throne. The other players, the *subjects*, together decide on a story to present in pantomime. Each *subject* is assigned a part and all go to the *king*, saying "Hail, O King." The *king* replies, "Hail! Where have you been?" The answer is "Far away in the forest." The *king* then asks, "And what have you been doing?" The group replies in pantomime and the *king* tries to guess the title of the story. If he guesses correctly, he remains *king*, otherwise he chooses a *subject* to take his place. This is similar to "Little White House on the Hill" and "Lemonade, what's your trade?" played by children in the United

Israel—Hail, O King.

States of America. The American versions include running when the pantomime is guessed.

Khuurak

Ages: teen
Players: 20 or more; two-group; informal
Place: out-of-doors

Supplies: not any
Activity—hunting: chasing, hiding, running
Appeal: competition, skill

A large playing area is necessary for this game. In Israel the players use the whole town and the surrounding country. The players are divided into two groups. A *home base* is established at a door or a tree. One group is assigned to remain at the *base* while the other group goes away and hides. After a stated time has passed the players at the *base* divide into small groups and begin a search for the hidden players. The object of the game is for the hidden players to return to the *home base* without being seen by the opposing group.

LEBANON

Bat and Stick Game

Ages: teen
Players: 2 or more; individual; informal
Place: out-of-doors

Supplies: sticks
Activity—athletic: batting, jumping
Appeal: competition, skill

This is a game that all Lebanese boys enjoy playing in their backyards or on the street.

A *bat* (stick) about the length but not as large as a baseball bat and a *ball* that is a piece of wood about 5 inches long are needed. The stick is rounded at each end so that it is egg-shaped.

The *batter* stands on the starting line and hits the stick on end to make it jump into the air and then hits it away from him as far as possible. After the stick lands, the *batter* must estimate the number of broad jumps his opponent will take to reach the stick. If the *opponent* fails to reach the stick in the number called by the batter, the *batter* gets that number and continues at bat. If the *opponent* reaches the stick in that number or less, the *batter* is out and the *opponent* takes his turn at bat. The *batter* estimates on the high side as he tries to increase his score and to remain at bat. 100 points wins the game.

This game with modifications is reported to have been played in Southern United States in the early twentieth century. There is little evidence of its being generally played there today.

My Bride Is Lost, What Is She?

Ages: 9–12
Players: 20 or more; group-and-one; informal
Place: home; schoolroom

Supplies: not any
Activity—pastime: guessing
Appeal: problem solving

One player, chosen to be *It*, leaves the room. The other players decide on an object, flower, etc. *It* returns and goes from one player to another, asking, "My bride is lost? What is she?" Each player asked replies with a question pertaining to the object selected by the group, for example, "Is she pink?" *It* continues to ask his original questions and makes a guess until he guesses correctly. Time limit and the number of guesses allowed *It* may be governed by the age of the players.

Oh, Neighbor, Have You Fire?

Ages: 9–12
Players: 5 or more; group-and-one; rectangle
Place: out-of-doors
Supplies: not any

Activity—hunting: chasing, dodging, running
Appeal: dramatization, problem solving

A rectangle about 30 by 20 feet is drawn. A player chosen to be *It* stands in the center. The other players are stationed at the corners of the rectangle. *It* approaches a player and asks, "Oh, Neighbor, have you fire?" The player answers, "No, my neighbor has fire." *It* then goes to another player, asking him the same question. The player being questioned must leave his base. Two other players may try to change during the questioning. *It* tries to catch one; if he succeeds, the player becomes *It;* if he fails he continues as *It. It* can tag a player only while he is running and cannot go to an abandoned base. Players may use trees as bases. This is often done by the Lebanese boys and girls. The game "Puss Wants a Corner," played by children in the United States, is similar in pattern, although different in conversational approach. The same is true of "How Do You Like Your Neighbor?" from Turkey.

Tabaat

Ages: teen
Players: 8 or more; two-group; line
Place: gymnasium; out-of-doors
Supplies: handball

Activity—athletic: batting, bouncing
Appeal: competition, skill

Players are divided into two equal teams. Each team stands behind a line parallel that is ten or more yards from the other. Opponents face each other. One team starts play, which consists of a series of six different plays of bouncing a ball. To win, one team must complete each of the plays. The ball must go beyond the line of the opponents' and must bounce before being caught by an opponent or batter out. The plays are:

1. Throw ball up with one hand; hit it with the other.
2. Throw ball up with one hand; hit with the same hand.
3. Bounce ball on the ground; hit it.
4. Throw the ball up; clap hands; hit ball.
5. Throw the ball under a leg, up; hit ball.
6. Throw the ball behind back, up; hit ball.

Each player on a team at bat gets a turn. The second player starts on the play that the first player lost and so on. When a team returns to bat, however, the team must start from the beginning.

SYRIA

Hockey

Ages: 9–12
Players: 6–12; group-and-one; informal
Place: out-of-doors

Supplies: curved stick, rag ball
Activity—athletic: running, striking
Appeal: competition, skill

Each player is equipped with a curved stick. A hole, called the *mother*, is made in the center of the field. One player is selected to guard it with his stick. The others try to drive a ball made of rags into the hole.

Hop Tag

Ages: 9–12
Players: 20 or more, group-and-one; informal
Place: gymnasium; out-of-doors

Supplies: not any
Activity—hunting: chasing, dodging, hopping
Appeal: skill

The one called *It* must hop to tag the others, who are privileged to run. The game "Getting the Bride Home," played by the children of the Sudan, is similar but with more drama.

Motion Tag

Ages: 9–12
Players: 20 or more; group-and-one; circle
Place: gymnasium; home; schoolroom

Supplies: not any
Activity—pastime: imitation
Appeal: competition

All sit in a circle on the floor. One chosen to be *It* makes some motion, such as taking hold of the ear of the player next to him. Each in the circle must follow this motion. If anyone laughs or speaks, he is eliminated from the game. The last one to laugh starts the next game.

Robbers

Ages: teen (boys)
Players: 20 or more; two-group; informal
Place: out-of-doors

Supplies: not any
Activity—hunting: chasing, dodging, running
Appeal: competition, dramatization

This game arises out of the practice of Bedouin robbers attacking peaceful travelers.

The *travelers*, a group of boys, pretend to lead a *donkey* from the village pastures; as they advance, a band of yelling *robbers* swoop upon them from under cover and a sham battle is waged.

TURKEY

Cops and Robbers

Ages: 9–12

Players: 20 or more; two-groups-and-one; line

Place: gymnasium; out-of-doors

Supplies: not any

Activity—hunting: chasing, dodging, running

Appeal: competition, skill

The players are in two teams, the *cops* and the *robbers*, and stand on safety lines about 60 feet apart. A *leader* stands at one end of a dividing line which is midway between the teams. The *leader* signals players numbered "one" on each side to advance to the dividing line. The players may not cross the line but each tries to tag his opponent with the right hand and return to his safety line before being tagged by his opponent. If tagged, the player caught is out of the game; if not caught, the one chasing is out. The winning team is the one that eliminates its opponents first.

How Do You Like Your Neighbor?

Ages: 9–12

Players: 20 or more; group-and-one; circle

Place: gymnasium; out-of-doors

Supplies: not any

Activity—hunting: running

Appeal: competition, dramatization

One player stands in the center of a circle formed by the other players who sit a few inches apart. The center player asks one of the seated players, "How do you like your neighbor?" The answer may be, "Not at all," or "Fine." If he says the former, the seated player immediately signals another in the circle to change places with him. The center one tries to get one of the vacant places. The odd player becomes the center one. This game was played in Constantinople as far back as the early seventeenth century—1649. It has been played in southern United States since early colonial days.

Kukla

Ages: teen

Players: 12 or more; group-and-one; informal

Place: out-of-doors

Supplies: beanbags or stones, can

Activity—hunting: chasing, throwing, running

Appeal: competition, skill

This game is a variation of the age-old game "Duck on a Rock," from Greece. Players, each holding a flat stone or beanbag, stand in a row and on the *home line*. The *goal line* is established 12 or more feet from the *home line*. A *tin can* is placed on the center of the *goal line*. A circle about a foot in diameter is drawn around the *can*. One player is chosen to be the *guard* by each player throwing his *beanbag* toward the *goal line*. The player whose *beanbag* is closest to the line is the *guard* and takes his place on the *goal line* and near the *can*.

The game is started by one of the line players throwing his *beanbag* at the *can*, trying to knock it over and as far away from the circle as possible. Each player has his turn at throwing and always at a low range. Should a player hit the *can*, each player whose *beanbag* is in front of the *goal line* must run to pick up his *beanbag*. The *guard* must replace the *can* in its circle and then try to tag the players as they recover their *beanbags*. If a *beanbag* lands behind the *goal line*, it may be used as a safety zone by its owner who stands on it until the *can* has been knocked over again. The player may then pick up his *beanbag* and run for *home*. A player who is tagged replaces the *guard*. The *guard* joins the team that lost its player.

Long Donkey

Ages: teen (boys)
Players: 10–20; two-group; informal
Place: gymnasium; out-of-doors
Supplies: not any
Activity—stunt: mounting
Appeal: competition, skill

The players divide into two equal groups. The *leader* of one team stands with his back against the wall. His teammates begin to form the *long donkey* in this manner; one player bends over and places his head against the stomach of the leader, another player puts his head against the rear of the first, a third player puts his head against the rear of the second, and so on until all members of the team have helped form the *donkey*. The opponents are *riders* and start the game by jumping on the back of the *long donkey*. The *leader* of the *riders* mounts near the head that is represented by the *leader* of the *donkey team*. When all *riders* are mounted their leader must audibly count to thirty before taking a breath. If he or a member of his team falls from the *donkey* before the count is completed, the two teams change places.

Mule

Ages: 9–12
Players: 10 or more; group-and-one; informal
Place: out-of-doors
Supplies: peg, rope, strip of cloth,
a stocking or towel
Activity—hunting: dodging, grasping, striking
Appeal: repetition, skill

A rope about 5 yards long is tied to a stick that is driven in the ground. "Swats" of towel, stocking, or old cloth are placed around the stick. One player, chosen to be *It*, grasps the end of the rope, and the action is started when the other players rush in and grab a "swat" and immediately use it to strike at the player holding the rope. *It* tries to tag the opponents. If he is successful he changes places with the player who is tagged and the game is started anew.

In North America a similar game, "Swat Tag," is played; in Africa the same pattern of play is called "Tied Monkey."

The Oil in the Church Has Given Out

Ages: 9–12
Players: 8–12; group-and-one; informal
Place: gymnasium; out-of-doors

Supplies: not any
Activity—stunt: pushing
Appeal: competition, dramatization

One player stands in front of a stone wall while perhaps ten others stand in front of him and press him against the wall to get a little oil. As soon as he shouts for breath they stop and another is pressed.

Whom Will You Take?

Ages: 9–12
Players: 20 to 30; two-group
Place: gymnasium; out-of-doors
Supplies: not any

Activity—hunting: chasing, pushing
Appeal: competition, dramatization

The players are divided into two equal lines about 30 feet apart and facing each other. The numbers of each line join hands. One side calls *"Bildim sizdar kim dosha"* ("Whom will you take?"). The other, *"Katheruna dosha,"* meaning "Katherine is wanted." (Any name may be called.) At that Katherine runs and tries to break through the arms of the opposing line. If she breaks through, she and another player of her group must join the opposing line. The game is continued until all on one line have been taken. The player whose name is called should want to gain admission to the opposite side.

This game is similar in formation and skill to "Forcing the City Gates" played by Chinese children but is exactly the opposite in object. It is played by both boys and girls in the United States of America as "Red Rover."

ARMENIA[1]

Dempig

Ages: 9–12
Players: 10 to 20; group-and-one; informal
Place: out-of-doors

Supplies: not any
Activity—hunting: chasing, dodging, running
Appeal: competition, skill

[1] Most of Armenia is now a part of Turkey.

It is chosen by casting lots. The other players crowd around him and suddenly one of them taps him on the back and runs away. *It* must run after him. If he catches the runner before another player tags the runner, the one caught becomes *It*. If he does not catch the runner before he is tagged by another, *It* must chase the last player who tagged the runner. Each time a runner is tagged by a player, *It* must run after the player who did the tagging.

Jumping or Donkey Game

Ages: teen
Players: 10 or more; single group; line
Place: out-of-doors

Supplies: handkerchief
Activity—athletic: jumping, leaping, stooping
Appeal: competition, skill

The players line up a certain distance from a designated goal. All players jump to the goal. The last one to reach the goal is the *donkey*. He stoops low and the other players jump over him as in "Leap Frog." The player gradually raises himself up to where he stands at his full height except that his head is dropped forward. If a player fails to jump over him the two players exchange places. If all succeed, they jump again. The jumping is made more difficult this time by placing a handkerchief on the head of the *donkey*. The players continue to jump until one of them causes the handkerchief to fall. The player who knocks the handkerchief down becomes the *donkey*. This game is excellent for development of agility and strength, and offers great challenge to the individual.

Tutush

Ages: 9–12
Players: 4–12; group-and-one; informal
Place: out-of-doors

Supplies: club, sharp stick
Activity—athletic: catching, running, striking
Appeal: skill

One player serves as batsman, the others are fielders. Instead of using a ball and bat, a long stick or club serves as the bat and a short stick sharpened at both ends and about five inches long takes the place of a ball. The batsman knocks the sharp stick into the air and strikes it a second time after which the fielders are allowed to catch it. The fielder who catches a fly goes to bat, otherwise the batsman continues. This game is similar to "One Old Cat" played in the United States and to "Bat and Stick" of Lebanon.

GAMES AND SPORTS—SOUTHERN ASIA

INDIA

Atya Patya

Ages: 9–12
Players: 10; two-group; line
Place: gymnasium; out-of-doors
Supplies: not any

Activity—hunting: chasing, dodging, running
Appeal: competition, skill

The court is the size of a tennis court and is divided into four sections with boundary lines clearly defined. A good number for this game is ten players; five on a side. One side is the aggressive side during the first round. The captain of this team stands on the middle line of the court and may go on the boundary lines on either side of him; the other players of this team may take each of the other four lines in their half of the territory. The opposing team lines up in this way also. The players, with the exception of the captains, must keep strictly to their places. The two captains shake hands as a signal to begin. The object of the aggressive players is to run to the far boundary line and back without being caught by the defensive team. A score of one is made for each player making the round. The sides change if a player is caught or goes out of boundary. The game usually consists of five innings.

Blind Man-Bee

Ages: 5–8
Players: 10 to 20; group-and-one; informal
Place: gymnasium; out-of-doors

Supplies: large handkerchief
Activity—hunting: chasing, dodging, running
Appeal: dramatization, skill

This is a form of blindman's buff in which the players taunt the blindfolded one by crying, "Touch, touch me quick, blind man-bee. Touch me quick."

Fist Ball

Ages: teen (boys)
Players: 6 or more; group-and-one; informal
Place: playground

Supplies: football
Activity—athletic: catching, striking, throwing
Appeal: competition, skill

The playing field is a rectangle 20 by 30 yards. In the center of one of the 20-yard lines a *base* two yards square is marked. One player is appointed to serve as *batter*. He stands on the base and holds a ball (usually a football). The other players are *fielders* and scatter over the entire field.

The game starts when the *batter* throws the ball to some part of the field, trying to place it so that it will hit the ground before it is caught by a *fielder*. When a *fielder* gains possession of the ball after it has touched the ground, he throws the ball, from where he stands, across the base so that it clears the ground and yet is not higher than the reach of the *batter*. The *batter* hits at the ball as it passes over the base, trying to knock it back into the field. If he is successful he remains on base until he strikes out.

The *batter* is out (1) if he strikes at the ball and misses it; (2) if he strikes the ball more than once; (3) if he bats a fly ball that is caught by a *fielder*; (4) if he bats the ball within the base or without the field; (5) if the ball falls outside the field on his first throw. In the case of (3) and (5) the *fielder* who secures the ball becomes the batter; at all other times the *fielders* follow a definite order of batting agreed upon before the beginning of the game. When put out the *batter* takes a place in the field and the game begins anew.

If a ball thrown by a *fielder* does not pass over the base properly, any player who secures the ball may throw it from the same place a second time.

Goodoo-Goodoo

Ages: 9–12
Players: 10 to 20; two-group; line
Place: gymnasium; out-of-doors
Supplies: not any

Activity—hunting: holding the breath
Appeal: competition, rhythm

The players are in two groups and are separated by a line drawn on the ground. One player from each side acts as *leader*. The *leader* of one side sends one of his men to cross the line and touch an opponent. As the player advances, he must repeat, without taking breath, the words, "Goodoo-goodoo." If he succeeds in returning to his place, without drawing breath, he is safe and the other side sends a player across the line. If he fails, he is a *dead man*, and is out of the game. The side having the most players at the close of the game wins.

Guli Danda

Ages: 9–12
Players: 6–12; transition
Place: out-of-doors
Supplies: one stick 1 yard long; one 10-inch stick

Activity—athletic: catching, running, striking
Appeal: competition, skill

A stick about a yard long is called the *danda* and serves as a bat. A shorter stick, about 6 inches long, serves as a *ball* and is called *guli.* A base is established from which the players take turns in batting a ball. The score is determined by the number of inches the *ball* falls from the base, the distance being measured by the length of the *bat.* The score may be 50 to 100 as agreed upon by the players. The player scoring the smallest number of points is the loser and becomes the *slave* of the victor. The lower score is subtracted from the higher and the *slave* has to serve his victor the same number of points by which he has been defeated. To do this he must recover the *ball* every time it is batted by the victor and return it to the base. Many victors do not enact the penalty of slaving upon the defeated player because they find it more pleasure to begin and play a new game. The game is also called "Ball and Bat Game."

Ha-do-do

Ages: teen
Players: 6–12; two-group; informal
Place: gymnasium; out-of-doors
Supplies: not any

Activity—hunting: chasing, dodging, running, holding breath
Appeal: competition, rhythm, skill

This game is one of the most popular in India, and is played not only by boys and girls but also by grown-up men. The playing area is a large rectangular court with a dividing line in the middle that serves as the *base.* The players are divided into two sides consisting of three or more players in each group. One group chooses a player to make an attack on the opponents. The attacker goes to the base line, inhales deeply, and enters the territory of the opposing side. He must make a sound like "kit-kit," "choo," or "ha-do-do" to signify that he is holding his breath. He tries to tag the members of the opposing side. When he tags a player that player is considered *dead* for the rest of the game. At the same time the members of the opposing side try to catch the attacking player securely before he has a chance to escape by touching the base with any part of his body. If he is caught, he is *dead* and must retire. If he should lose his breath while in the enemy's territory, he is considered *dead.* The sides take turns in sending players to the opposite court. The side having the greatest number of players at the close of the game wins. The height of excitement occurs when a player falls prone and tries to touch the base with extended hands or feet.

Kauri Karel Wail

Ages: teen
Players: 20 or more; two-group circle
Place: gymnasium; out-of-doors

Supplies: not any
Activity—hunting: mounting, running
Appeal: competition, rhythm, skill

The players form a double circle with partners facing the center. The outer circle players are *riders* who mount the backs of the inner circle players or *horses*. One *rider* is chosen to dismount and run around the circle. As he runs he must utter a continuous sound, as "*Kauri Karel Wail, Bennum Gitta Laon Tail,*" to indicate that he is holding his breath. The object of the game is for the *rider* to encircle the ring and return to his mount before he renews his breath. If he is successful the next *rider* repeats the procedure. The play continues in this manner until a *rider* fails. Then the *horses* and *riders* change places. If all *riders* succeed, they are given a ride to a designated goal.

Khokad

Ages: 9–12
Players: 12–16; two-group; line
Place: gymnasium; out-of-doors
Supplies: not any

Activity—hunting: chasing, dodg-
ing, running, stooping
Appeal: competition, skill

The players are divided into two groups with a *captain* for each group. Six to eight in a group is a good number. The *captain* of Group I stands at the end of the line of players who are about 3 feet apart. Beginning with the first player, every other player faces at right angles to the *captain* and all players squat on the ground. The members of Group II take their places midway between the squatting players. The *captain* of Group I encircles his line three times, cries "Ready?" and then quickly runs down the line, with outstretched arm, trying to tag the players of Group II. The players may dodge out of line, but must get back in place immediately. The *captain* may mislead the players by running around the line without trying to tag a standing player. As he passes the end players, he must touch them on the head. He is not allowed to intersect the line, nor can he start down the line and then reverse his direction. He must go the length of the line and touch the end player before retracing his steps.

When a standing player is tagged he drops out of the game. The players change places when all standing players are caught. The *captain* of the squatting players has the privilege of calling on one of his men to take his place, saying, "Khok" and the player's name. The *captain* can use this privilege only after one player has been caught and he must be at the end of the line before he calls his teammate's name. When he takes the place of the squatting player, he must go down the line and to the back of the player whom he has called. As soon as a player is called, he may rise and catch any standing player who is near. If the seated side makes an error during play, one who has been tagged may return to his stand.

Kittuppullu

Ages: 9–12

Players: 4–12; group-and-one; informal

Place: out-of-doors

Supplies: bat, small stick

Activity—athletic: catching, running, striking

Appeal: skill

This game of South India is a type of cricket that comes from ancient times. One player is chosen to be the *striker*. He holds the

India—Kituppullu.

bat, a long stick, and the *pullu* or short stick. He strikes the *pullu* to make it go high in the air and the others try to catch it as it falls to the ground. The player who catches the *pullu* is the next *striker*.

Nurse and Child

Ages: 5–8
Players: 10 or more; group-and-two; informal
Place: schoolroom

Supplies: not any
Activity—pastime: guessing, walking
Appeal: problem solving

One player, chosen to be the *nurse*, sits on the ground. A second player, the *child*, sits on the nurse's lap and spreads her legs apart. Her eyes are blindfolded by the *nurse's* hands. One by one the other players step over the extended legs of the child. The object of the game is for the child to guess the name of a player as she crosses over her legs. If the child succeeds in guessing correctly, she becomes the *nurse*, the player becomes the *child*, and the *nurse* joins the group. The *child* does not become the *nurse* until she guesses correctly.

Phugadi

Ages: 5–8
Players: any number; couple; informal
Place: gymnasium; out-of-doors

Supplies: not any
Activity—stunt: grasping, whirling
Appeal: rhythm

Two players stand facing each other with their toes touching and their hands clasped and crossed at the wrists. They lean back stiffly and start turning as fast as they can, continuing to do so as long as possible. In the United States of America this is called "Stiff Starch."

Throwing to the Stars

Ages: teen (boys)
Players: unlimited; transition; informal
Place: gymnasium; playground

Supplies: tennis ball
Activity—athletic: balance, catching, running, throwing
Appeal: competition, skill

The ball is thrown high into the air by one player. He and all other players immediately rush to catch the ball on the fly. Should a player catch the ball before it touches the ground, he throws it up again. Play continues in this manner until the ball is missed, whereupon all players scatter with the exception of the one who last threw the ball. He then picks up the ball and throws it at the other players. If no one is hit the player must throw again. Should he hit a player he then becomes a *rider* and mounts the *horse* or the player whom he hit. If in trying to catch the ball a player misses it but is touched by the ball, he becomes a *horse* for the player who threw the ball. The *horse* places his hands on his knees and allows the *rider* to mount. The *rider* then throws the ball and he along with the other players attempts to catch it. The player who succeeds in catching the ball changes places with the *rider*. The *horse* may try to catch the ball. If he succeeds he changes places with his *rider*. If a *rider* touches the ball but fails to catch it, he and his *horse* change places. Should the ball be missed altogether, the *horse* gets the ball and throws it at the other players who have scattered over the field. The player hit by the ball starts the game anew by throwing the ball in the air.

4

Australia and New Zealand

AUSTRALIA

Australia, the smallest continent, is about the size of the United States of North America. It, like Canada and New Zealand, is a self-governing member of the British Commonwealth of Nations. The peoples of Australia are predominantly of British or European origin. So are their games and sports. The European-Australian children play much the same traditional games as do the children of England, Ireland, Scotland, and Wales. Consequently their play is similar in pattern to much of the play of the children in the United States of America.

Australians develop great skill in outdoor sports. They enjoy their sports through participation. Generally when there are competitive games, track events, and rowing races among the schools only friends, family, and students attend them.

The sports that do hold nation and worldwide interest among Australians are the Davis Cup Tennis Matches; the world-famous Australian horse races; and the England-Australian cricket matches. More than 60,000 members are registered in the New South Wales Tennis Association. Boxing, swimming, and track have also attracted many Australians into the professional sports level.

Riding the breakers and surfing are favorite activities with children and adults. The Australians take their water sports seriously and provide well for safety. There are over 10,000 volunteer members of the Surf Life-Saving Association. Each beach has its own life-saving club.

Football, played in four different ways, is popular among Australians. The best liked form is "Australian Rules," which was developed on the continent.

A form of bowling that is called "bowls" is quite popular with boys and men. It is played by rolling balls, which are not quite round, near a white stationary ball called a "jack." Blind veterans participate in the game as others call the plays for them.

ABORIGINES OF AUSTRALIA

The Aborigines or tribesmen of Australia are comparable to the North American Indian in skill and ingenuity. Today they, like the Indian in North America, are a fractional part of the Australian population. Their string games are unique and have been recorded in detail by Daniel Sutherland Davidson (*Proceedings of the American Philosophical Society,* "Aboriginal Australian String Figures," 1941).

String games seem to have come out of antiquity. Their appearance in practically all parts of the world is not uncommon today. It is their universality that justifies their being given a place in this worldwide collection of games. Australia is the first continent from which string games were reported, though it cannot be claimed that the distribution of the games there was completely continental.

NEW ZEALAND

The peoples of this lonely and lovely land are beacon lights of dramatic chivalry, customs, and cooperation in social living. The New Zealanders' adaptation to the remoteness of their geographic location; their appreciation of the scenic beauty of the land; their peaceful co-existence among varied cultural groups; and their deep and active concern for the welfare of all of their peoples places them in the zenith of human societies today.

The New Zealanders' love for the out-of-doors, induced by favorable climatic conditions, has led to their participation in many sports. Rugby football is the favorite sport in winter, cricket in summer. Other sports enjoyed by the people of this island are golf, tennis, skiing, basketball, soccer, baseball, hunting, fishing, and swimming. Bicycle riding is a popular activity. It is also a chosen mode of transportation for many working people and school children.

Horse races are held every day of the year except Sundays, Easter, and Christmas. Boxing Day, a big social event, is the most important day of racing. It is on this day that the Auckland Cup meetings are held.

The games heritage of the New Zealand children is rich. Its roots, like those of games from the United States of North America, reach deep into Western Europe. The European-New Zealand children play traditional games popular in England, The Netherlands, France, and the United States.

THE MAORI

Today's children of the Maori (MAH-aw-ree), the early settlers of 1350 from Tahiti, have also inherited many interesting play patterns. The more popular ones are in this collection as suggested adaptations for pleasurable activities today.

GAMES AND SPORTS—AUSTRALIA

Aboriginal String Games. The games are grouped in three classes:

String tricks and catches
Cat's cradle
String figures

All of the classes have similar characteristics yet each class, like the peoples who created them, has distinctive patterns. String tricks and string figures are given in the material that follows.

The *string tricks and catches* are simple and readily learned. Their appeal is the element of surprise, first, the sudden "falling apart" of some of the complicated arrangements, and second, the string unexpectedly catching a hand or finger.

The *Cat's Cradle* is somewhat monotonous and noncreative. It usually requires the skill of two players who take turns at removing a design off the hands of the other. This string play seems to have been in the Far East and to have traveled to Western Europe with the expansion of the tea trade.

The *string figures* are complex and intricate. They include some tricks, catches, and cat's cradle along with some distinct characteristics of their own. One person usually performs the figure, though he may use his toes, knees, elbows, and hands and feet.

Terms Used:

The string: a single string; doubled string
Openings: initial arrangements of the string
   a. First position
   b. Opening A
   c. "Little Fishes" Opening
Navaho: a simple movement used in many string games
Release: converting to the original loop

FIRST POSITION. The most common of all openings throughout the world is the "First Position." It is not only the opening from which many figures are developed directly; it is also the basis for executing

Opening A. It is assumed in this way. Place a loop back of each thumb, then take the string across each palm and back of each little finger. Draw the string taut (Fig. 1).

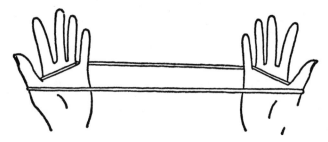

Fig. 1. First Position.

OPENINGS. *Opening A.* Opening A is extremely common in all parts of the world. The steps in its construction are reminiscent of Cat's Cradle, but the initial arrangement of the strings is not the same.

1. *Both hands.* First position.
2. *Right hand.* With back of index finger pick up from below the left palmar string and return to position.
3. *Left hand.* With back of index finger pick up from below the right palmar string between the strings of the right index finger loop. Draw out and return to position (Fig. 2).

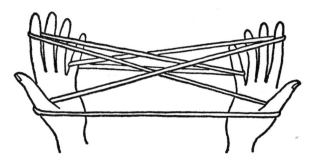

Fig. 2. Opening A.

"Little Fishes" Opening. This opening, although not as common as Opening A, is widely distributed in the world.

1. *Both hands.* Pick up strings between tips of thumb, index, and middle fingers, hands about 10 inches apart. Make a loop in the string by bringing the hands together, the right hand a little forward of the left. Insert the index finger into this small loop from

the far side until string is at base of finger. Press middle finger against index finger to prohibit string from sliding up finger. Close ring and little fingers loosely over pendant string. Reach index finger toward you into long hanging loop and seize between tips of thumb and index finger the string that runs across hand to the far side of the little finger. Extend the hands, slowly playing out this string between the thumb and index finger and keeping the first loop picked up well at the base of the index finger. When the hands are fully extended keep the strings taut, remove all fingers except index finger from strings, and rotate index finger inward and upward by lowering elbows and extend (Fig. 3).

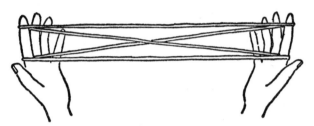

Fig. 3. "Little Fishes" Opening.

Other Movements. *Navaho.* The movement is simple. It consists of lifting a lower string over an upper string on the same finger and dropping it on the other side of the finger. Some persons use the lips or teeth to lift the lower string; some grasp the string between the tips of the thumb and index finger of the other hand, closing the other fingers on that hand to secure the strings.

Release. The term "normal release" means the process of converting to the original loop without entangling the strings. This is achieved by carefully placing the figure on the lap, withdrawing the fingers, and then drawing out at bottom and top the main cross strings at their center positions.

String Tricks.

Fingers Caught

Ages: 9–12

Players: any number; individual; informal

Place: home; schoolroom; out-of-doors

Supplies: string

Activity—pastime: manipulation of fingers

Appeal: skill

1. *Left hand.* Hold hand with fingers and thumb outward.
2. *Right hand.* Hold loop over left thumb and hand and withdraw right hand. Insert index finger from the left under near thumb string, reach between thumb and index finger, and pick up from

the right with ball of finger the far thumb string. Draw out to the left of near thumb string to form a small loop, rotate index finger inward and upward to give loop a twist, and place it over left index finger.

3. *Right hand.* In a similar manner pick up the far hand string between the index and middle fingers and place, after twisting, on the left middle finger.

4. *Right hand.* Proceed similarly by drawing out and twisting a loop from between the middle and ring fingers and placing on the left ring finger, and from between the ring and little fingers and placing on the little finger (Fig. 4).

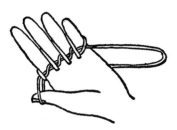

Fig. 4. Fingers Caught.

5. *Right hand.* Draw taut the two long hanging strings. Lift left thumb loop off thumb and drop. Now pull on the near long hanging string and all the strings will come off the fingers.

Cutting Off the Head

Ages: 9–12

Players: any number; individual; informal

Place: home; schoolroom; out-of-doors

Supplies: string

Activity—pastime: manipulation of string

Appeal: skill

1. *Right hand.* Place string over head so that a long loop hangs in front of body.

2. *Both hands.* With thumb and index finger pick up middle of string of pendant loop. Raise hands to level of mouth and cross them with strings tightly drawn. Pick up with teeth the intersection of crossed strings and bring hand back to a position directly in front of shoulder. Extend index finger so that string becomes a thumb loop (Fig. 5). Swing hands upward and backward to toss far thumb string over head to nape of neck. Retain loop on thumb and return hand to shoulder position. Palms outward, fingers upward. Bring hands suddenly together with a loud clap and at same time release strings from teeth. Both strings now appear on back of neck.

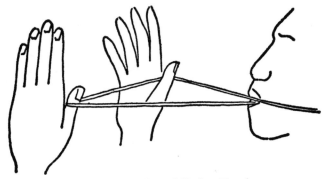

Fig. 5. Cutting Off the Head.

Threading the Needle

Ages: 9–12
Players: any number; individual; informal
Place: home; schoolroom; out-of-doors

Supplies: string
Activity—pastime: manipulation of string
Appeal: skill

A single piece of string is better for this widely distributed catch, although a loop used as a single string will do.

1. *Right hand.* Place string over left thumb, palm inward, fingers to right, so that about ten inches of string hangs on the far side of thumb. With right thumb and index finger pick up the near thumb string and wind several times around thumb. Make a small loop in the remainder of string held in right hand and place this between left thumb and index finger so that the long hanging part of the string is near the base of the left thumb.

2. *Right hand.* With tips of right thumb and index finger pick up the hanging end of the original far thumb string and draw to right without pulling taut. Hold this string as if you were threading a

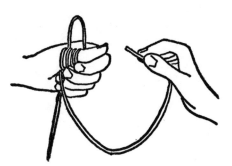

Fig. 6. "Threading the Needle."

needle and make several passes toward the loop (Fig. 6). Finally draw this string tight and allow it to pass upward between the left thumb and index finger at the same time as you pass the right hand quickly over the left hand. This movement draws the string up into the loop but gives the impression that it has been passed through the loop.

String Figures.

Two Water Holes

Ages: teen

Players: small group; individual; informal

Place: home; schoolroom; out-of-doors

Supplies: doubled string

Activity—pastime: manipulation of string

Appeal: skill

1. *Both hands.* Use doubled string or short loop. First position.
2. *Right hand.* Pick up from above with index finger the left palmar string. Rotate the index finger toward you to give a half twist to the index finger loop. Extend.
3. *Right hand.* Pick up from below on back of thumb the near index finger string.
4. *Left hand.* Pick up from below with thumb the near little finger string. Bend index finger over palmar string and pick up from below the far thumb string. Return to position.
5. *Both hands.* Navaho thumb strings. Drop little finger strings and turn hands palms downward.
6. *Left hand.* Rotate downward, then upward to the right until palm is facing upward and back of left wrist touches back of right wrist.
7. *Right hand.* In conjunction with Movement 6 move right hand to left and turn palm upward (Fig. 7).

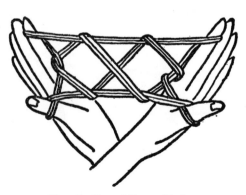

Fig. 7. Two Water Holes.

Two Kangaroos

Ages: teen

Players: small group; individual; informal

Place: home; schoolroom; out-of-doors

Supplies: string

Activity—pastime: manipulation of string

Appeal: skill

1. *Both hands.* Opening A. Pass little, ring, and middle fingers and thumb from below into index finger loop that thus becomes a wrist loop.
2. *Both hands.* Insert index finger from above into little finger loop, bend it toward you, and insert from above into thumb loop. Pick up with back of index finger the far thumb string and draw it up through the little finger loop. Extend.
3. *Both hands.* Drop thumb loop. Insert thumb from below into index finger loop and withdraw index finger.
4. *Right hand.* Hold strings secure, reach over back of left hand, and with thumb and index finger pick up left wrist string, lift off left hand, and place on left thumb and index finger as in first position.
5. *Left hand.* Repeat Movement 4 with left hand.
6. *Both hands.* Repeat Movement 2.
7. *Both hands.* Hold strings slack and drop little finger loops. Extend. Reach little finger forward and pick up from below with its back the near index finger string. Return to position and drop index finger strings.
8. *Both hands.* There are now two loops on the thumb and one on the little finger. On each palmar string is a loop one string of which runs directly across figure to other palmar string. Bend the index finger down over palmar string and with its ball pick up from the far side this horizontal string. Return to position by rotating the hands toward you and lowering slightly the elbows, thus placing a loop on the back of first joint of the index finger.
9. *Both hands.* Drop thumb loops. Turn palms downward and draw out working strings slowly until figure is obtained (Fig. 8).

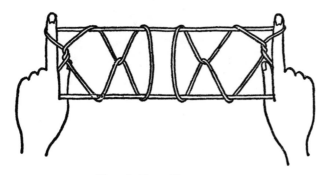

Fig. 8. Two Kangaroos.

Turtle or Spider Net

Ages: teen

Players: small group; couples; informal

Place: home; schoolroom; out-of-doors

Supplies: double loop string

Activity—pastime: coordination; manipulation of string

Appeal: skill

1. *First Person. Both hands.* "Little Fishes" opening.
2. *First Person. Both hands.* Treat the double loop as a single string and execute again the "Little Fishes" opening to place a quadruple loop on the index fingers.
3. *Second Person. Left hand.* Insert index finger from above into loops held by first person near his right hand and remove from his right index finger.
4. *Second Person. Right hand.* With palm downward pick up from above with ball of ring finger one of the near strings a few inches from left index finger of first person and draw out slightly. Pass index finger over this string, pick up from above with its ball a second string, and draw out over first string.
5. *Second Person. Right hand.* Straighten index finger until the back of the first joint rests under ring finger string. Move thumb along

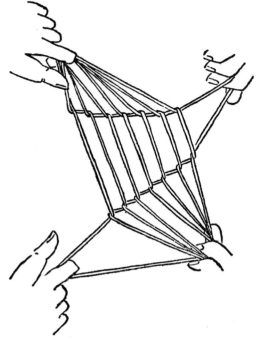

Fig. 9. Turtle.

ball of index finger to catch palmar index finger string on back of first joint of thumb. Separate thumb and index finger slightly. Pass index finger forward and pick up from above with its ball a third string. Draw this string out over second string.

6. *Second Person. Right hand.* Proceed similarly to Movement 5 and pick up the fourth near string and each of the four far strings of the quadruple loop. When the eighth string has been drawn out on the ball of index finger pass the index finger outward under all strings toward right hand of first person.

7. *First Person. Right hand.* Pass index finger downward into loop on right finger of second person and take off.

8. *Second Person. Right hand.* Pass index finger downward into ring finger loop and take off.

9. *Both Persons. Both hands.* Extend hands slightly to draw strings taut (Fig. 9).

Maori—Top Spinning.

GAMES AND SPORTS—NEW ZEALAND

THE MAORI

Haka-Pai (HAR-kar PA-i)

Ages: 9–12
Players: 6–12; two-group; line
Place: home; schoolroom

Supplies: small ball, string
Activity—pastime: swaying body
Appeal: rhythm

The *haka-pai* or ball-dance is a rhythmic movement of hands and body. This activity is especially popular among the girls. The girls are seated in a line. Each girl holds in her hands a short string to which is attached a small ball of dried flax stuffed with down from a wild reed. As the girls sway their bodies to some rhythmical accompaniment, preferably 6/8 time, they also move the hands so that the balls lightly bounce off the wrists.

Top Spinning

Ages: all
Players: 6 to 30; individual; informal
Place: out-of-doors

Supplies: string, tops
Activity—pastime: top spinning
Appeal: competition; rhythm

All Maori, old and young, have enjoyed spinning tops. The skilled player may use a whip of long flax strings attached to a short stick to make his top spin faster. An individual "knock-out" is achieved when a player whips his top close enough to the top of another player to knock it over. Group contests may be held also.

5

Europe

The influence of the peoples of Europe is far-reaching in time and territory. Centuries ago and throughout the years, the kingdoms, the governments, and the rulers of the old world countries established their ideas within many and vast new lands. So it was with the common people who, in due time, were transplanted to the new worlds—except that the business of the common people was adjusting to the problems of everyday living. As they become a part of new worlds whether in North America or in Africa, these valiant people established many of their beliefs and customs into the work, worship, and play of the peoples around them. Thus the folkways of many peoples were finally merged into new, yet related, patterns. This was especially true of European play and games, with the exception of those from Eastern Europe. The regions and their countries contributing to the global collection of games are:

CENTRAL EUROPE
Germany   Switzerland

EASTERN EUROPE
Poland   Russia

NORTHERN EUROPE
Denmark   Norway   Sweden

SOUTHERN EUROPE
Greece   Portugal
Italy   Spain

WESTERN EUROPE
Belgium   The Netherlands
France   United Kingdom
                 England   Scotland   Wales
                 Republic of Ireland

CENTRAL EUROPE

The climatic conditions of both Germany and Switzerland are conducive to vigorous activity. Traditional influence seems more predominant in the games from Germany than in those from Switzerland. The specific observations that follow apply briefly to pre-World War II Germany and more fully to West Germany of today.

GERMANY AND SWITZERLAND

The existing folk games of Germany are popular with North American children. The scarcity of traditional games is no doubt due to their exclusion from play programs in German schools to make room for the emphasis placed on physical exercise.

At the turn of the eighteenth century German educators started the process of leading children and youth toward the goal of the highest physical performance possible. The progression was from Greek physical exercises, climbing and balancing, and exercises for the joints to complicated acrobatic exercises that were executed in gymnastics sports clubs and associations. A program of compulsion was carried out by National Socialism, and finally the sports activities of German children and youth evolved into its present status.

Soccer is the favorite team sport; hand ball and badminton are the two most popular recreational games in Germany today. Germans had rather participate in sports than watch them. Educators in West Germany are using sports and games as a training medium through which the children and youth of Germany will "not only learn the rules of the game of democracy but also digest its human dignity and beauty."

Skiing, ice-skating, sledding, and tobogganing are favorite activities of children and adults in Germany and Switzerland. Often grandparents lead the way in skiing contests when the whole family participates. Family hikes and picnics are a part of every Sunday and holiday events.

The four games described in the "Games from Switzerland" are delightful patterns of play. They indicate a dramatic fun-loving approach to play, and they provide a challenge to the alertness of all participants.

EASTERN EUROPE

The traditional play patterns of Eastern Europe may be numerous, yet few of them are known to peoples in other parts of the world. Why, one might ask, are there so few folk games from peoples who are rich in legend and folk-living? The answer may fall into two categories. Either the play life of the everyday people, children especially, has been drained (through the centuries) of its fun-loving element and therefore has faded out; or the life of the plain peoples in Eastern Europe has undergone such violent changes the past several decades that games and play patterns that might have existed have been excluded from all plans used to put the Communist wheels into motion.

POLAND AND RUSSIA

The game from Poland is interesting yet not sufficient basis for a conclusion as to the traditional play life of Polish boys and girls. Their dances, however, are gay and resemble square dances of the United States of North America.

The young people of Poland today are enthusiastic about sports. They enjoy soccer, swimming, boxing, track and field, cycling, fencing, and skiing.

The games from Russia indicate that play and games may have had, at one time, a place in the life of the boys and girls. The similarities of several of the Russian games to the games from other lands point out again the universality of play regardless of differences in societies and influences of political leaders.

The play life of the boys and girls in present day Russia is not planned for fun and free choice of activities and so it has been since the days of Joseph Stalin. He used and misused play, games, physical education, and sports to gain control of the children, the boys and girls, and the youth of Russia. Premier Khrushchev and his followers are going a step further, for Russia is working hard and succeeding in many situations, to establish superiority in worldwide athletics. This is being done for several obvious reasons. First, Russia is building self-confidence within her own youth; second, she is trying to dominate athletic competition of the countries of the free world, especially that of the United States of North America; and third, she is teaching her youth that strong healthy bodies are necessary as preparation to taking over the world for Communism. Because of these reasons the Russians—children, youth, and adults— show a definite seriousness in their games that goes deeper than the desire for companionship, for competition, and for public acclaim. The Russian attitude, that of girls and women as well as that of boys and men, is Spartan-like in its intensity and devotion to winning. For example, *footbul* (football) is the favorite Soviet sport. It is a kind of soccer and not football as played in the United States. The Soviets take the game solemnly, never cheering an outstanding play of an opponent; and only clapping, never cheering, their own team.

NORTHERN EUROPE

Regardless of the general climatic coldness of the Scandinavian countries, the peoples of other and warmer lands find that the friendliness of the Danish, the Norwegian, and the Swedish people overcomes all extreme weather conditions. The games from these countries are patterns of friendly play and competition. Although the majority of the games are outgrowths from practices and legends of a strenuous past, they present a delightful picture of a happy play heritage not common to all societies.

DENMARK

There are fewer restrictions of etiquette on social life in Denmark than in most countries, and consequently less extremes in the modes of life and fewer grades—social distinctions. Though hard workers, the Danes are a pleasure-loving people. There are many parks and open spaces that in spring and summer are the scenes of gay amusements. Circuses, yachting, wrestling matches, cycle races—all go to make up the recreational life of the average Dane. Swimming is the favorite pastime of every Danish boy. There are supposedly more bicycles per capita in Denmark than in any other country of the universe, indicating that everybody cycles in Denmark.

Along with polo and hockey, football is a popular summer sport. Lawn tennis consumes a large part of the leisure time of the Danes during the summer months, with croquet being a particular favorite of the girls and women. In winter, theaters, music halls, and concert halls re-open. Dinner parties are the chief social entertainment, with dancing coming in for its share of leisure time employment. "Bandy," a game similar to ice hockey, is a favorite during the winter months. With such a variety of sports activities in which whole families may participate there is little wonder at the scarcity of traditional games from Denmark.

NORWAY AND SWEDEN

The Norwegian children do not enjoy the freedom of year-round play as the children in the United States do because of the long winters. They know little about out-of-door games and sports such as cricket, football, golf, hockey, or tennis because the snow-covered ground does not provide opportunity for such activities. Skating, skiing, and tobogganing are the Norwegian winter sports. During the month of March a week-long series of ski events, the *Holmenkollen Week*, is held just outside of the city of Oslo. A ski-jump contest held on the last day climaxes the occasion. In the summer the Norwegian youth fish in the lakes and rivers and go for long walks in the mountains. When the weather permits the children enjoy outdoor games and most of them may be classed as singing games and folk dances. "Blindman's Buff," "Forfeits," and "Hunt the Slipper" are played in Norway as they are played the world around. "Hop-in-Paradise," which is a form of "Hop-Scotch," is a favorite game with Norwegian boys and girls.

The present generation of Sweden manifests the courage of its Viking ancestors in the choice of active and vigorous sports and pastimes. Swedish legends tell that the Viking warriors often engaged in tests of skill and strength with the bow and arrow and with the javelin and sword. Wrestling and jumping were also popular sports.

Today the Swedes practice curling and football as learned from other countries. The national sport is skating, whereas the most popular and very useful form of sport is skiing.

Swedish boys and girls play many games that are similar to those enjoyed by North American children. The outstanding characteristic of all the Swedish play activities is that there is no evidence of roughness. The players enter into the game with the desire to share the fun with others and thus gain a great deal of pleasure in a simple and natural way.

SOUTHERN EUROPE

The people of Greece, Italy, Portugal, and Spain reflect their love for life in their folk games. The cruelty of ancient life and the demands of survival activities among these peoples are faintly evident in many of the play patterns. Yet through the years there has evolved a healthy and relaxed attitude toward play, games, and sports.

GREECE

The Greeks' love of contests in sports has influenced the peoples of the world for centuries. The greatest evidence today is seen in the Olympic Games now held every four years.

In ancient days the young Greek boy often played "Blindman's Buff" and "Tug-of-War." He also enjoyed a peculiar test of balance that consisted of jumping on an inflated skin made slippery with grease. Ball games were a favorite pastime with Greek children.

As the Greek boy reached seven years of age his serious education began. The beginning consisted chiefly of classes in gymnastics and activities such as wrestling and running that would develop swiftness of foot and eye. Long and high jumps, with and without a run, and throwing quoits and spears at targets, were taught the young Greek. These accounts of the physical training of the boy point to the Greek idea that the development and discipline of the body should be the main purpose in life.

The modern adaptations of early Greek games are very popular with North American children today. The games "Duck on a Rock," "Black and White," and "Hand Tag" are games that have been derived from ancient play patterns of the early Greeks.

ITALY, PORTUGAL, AND SPAIN

The freedom-loving people of Italy enjoy holidays and festivals that are enlivened by dances, music, and games. They are equally as enthusiastic about art museums and opera as they are about golf and bathing beaches. The sports program of the Italian Youth survived the trauma of the Fascists' dreams of world superiority in athletics. Games and sports are enjoyed today for their contribution to companionship, to developing strong bodies, and to healthy competition at home and abroad.

In Italy many of the children's games are quite similar in character, if not in name, to the games of the North American children. Marbles, kite-flying, and ball-playing come in for the greater part of the children's play. There is a game similar to "Duck on the Rock," popular in Greece and in the United States.

The chief recreational interests of the Portuguese boys and girls consist of folk music. This includes the lively dancing songs, as well as the sad songs, done to the accompaniment of a guitar. Two of the folk games from Portugal demand a quick and agreeable response to the surprise-element within the game patterns; the other game is suggestive of the "Cops and Robbers" theme so popular the world over.

The young Spanish girls and boys often play together. Their games are usually simple, gay, and enacted to a song or nursery rhyme. The market game in which each child takes the part of a woven basket, a clay jar, or a vegetable is a favorite with the young girls. In another game enjoyed by them each player takes the part of a bottle of perfume, a comb, or a flower for the hair.

Boys play at soldiers and warfare, but their chief delight is to play bullfight. The Anglo-Saxon sports of football and baseball are becoming popular with Spanish boys and men.

WESTERN EUROPE

The lifeline of many play patterns popular today with boys and girls throughout the world can be traced directly to the peoples of Western Europe. The cultural patterns of each country are unique and so it is with the games and play. Many sports so popular in the United States of America today have their roots in the old world.

BELGIUM AND FRANCE

The Belgians enjoy many sports including basketball, soccer, archery, quoits, and cycling. The game "Tap the Line" is an adaptation from a Belgian folk tale of long ago. The description of the game would indicate that the play patterns of this country are rich in dramatic as well as physical activity.

The children of France have been, and still are to a large degree, closely supervised in the home and at school. This may have adversely influenced the spontaneity of play; it may, too, be an indirect cause of the scarcity of French folk games. In the past the children seem to have acquired a reserve that is unnatural to childhood. Recently strides are being made in establishing a desire for sports and physical education activities among the children and youth of France. There is a program of "natural" activities and games of low organization that lead to sports. Emphasis is first placed on track and field, then on swimming, these being considered basic activities.

In the cities, football and tennis are popular among the French youth. Bicycle riding and racing are favorites with all. Bull fights are also enjoyed. Men in the villages like the game of "bowls," which is played with a wooden ball rolled on a lawn or even on a street.

THE NETHERLANDS

Since this country's chief industries depend primarily upon the sea, the logical conclusion is that many of her children's games are relative to the sea, and so they are. The Netherlanders focus their interests on water activities such as swimming, rowing, sailing, and fishing. The team sports of basketball and soccer are popular.

The most popular sport in The Netherlands is ice skating. Some of the skaters hold little sails that carry them, with the aid of the wind, over the ice very rapidly. The schools declare a holiday each winter when the canals freeze hard enough for skating. Many of the people enjoy sleigh-riding, often using coasting sleds that are low in front and guided by a stick and a rope.

Other popular game activities are "bowling on the grass," "tick-tack," and "tock." "Tick-tack" is a complicated game similar to backgammon. "Tock" is played with an ivory ball that is knocked under wire wickets with a cue.

Marbles, hoops, tops, and balls, are commonly used play equipment among the chilldren. Hop-scotch, tag games, leapfrog, kite flying, egg rolling (on Easter), and rope jumping are favorites with young boys and girls.

The Netherlands—Ice Skating.

UNITED KINGDOM

ENGLAND

The games played by the English children are active and suggest the Englishman's traditional love of sports and outdoor activities.

The folk games of England bear evidence of early beliefs and customs. The games "Hunt the Fox," "Jingling Match," "Pell Mell," "Smugglers," and "Stool Ball" have their origin in folkways of old England. These games and many others have given rise to game patterns played by children in all lands where the English established themselves as a ruling authority.

Much in contrast to the English attitude toward play today is the story of old London and the love of its citizens for football, wrestling, and sham fights held outside the city. The game of football was extremely popular in England, and especially in and around London, during the reign of King Edward II. The King, who wanted his people to become skilled at archery and to help spread England's fame in the sport, made a law to stop the playing of football and other "dishonest" games. Today soccer, cricket, and rugby are well-established sports in England, with many lead-up games of skill being a part of the play among young children.

SCOTLAND AND WALES

Golf is the favorite sport of Scotland. Its world famous courses attract many internationally known players each year.

Many games played by the children of Scotland are similar to the games of the English children. The Scotch games differ only in name from the English games of similar organization. One outstanding difference in some games popular with the Scotch children is that their play often suggests warfare.

Rugby and soccer are the favorite team sports of the kind, hospitable, and game-loving people of Wales, a small mountainous part of Great Britain. The Welsh rugby teams often enter international competitive events. The universal sports of tennis, lawn bowling, golf, fishing and swimming, and boxing are enjoyed by the youth and adults. Families enjoy singing together many evenings. Their fondness for their traditional songs bespeaks of their devotion to their country's rich heritage of folklore.

Games from Northern Ireland are not available.

REPUBLIC OF IRELAND

Although the game "Blarney Stone" is not a traditional Irish folk game, it does its part in upholding the Irish legend of old Blarney Castle. This legend has not only provided the pattern for an attractive game, but for many years it also provided an attractive income to Sir George Calthrust, the owner of the castle. Many folk, tourists especially, paid a shilling to kiss the famed stone.

GAMES AND SPORTS—CENTRAL EUROPE

GERMANY

Alpine Tag

Ages: 9–12

Players: 21 or more; transition

Place: gymnasium; out-of-doors

Supplies: playground ball

Activity—hunting: chasing, dodging, grasping, running

Appeal: competition, dramatization, problem solving, repetition, skill

One player, chosen to be the *king*, carries an *Alpine stick*, which may be a long paper wand or a stick. The other players are divided into four groups with a *goat* leader for each group. The players form a large hollow square with each *goat* at the head of his line. A large, soft ball, the *yodel ball*, is placed in the center of the square, very near the *king*.

The game begins when the *king* taps three times with his *Alpine stick*. Then the four *goats* start leading their lines anywhere they want to go, but not too far from the *yodel ball*. The *king* remains still and keeps his eye on the ball. Suddenly a bugle call or other signal is given and the *goats* rush for the ball. The one to reach it first grabs it and runs. The *king*, the other three *goats*, and the line players, all yodeling and shouting, chase him.

The *goat* with the ball may roll it to any player in his own line by hitting the ball with his hand, but never kicking it. If the chase lasts unusually long, a signal to stop may be given, the player with the ball becomes *king*, and the former *king* takes the player's place in the line.

All of the *goats* and their players try to keep the *king* from getting the ball. If the *king* does get the ball and immediately taps the player who last held the ball with his stick, all of the players must return to their places in lines and start the game as before. If a player or *goat* gets the ball from the *king*, he becomes *king* and the former *king* is out of the game. In every case the new *king* chooses four new *goats* to lead the lines and the game continues as before.

Barley Break

Ages: 9–12

Players: 20 or more; two-group; informal

Place: gymnasium; out-of-doors

Supplies: not any

Activity—hunting: chasing, dodging, running, stamping

Appeal: competition, problem solving, skill

This lively game is centuries old and was played at harvest time around the stacks in the cornfields.

A strip of ground is divided into three equal squares, each measuring from 10 to 50 feet, the size depending upon the number of players. The center square is called the *barley field* and is occupied by two *guards* who link arms and face in opposite directions. The other players are divided into two teams of *barley breakers* who also form in couples but face the *barley field*. The *barley breakers* enter singly or in couples with linked arms and tramp the barley, thus taunting the *guards* who try to catch them. Any *barley breaker* caught must stand in the *barley field* until his partner is tagged; then the two become *guards*, and replace the former *guards*. Any individual *barley breakers* who have been caught return to their own field and the game goes on as before. The *guard* must remain within the field.

Baste the Bear

(See Denmark.)

Carnival Game

Ages: 9–12; teen
Players: any number; couples; informal
Place: out-of-doors

Supplies: sausages
Activity—contest; pastime: eating
Appeal: competition

Each of two players takes in his mouth one end of a long string of linked sausages and have an eating race. The winning player is the one who eats the most sausage before his nose touches that of his opponent.

This game is played as a favorite during *Fasching*, a Munich carnival celebration, which lasts from January until Shrove Tuesday, which is sometimes in late February or early March.

Crown the King

Ages: 9–12
Players: 20 or more; two-group-and-one; circle
Place: gymnasium; out-of-doors
Supplies: not any

Activity—hunting: bending, climbing, grasping, reaching
Appeal: competition, problem solving, skill

One player is chosen to be *king* while the others are divided into two groups. One group guards the *king*, while the others, the *aggressors*, attempt to crown the *king*. The *guards* form a protective wall about the *king* by clasping each other around the waist and bending over. The *aggressors* take turns at trying to touch the *king*

Germany—Carnival Game.

by wriggling over the backs of the *guards,* who do all they can to shake off their opponent. If he touches the *king,* a point is scored by his side. If he falls off, he loses his right to try to crown the *king.* When all of the *aggressors* have had their turn, they change duties with the *guards* and the former *guards* take their turn at crowning the *king.* The side having the highest score wins. If the group is small, as each player succeeds in touching the *king,* he becomes the *king* and the former *king* becomes a *guard.*

The game originated with German peasants who showed a definite dislike for tyrannical kings.

Dog Collar

Ages: teen (boys)
Players: any number; couples, line
Place: gymnasium; out-of-doors

Supplies: loops of strong cloth
Activity—contest: pulling
Appeal: competition, skill

German backs are strengthened in this unique game. The players are in two lines facing each other. With a dividing line between the two sides, a loop of strong cloth or soft rope is placed back of the neck of each couple of opposing players. The contestants kneel and, at a signal, try to pull each other by the head across the dividing line. The team pulling the most opponents over the line within one minute wins.

German Egg Game

Ages: 9–12
Players: any number; couples; informal
Place: gymnasium; out-of-doors; schoolroom
Supplies: colored eggs, cotton, two baskets
Activity—hunting: running
Appeal: problem solving, skill

This game is most interesting when played by only two, letting the others watch until their turn comes. Two baskets, some cotton or shavings, and several pretty colored eggs are needed. One basket is shallow and filled with the shavings. The other contains the eggs. One player is chosen to be the *runner* while *the other* tends the baskets. The *runner* rushes from a starting place and back; during that time *the other* player tries to transfer the eggs from the egg-basket to the shallow one. The children then change places and play again. The score depends upon the number of eggs transferred. The eggs may be given to the player having the best record. This game is sometimes known as "Easter Game."

Going to Jerusalem

Ages: 9–12
Players: 20 or more; transition
Place: gymnasium; home; schoolroom
Supplies: cane, chairs
Activity—pastime: running, walking
Appeal: dramatization, problem solving, skill

This game was devised in Germany to meet the scarcity of partners for girls as a result of the great loss of lives in the Thirty Years' War. It is sometimes played in the United States by the same name and as "Musical Chairs." In Germany it is also called *Mauer Blümchen* or "Wall-Flower." It is most enjoyable when played with musical accompaniment.

Chairs are placed in a row in the center of the room so that alternate chairs face in opposite directions. The number of chairs should be one less than the number of players. One player is chosen to be the *leader* and stands to one side while the others are seated in the chairs. The *leader*, carrying a cane, starts the game by walking around the row of chairs as the music begins and chants, "I'm going to Jerusalem! I'm going to Jerusalem!" Suddenly he stops at the back of a chair and taps his cane on the floor. The player sitting in the chair must immediately rise and follow the *leader*. The *leader* continues to recruit the players for his trip to Jerusalem until all are following him in a single file.

When the music stops, or upon some other signal, the players rush for chairs. The player without a chair is out of the game and takes with him one of the chairs. The game continues until there are only two players encircling one chair. The player who secures it wins.

Schlagball

Ages: teen
Players: 12 or more; two-group; informal
Place: out-of-doors

Supplies: a softball, bat
Activity—athletic: batting, pitching, running, throwing
Appeal: competition, skill

This game is something like baseball except that each team has a goal instead of bases. The players are in two teams. The batter hits a ball, about the size of a baseball but softer; he then runs to the goal. If he makes it without being hit by an opponent who may pick up the ball and throw at him, he scores one point. If he is hit by the ball, the opposing team goes to bat.

SWITZERLAND

Blinzlis (Blintz-lis)

Ages: 9–12
Players: 30 or more; two-group-and-one; circle
Place: gymnasium; out-of-doors

Supplies: not any
Activity—hunting: alertness, batting the eyes, running
Appeal: dramatization, strategy

Blinzlis, meaning "batting the eyes," is a game for a large group. The players stand in two circles, an *inner* and an *outer* one, with all facing the center of the circles. One player stands in the center and has to bat his eyes at one of the *inside circle* players. This is the player whom he wishes to join him. Each player in the *outside circle* has to be careful that his partner does not run away. He may hold him when he does try to run. If a player is not paying enough attention and his partner succeeds in running toward the one with the batting eyes, the player left in the *outside circle* has to stand in the center and bat his eyes at some other player, thus trying to regain a partner.

Fuul Ei (Fool-i)

Ages: 9–12
Players: 20 or more; two-group-and-one; circles
Place: gymnasium; out-of-doors

Supplies: handkerchief
Activity—hunting: chasing, dodging, running
Appeal: dramatization, skill

The players stand in a double circle, except one, the *fuul ei* or *rotten egg*, who is without a partner. This player has a handkerchief and runs around outside of the circles. He tries to drop the handkerchief unnoticed behind one of two partners, then proceeds on his course. If he succeeds in going around the circle until he reaches the handkerchief without the person behind whom it was dropped noticing it, he calls out, "Rotten Egg." The new *rotten egg*, that is the circle player, has to take the handkerchief and start the game anew. The first *rotten egg* takes his place in the inner circle. If the partner of the outside player has noticed the dropped handkerchief in time, he picks it up quickly, chases the *rotten egg*, and if he catches him before he has reached his place, the *rotten egg* must try again.

Hallihallo (HAH-li HAH-lo)

Ages: 9–12
Players: 10 or more; group-and-one; row
Place: home; schoolroom

Supplies: ball or beanbag
Activity—pastime: alertness, catching, throwing
Appeal: suspense

The players sit in a row and one, the *leader*, stands in front of the group with a ball in his hands. He says, "It is an animal, starting with 'B'" (buffalo perhaps) and throws the ball to the first player sitting in the row. The player replies by trying to guess the name of the animal starting with "B" and throws the ball back. If his guess is right, he then becomes the *leader* and stands in front of the group. The first *leader* sits at the end of the row. If the player does not know the answer, he throws the ball back to the *leader* and the play continues to the second player in the row. If at the end of the row no player has guessed the name of the animal, the *leader* this time has to say the second letter of the animal, as "Bu" and so on. He may ask anything such as the name of a town, country, river, mountain, car, etc. A player should not be allowed too long a time to think, but should throw the ball back rather quickly.

Pussy Cat Makes Miau

Ages: 9–12
Players: 20 or more; group-and-one; circle
Place: home; schoolroom

Supplies: not any
Activity—pastime: self-control
Appeal: dramatization

The players stand in a circle. One of them, the *pussy cat*, stands in the center, and starts the game by kneeling or cowering before a circle player. The kneeling player imitates the voice of a hungry, lonely cat. The circle player must caress the *pussy cat* and say, "Poor pussy cat." If the circle player says this three times without smiling, the poor *pussy cat* must try his chance with another player, and so on until he finds someone who smiles at him. When the *pussy cat* does get a player to smile, he exchanges places with the player who then has to go into the center of the circle and become the *pussy cat.*

GAMES AND SPORTS—EASTERN EUROPE

POLAND

Grandma Is Blind

Ages: 9–12
Players: 20 or more; group-and-one; circle
Place: gymnasium; out-of-doors

Supplies: blindfold
Activity—hunting: chasing, dodging, running
Appeal: dramatization

One player, the *blind grandma,* is blindfolded and turned about. The others, in a circle formation, ask, "Grandma, grandma, where are you?" *Grandma* replies, "On a barrel." The players then ask, "What does the barrel hold?" "It is full of fish," *grandma* answers. The players ask, "Grandma, are you as nimble as the fish?" "Indeed, I am," says *grandma.* "Then grandma, catch us if you can," the players shout and run about the area as *grandma* tries to catch them. The first one caught is the next *blind grandma.*

RUSSIA

Czars

Ages: 9–12
Players: 20 or more; group-and-one; informal
Place: gymnasium; out-of-doors
Supplies: not any

Activity—hunting: guessing, chasing, running
Appeal: dramatization, problem solving

One player is chosen to be the *Czar.* The others are his *subjects* and agree upon some pantomime that they will present to the *Czar* as he approaches them saying, "Well, my subjects, what have you been doing?" If the *Czar* guesses correctly all *subjects* turn and run to a designated goal, trying to escape being tagged. If a *subject* is caught, he takes the *Czar's* place, otherwise the *Czar* must try again.

"Hail! O King" from Israel and "Little White House on the Hill" from the United States of America are similar games.

Golden Gates

Ages: 5–8
Players: 20 or more; two-group; line
Place: gymnasium; out-of-doors
Supplies: not any

Activity—hunting: guessing, holding
Appeal: dramatization, problem solving

This game is the same as "London Bridge" played by children of the United States. The Russian children chant,

> Go through the golden gates, go, go,
> Go through the golden gates, go, go, etc.

The game is ended with a tug-o-war or some other contest.

Gorelki

Ages: 9–12
Players: 13 or more; couples-and-one; lines
Place: gymnasium; out-of-doors
Supplies: not any

Activity—hunting: chasing, dodging, running
Appeal: dramatization, problem solving

The formation and object of this game is the same as "Widower's Game" of Sweden, "Two Friends" of Ghana, and "Last Couple Out" of the United States. In the Russian game "Gorelki" the *leader* says:

> Burn bright, burn bright,
> Fire must not die tonight,
>   Look above the sea,
> Birds are singing,
> Bells are ringing,
>   One, two, three.

As the *leader* says *three*, the last couple separates, runs out, and tries to clasp hands in front of the *leader*. If they succeed, they go to the front of the files. If one of the couples is *caught*, he is the *leader's* partner. The other member of the couple becomes the *leader*.

Russian Hole Ball

Ages: 9–12
Players: 3–10; single-group; informal
Place: out-of-doors

Supplies: small ball, beanbag, or stone
Activity—pastime: pitching
Appeal: competition, skill

The players are numbered 1,2,3, etc. As many holes as there are players are dug in the ground. The holes, in a straight line and 3

Russia—Gorelki.

feet apart, are large enough to contain the ball. Each hole is numbered consecutively beginning with one. The first player toes a line
10 feet away from the first hole. He pitches the ball for one of the
holes. The score of the pitch is according to the number of the hole
in which the ball falls. The next player is also designated by the
number. For example, if the ball falls in hole four, the first player's
score is four; this player gives his place to Number Four, who has
his turn at pitching for a hole. The winner of the game may be determined by the player holding the highest score at the end of a set
time limit; or he may be the player who first scores 25 to 50. This
game is adaptable to snow and to the sand of the seashore.

"Ring and String Game" and "Rouble Game" are mentioned in
Tolstoy's *War and Peace* as being popular with Russian boys and
girls.

The Sea Is Getting Stormy

Ages: 9–12; teen
Players: 20 or more; group-and-one; circle
Place: home; gymnasium; schoolroom

Supplies: chairs
Activity—pastime: running, talking, walking
Appeal: dramatization, problem solving

This game is similar to "Going to Jerusalem" from Germany. The difference in the Russian version is that the *leader* walks about the room telling a story. From time to time he calls the different players from their chairs to join him. After all are walking behind the *leader*, he suddenly calls, "The sea is getting stormy," whereupon all rush for chairs. The odd player becomes the *leader* and begins to tell a story.

Ting-a-ling

Ages: 9–12
Players: 20 or more; group-and-one; square
Place: gymnasium; out-of-doors
Supplies: bell, box

Activity—hunting: chasing, dodging, listening, running, passing
Appeal: dramatization, problem solving, rhythm, skill

This game is adapted from a very old Russian legend, a tale of Moscow, often known as the city of bells.

The players stand on the lines of a large square, all facing the center. A small square is in the center of the large one. Straight lines are drawn diagonally from corner to corner through the big square.

One player is chosen to be the *clapper* and takes his place in the small square that is called the *steeple*. The clapper holds a small box or basket in his hands, a box large enough to hold a small bell that has been given to one of the line players. A *captain* is chosen to lead the lines. At the signal, he starts walking along the lines of the big square or up and down the diagonal lines. The others must follow the path of the captain. In the meantime the child with the bell rings it softly and passes it to another player as they follow the captain. As they march along each player who receives the bell rings it softly and passes it on. The *clapper* tries to detect who has the bell by watching closely from the *steeple*.

He suddenly claps his hands, the children stop quickly, break rank, and encircle the *clapper* as fast as they can. The player who holds the bell drops it into the *clapper's* box and runs as fast as possible while the *clapper* chases him. The chase must be confined to the inside of the square. The other children may follow the *clapper.* If a player gets close enough to the *clapper* to grab the bell out of the box, he may do so. Then the *clapper* must chase the player who has the bell. The player may escape by passing the bell to any other player and again the *clapper* chases the player with the bell. The chase continues until a signal to stop is given. The player holding the bell at this time is the *clapper* for the next game.

GAMES AND SPORTS—NORTHERN EUROPE

DENMARK

Baste the Bear

Ages: 9–12
Players: 10 or more; group-and-two; circle
Place: gymnasium; out-of-doors
Supplies: rope, stool

Activity—hunting: dodging, striking
Appeal: problem solving, repetition, skill

The *bear* sits on a stool in the center of the circle and holds one end of a two-foot rope knotted at each end. His *keeper* holds the other end of the rope in the circle. The players may only try to tag the *bear* or his *keeper* when the *keeper* calls, "My bear is free!" If they tag at any other time that player becomes the *bear;* the former *bear* is the *keeper;* and the *keeper* joins the circle. The players try to tag the *keeper* (who tries to protect the bear by dodging around him) or the *bear* without being tagged themselves by either. Should a player be tagged the player becomes the *keeper* and the *keeper* joins the circle.

If a rope is not available the *bear* and *keeper* may hold hands, or a small circle may be drawn in which the *bear* and *keeper* must remain, or the *keeper* may be allowed to go two steps and no more away from the *bear.*

Danish Rounders

Ages: teen
Players: 8–20; two-group; informal
Place: gymnasium; out-of-doors
Supplies: tennis ball

Activity—athletic: catching, running, striking
Appeal: competition, problem solving, skill

This game is very popular in Denmark. It is especially good for small teams. The playing rules are simple, as follows:

1. Two teams, of any number of players, who play on a regular tennis court, marking squares at each corner of the court—similar to bases in ball games.
2. The "in" team is that which is batting, the "out" that which is fielding.

Denmark—Baste the Bear.

3. The pitcher, of the out-team, has to throw the ball above the head of the batter, who hits with her hand and runs to the first square.
4. A point is scored when a player has run all around the field or room, passing through each square.
5. The fielders try to return the ball as quickly as possible to the pitcher, who grounds it in the pitching circle and calls "Down!" The ball must be in her hand.
6. When "Down" is called, any player running between squares is out.
7. To be in the squares, any player must be grounded, not in the air.
8. If the ball is caught from a hit, the player who hit it is out and anyone running between squares is out.
9. Any number of players may be in a square at the same time, and the running need not be in consecutive order.
10. The players need not run every time the ball is hit, but at their own discretion.

11. If the hitter misses the ball, she runs anyway. (With small children, two tries at hitting may be allowed.)
12. Points may go to side or individual.
13. Teams should have an even number of innings, or play to time.
14. The last one to bat when no one else is waiting can have three tries but must run to first square each time and can be put out. The other players can run for each hit.[1]

Dog and Hare

Ages: 5–8
Players: 20 or more; group-and-two; circle
Place: gymnasium; out-of-doors
Supplies: not any

Activity—hunting: chasing, dodging, galloping, running, skipping
Appeal: dramatization, problem solving, repetition

The players form a circle and join hands. Two players are chosen from the ring, one to be the *hare;* the other the *dog.* The *hare* pretends to be asleep in the center. He crouches on all fours and places his head low to the ground. The circle players start walking slowly around and around the *hare.* They gradually increase their speed by running, galloping, or skipping. The *hare* awakens and hops about, occasionally sitting up to wiggle his long ears that are represented by his hands placed at either side of his head. Meanwhile the *dog* is outside the circle, awaiting his opportunity to chase the *hare.* His chance does not occur until the circle players suddenly stop moving. Even then they may crowd together to help the *hare,* although they must not stoop or sit. When the *hare* is caught he chooses a circle player to take his place and he becomes the *dog.*

Guard the Blind

Ages: 9–12
Players: 10 or more; group-and-two; circle
Place: gymnasium; out-of-doors

Supplies: handkerchief
Activity—hunting: running, statue
Appeal: dramatization, problem solving

It, who is blindfolded, stands with his *guard* in the center of ring formed by the other players. The *guard* tries to keep the circle players from tagging *It.* When *It* is tagged he commands "Stop!" and each player must hold the position he was in at the time of the command. Then *It* tries to guess which player tagged him. If he succeeds, the player becomes *It.* If he fails, the *guard* becomes *It* and another *guard* is chosen from the ring.

[1] Campbell, Antoinette, "How We Do It," *Journal of Health and Physical Education.* Vol. **IX** (May, 1938), p. 312. Quoted by permission of the publishers.

Ocean Is Stormy

Ages: 9–12
Players: 20 or more; transition
Place: gymnasium; out-of-doors
Supplies: not any

Activity—hunting: listening, memory, running
Appeal: dramatization, problem solving

The players are in couples and stand within small circles marked on the floor about the room. There is one more couple than circles. Each couple quietly selects the name of a fish with the exception of the odd couple. They are the *whales* and walk about the room, calling the names of the fishes. When a couple's name is called, they leave their circle and walk behind the *whales*. After all names have been called or after the *whales* have called all the names they can think of, they cry, "The ocean is stormy." All *fishes* and the *whales* heed the warning by rushing to find a circle. The odd couple without a circle becomes the *whales* for the next game.

Robbers and Soldiers

Ages: 9–12
Players: 20 to 30; transition
Place: out-of-doors
Supplies: not any

Activity—hunting: chasing, dodging, hiding, running
Appeal: competition, problem solving, skill

This is an interesting version of "Hide and Seek." The players are divided with a proportion of one *robber* to five *soldiers*. The *General* is the leader of the *soldiers* while the *robbers'* leader is called the *Captain*. The *soldiers* stand at the prison until the *General*, who allows the *robbers* five or ten minutes' start, gives a command for the *soldiers* to search. The *robbers* may hide in any place they wish and may resist all the capture possible when found. Several *soldiers* may be required to bring a single *robber* to prison. A *robber* may resist all the way and perhaps escape before they reach the prison. Prisoners may escape if not prevented by the guard who is appointed by the *General*. *Soldiers* may use any means to capture a *robber* besides a simple hunt. The game is over when all *robbers* are prisoners. *Soldiers* may signal for help at any time.

Robin's Alive

Ages: 5–8
Players: 20 or more; single-group; circle
Place: gymnasium; out-of-doors; schoolroom

Supplies: ball or beanbag
Activity—hunting: passing
Appeal: dramatization, repetition

It is said that games in which an object is passed around the circle from hand to hand come from an old Danish tale. Centuries ago there lived a Danish nobleman who possessed a pet bird of which he was very fond. When the nobleman was called to war, he left the bird with a peasant and cautioned him to take good care of it. Unfortunately the bird died and the peasant was severely punished. The game known as "Robin's Alive" is based upon this tale and is played by children in Denmark.

The players stand in circle and pass from hand to hand a burning torch of paper or wood, saying, "*Lad ikke min Herre Fugl doee*" (Let not my Lord's bird die). The unfortunate player who holds the torch when the fire goes out pays a forfeit.

A variation of this game is to have the group chase the unlucky player. The one who catches the runner starts the next game. A ball or beanbag may be substituted for the lighted paper or wood and a signal be used to stop the passing of the object.

Slipper Slap

Ages: 9–12

Players: 20 or more; group-and-one; circle

Place: gymnasium; home; out-of-doors; schoolroom

Supplies: folded paper or slipper

Activity—hunting: passing, striking

Appeal: competition, repetition

One player stands in the middle while the others stand shoulder to shoulder around him so that he cannot see behind their backs. The players pass the slipper (a folded piece of paper several thicknesses) from hand to hand, slapping the one in the center whenever the opportunity presents itself. If the player in the circle is caught with the slipper in his hand by the center player, the two must exchange places. As soon as a player slaps the center person, he must instantly put the slipper behind his back and pass it to avoid being caught. The center player may be misled by the others who may pretend to pass or to slap.

NORWAY

Scitter-Scatter

Ages: 9–12

Players: 30 or more; two-group; circle

Place: gymnasium; out-of-doors

Supplies: not any

Activity—hunting: running, walking, whirling

Appeal: competition, rhythm, skill

This game comes from an ancient folk tale and has been popular for ages. The real name of the game is *Slaengkompas* or "Scatter-Compass."

The players form two circles of equal numbers. A captain known as *komy* is selected for each circle. The players join hands and face the center of the circle. The two circles are several feet apart and each *komy* starts walking slowly around his own circle and counts as he walks. The players listen closely and walk just as their *komy* walks.

The two *komys* may count as they wish, fast or slow, and in any order as: "One-three; two-one; three-four; three-two"; but as soon as a *komy* calls "Five!" the players in both circles drop hands quickly and whirl completely around five times as fast as possible. Then each player leaves his own circle and rushes to find a place in the opposite circle. When either *komy* shouts "Scitter-Scatter!" each player must face the center and join hands with the players near him. The *komys* try to get in the circle too. If any player in either ring is not standing thus, he must stand in the center of the ring.

The game goes on as before with each *komy* leading his players first slowly and then going faster and faster until the shout "Five!" is given. The players who are in the center of the rings may now try to get back into a circle as the players are whirling five times and exchanging places. Again any player caught out of the circle at the shout "Scitter-Scatter" must stand in the center and await his chance to get in the ring.

One object of the game is to catch a *komy* out of the circle. If a *komy* is caught not joining hands and facing center, the players rush to touch him. The first player to touch him becomes the new *komy* or captain for the next game. The players must watch both *komys* and the players in the center and try to keep them from joining in again.

SWEDEN

Blind Man's Buff, Number 1

Ages: 9–12   Supplies: can, large handkerchief
Players: 10 or more; group-and-   Activity—hunting: conversation,
  one; circle   guessing
Place: gymnasium; out-of-doors   Appeal: problem solving

The players sit or stoop in a circle. The blindfolded person stands in the middle of the ring, holding a cane in his hand. He points toward one in the ring. The one chosen must rise and put one end of the cane to his mouth as if speaking to the blind man through the telephone. The two hold a conversation, and the blind man guesses who is talking to him. If he is successful, he changes places with his victim; otherwise he returns to the center of the ring and continues as before.

Blind Man's Buff, Number 2

Ages: 9–12
Players: 10 or more; group-and-
one; circle
Place; gymnasium; out-of-doors

Supplies: large handkerchief
Activity—hunting: walking
Appeal: problem solving

The players sit on chairs in a circle. The person who has been blindfolded walks around and around and finally sits in the lap of one of the players. If he guesses the player's name correctly, that player is blindfolded. If he fails, no words are spoken, and the player whose lap he is sitting on spanks him and sends him on.

Lend, Lend, Fire

Ages: 9–12
Players: 20 or more; group-and-
one; circle
Place: gymnasium; out-of-doors

Supplies: cane
Activity—hunting: chasing,
dodging, running
Appeal: competition, skill

All the players except one sit on chairs in a circle. The one who is standing in the center of the ring walks up to one of the circle players, taps on the ground with a cane, and says: *"Lana, lana, eld"* (Lend, lend, fire). The player replies: *"Ga till mastra gannen"* (Go to the next neighbor), whereupon the one standing passes to the next player. The game continues in this manner and at the same time the players are exchanging chairs with one another. The questioner must be on the alert to get into a vacant chair. The player deprived of the chair must take the cane and go in search of fire. This game pattern is almost universal. However, it varies enough in the countries where it is played to bring forth conjectures as to its origin. In Lebanon it is called "Oh! Neighbor, Have You Fire?" The significance of the fire-theme is not verified as having grown out of the midsummer or midwinter fires of European custom, although it is entirely possible that therein lies the roots of this and similar games. In Turkey and the United States of North America the game is known as "How Do You Like Your Neighbor?"

Schlag Tag

Ages: 9–12
Players: 20 or more; group-and-
one; circle
Place: gymnasium; out-of-doors

Supplies: not any
Activity—hunting: bow, curtsy,
running
Appeal: skill

The players form a circle with *It* on the outside. He walks around the circle and finally stops before one player. If *It* is a girl, she curtsies, if a boy, he bows, and then runs around the circle, while the circle player chases him. The object is for *It* to try to return to the other's place in the ring before being tagged. If tagged, he is *It* again; otherwise the other player becomes *It.*

Stealing the Bone

Ages: 5–8

Players: any number; group-and-one; circle

Place: gymnasium; out-of-doors

Supplies: small object for a bone

Activity—hunting: chasing, dodging, running

Appeal: competition, skill

It or *Doggie Doan* sits with his eyes closed in the center of the circle of players. The *bone* is placed behind *Doggie Doan.* The circle players skip as they say,

> You'd better watch the bone,
> Doggie Doan, Doggie Doan,
> I'll take it for my own, for my own
> When I've snatched it and away I've gone.

The player nearest the *bone* when the word "own" is sung snatches it and runs. *Doggie Doan* immediately chases this player. If the player with the *bone* returns to her place without being tagged, the same player is *Doggie Doan* for the next game. If the runner is tagged, she is *Doggie Doan* for the next game.

Widower's Game

Ages: 9–12

Players: 13 or more; group-and-one; file

Place: gymnasium; out-of-doors

Supplies: not any

Activity—hunting: chasing, dodging, running

Appeal: competition, dramatization, skill

The players stand in pairs, a boy and a girl, one pair behind the other. An odd player representing the *widower* stands in front with his back to the rest. He calls, "The widower's game, last pair out!" The last pair then separates and runs forward in a large circle. The *widower* runs forward at the same time and tries to catch the girl. Since he is not allowed to look back he does not always know from which side the girl is running, for sometimes the boy and girl exchange places. In this way, the *widower* often contacts the boy instead of the girl. If he succeeds in catching the girl, the other boy is the *widower;* if he fails, he must try again. The pair that has just run joins the front ranks.

It is thought that this game is an outgrowth of ancient methods of marriage by capture. The game is called "Last Couple Out" by children in the United States, "Two Friends" in Ghana, and "Gorelki" in Russia.

GAMES AND SPORTS—SOUTHERN EUROPE

GREECE

Blind Man's Buff

Ages: 5–8
Players: 10 or more; group-and-one, circle
Place: gymnasium; out-of-doors
Supplies: not any

Activity—hunting: dodging, guessing, reaching, running
Appeal: problem solving, repetition, skill

The players encircle and run around a player *It,* whose eyes are closed and whose left hand is on his head. As the players tap *It* lightly on the shoulder, he tries to grasp someone with the right hand. If a player is caught he must permit *It* to guess who he is. When a player is caught and recognized, he becomes *It* for the next game.

Brazen Fly

Ages: 9–12
Players: 10–20; group-and-one; circle
Place: gymnasium; out-of-doors
Supplies: large handkerchief

Activity—hunting: clapping, dodging, skipping
Appeal: problem solving, repetition, skill

One player is blindfolded and all other players form a ring around him. They skip around him until he claps his hands three times. Then they must stop so that he may point to one who in turn steps into the ring with the blindfolded player. Immediately the blindfolded player tries to catch him. If he catches him and can name him, the two exchange places; if not, the same person must continue to be blindfolded. The one called into the circle will naturally try to escape but must submit when caught.

Another version of the game is that the blindfolded player chases the others and says, "I'm hunting a brazen fly." Meanwhile the players strike at him with a leather strap and say, "You may hunt but you won't catch."

Centipede

Ages: 5–8
Players: 6–20; group-and-one; circle
Place: gymnasium; out-of-doors

Supplies: knotted handkerchief
Activity—hunting: chasing, dodging, guessing, running, striking
Appeal: problem solving

All players sit in a circle with feet stretched out and mingled in a pile. A *leader* stands outside the circle and touches one foot or marks it with chalk. The *leader* calls someone to name the owner of the foot. When this player has named someone the owner stands.

If the guess is wrong, the guesser is chased and whipped with a knotted handkerchief. If the guess is correct, the guesser sits at one side from the circle and chooses the next one to be the *leader*. The one who was the *leader* takes a place in the circle.

Another version of the game is that if the guess is right, the player (guesser) takes the *leader's* place and the *leader* joins the circle.

Chili Chelone

Ages: 5–8
Players: 20 or more; group-and-one; circle
Place: gymnasium; out-of-doors

Supplies: not any
Activity—hunting: chasing, dodging, running
Appeal: dramatization, skill

This game was a favorite with young Greek girls. One girl called the *tortoise* sits in the center of a ring formed by the others. The circle players run around her and inquire, "Tor-tortoise what art thou doing there in the middle?" "Spinning wool, the thread of Milesian wolf," she replies. "And how," they ask, "was the son engaged when he perished?" The answer is, "He sprang from his white horse into the sea." The *tortoise* then springs up and tries to tag one of the questioners.

Chytrinda

Ages: 9–12 (boys)
Players: 10–20; group-and-one; circle
Place: gymnasium; out-of-doors
Supplies: box or pot

Activity—hunting: dodging, reaching, running, striking
Appeal: dramatization, repetition, skill

One player is chosen to be the *chytrinda* or *pot,* and sits in the center of the ring formed by the other players. The circle players run around and close to the *pot,* plucking, pinching, or striking him as they go. The *pot* tries to tag them. If he succeeds, the one caught becomes the *pot* and must sit in the center. This game was popular with Greek boys.

A variation of this game requires the one in the center to move about with a *pot* on his head. He holds the *pot* with both hands. The circle players cry out, "Who has the *pot?*" The one with the *pot* replies, "I, Midas," and tries all the while to reach someone with his foot. The first one caught carries the *pot* next.

Duck on a Rock

Ages: 9–12
Players: 20 or more; group-and-one; informal
Place: out-of-doors
Supplies: beanbags or stones

Activity—hunting: chasing, dodging, running, throwing
Appeal: competition, problem solving, skill

This is a modern version of the age-old game. A number of players, each having a *duck* (a stone or beanbag) stand on a throwing line; 25 feet away is *duck rock* or post on which a player called the *guard* places his duck and stands to either side of the *duck rock*. The object of the one who throws is to knock the *guard's duck* off of the *rock* if possible and to recover his own *duck* and get to the throwing line before being tagged by the *guard*. If the *guard's duck* is knocked off he cannot tag another player until first he has replaced his own *duck*. If a player goes to secure his *duck* and places one foot on his *duck* he cannot be tagged. But once he picks up his *duck* he cannot put it down again. A player may stand on his *duck* as long as necessary. Several players may be within the throwing line at the same time. If a player is tagged he becomes the *guard*. If a stone falls within a hand span of the *duck rock* without knocking the *duck* off, the thrower becomes a *guard* and the *guard* goes to the throwing line. If a *guard* tags a player, he must run so that the tagged player cannot tag him in return.

The *guard* may be determined by having the boys throw their *ducks* at the rock. The boy whose *duck* falls nearest the *rock* is the *guard*. The modern Greeks play the game by placing the *guard's duck* on a pile of stones instead of on the one *rock* or stake. As the players throw and hit the *duck*, the entire pile is often knocked over and the *guard* must rebuild them before he can chase the players.

A popular form of the game with American boys is "Stake Guard." The chief difference lies in the fact that the guard is confined to a limited territory in "Stake Guard." The game is often called "Duck Stone," "Ducks and Drakes," or "Duck on Davy."

Ephebike and Epikoinos

Ages: teen	Supplies: playground ball
Players: 20 or more; two-group; informal	Activity—athletic: catching, running, throwing
Place: gymnasium; out-of-doors	Appeal: competition, problem solving, skill

A line called the *Skyros* is drawn on the ground. Parallel to this line and equal distances from it, two *base lines* are drawn. The ball is placed in the center of the *Skyros*. The players are divided into two teams. Each team stands on a *base line*. At a given signal all players rush forward to seize the ball. The player who gets possession of the ball throws it toward the *base line* of the opposing team. Should the opponents intercept the ball, they immediately throw it toward their enemy's *base line*. The object of the game is to get the opposing team to overstep the *Skyros* or the *base lines*, either by force or by cunning.

The ancient Greeks used a ball made of bull's bladder blown tight and covered with a thick layer of leather.

Epkedrisnos

Ages: teen

Players: 10–20; single-group; informal

Place: out-of-doors

Supplies: large handkerchief, playground ball, large stones, small stones

Activity—athletic: balance, throwing

Appeal: competition, skill

The *Dioros*, a large stone, is placed at a certain distance from the *base line*. The players stand on the line and try to hit the *Dioros* with small stones. The player who first hits the stone mounts the back of a player who misses. The unsuccessful player is blindfolded and must carry his burden from the base line straight to the *Dioros*.

Greek Ball Game

Ages: 9–12

Players: 20 to 30; two-group; line

Place: gymnasium; out-of-doors

Supplies: playground ball

Activity—athletic: catching, running, throwing

Appeal: competition, skill

This is a modern adaptation of *Epkebike and Epikoinos*. Two lines are drawn as *base lines* on which players stand in lines. The ball is placed in the center. At a signal the opposite end members of each team run to the ball. The first one to reach it tries to throw it over his opponents' base line. If he succeeds, he scores one point for his team. The ball is kept in play until one side sends it over the *base line* of the other. The ball is then returned to the center. The players who have just run to the center go to the foot of the line, thus making two new runners. The game may be scored for a certain number of points, possibly 15, or until every player has had his turn at center. A space of 60 feet for a class of thirty children would be necessary.

Hunt the Slipper

Ages: 9–12

Players: 20 or more; group-and-one; circle

Place: gymnasium; out-of-doors

Supplies: slipper

Activity—hunting: passing, running

Appeal: problem solving, skill

The players form a circle and sit on the floor with the feet drawn up so that a slipper may be passed from one player to another under the lifted knees. One player is sent away from the circle for a few seconds and then returns to try to find the slipper. This is an ancient game.

Other versions of the game call for the odd player to run around on the outside of the circle and to try to tag the player who has the slipper. The odd player may stand in the center and guess who has the slipper. If he is successful using any of the three methods, he then changes places with the circle players.

Mount Ball

Ages: teen (boys)
Players: 20 or more; two-group; circle
Place: out-of-doors

Supplies: basketball
Activity—athletic: balance, catching, passing, throwing
Appeal: competition, skill

This is another game from ancient Greece that is popular today. The players are grouped in pairs, the two being about the same size. They form a double circle, and all face the center. The *outside player* of each couple mounts on the shoulders of the *inside player* who steadies his partner by taking his own arms back of the legs of the rider and clasping them in front of his own body. The mounted players throw a basketball to each other until one of them drops the ball. He then changes places with the player on whose shoulders he is riding. This game provides lively amusement but care should be taken to see that a boy does not support another who is much heavier than he. The team having the greatest number of mounted players after 10 minutes of play wins the game. The game has come down to us from the old Olympic games.

Olympic

Ages: 9–12
Players: 20 or more; two-group; line
Place: gymnasium; out-of-doors

Supplies: basketball
Activity—athletic: catching, passing, throwing
Appeal: competition, skill

The players form two teams. Each team divides into two lines facing each other and tosses a basketball back and forth between the lines for a period of three minutes. If a player lets the ball touch the ground, the opposing team scores five points and the offender drops out of the game. A game consists of 50 points. Although this game has come down from the ancient Greek Olympic Games, it offers excellent opportunity for practice of some of the skills of modern basketball.

Oyster Shell

Ages: 9–12
Players: 30 or more; two-group; line
Place: gymnasium; out-of-doors

Supplies: oyster shell or cardboard
Activity—hunting: chasing, dodging, running
Appeal: competition, repetition

The description here is a modern version of an old Greek game said to have originated from the practice of exiling wrangling politicians. The names of the opponents were written on an oyster shell; the shell was tossed into the air and the man whose name fell uppermost was sent from the city. The popular games "Day or Night," "Black and White," and "North or South" are supposed to have arisen from the custom.

Two parallel lines are drawn 10 feet apart and are known as the *starting lines*. The territory between the lines is the *neutral area*. At a greater distance beyond each starting line a *goal line* is drawn for each side. The players divide into two teams. One team is the *light* and the other the *dark* as decided. Leaders of alternate turns of captains toss an oyster shell in front of both teams as they stand on the starting lines. If the oyster shell falls dark side up, then the light team runs for its goal as the dark team chases them. If a player is caught, he must bring his captor home on his back. A team scores one point for each prisoner. The game may be scored 50, 100, or any number of points. It is advisable to adopt some means for opponents to be of equal size. The game continues with the fate of the oyster shell, whether it falls dark or light the majority of times, influencing the chance of winning.

Pebble Chase

Ages: 9–12
Players: 20 or more; group-and-one; line
Place: gymnasium; out-of-doors
Supplies: pebble
Activity—hunting: chasing, dodging, running
Appeal: competition, skill

The children are in line formation and all hold out their hands with palms together. The *leader* has a pebble in his hand. As he walks down in front of the line, he pretends to drop the pebble into the hands of each player. When he does drop it, the child who has it must run to a designated place (40 to 60 feet away) and back and give the pebble to the *leader*. All the others chase and try to catch the runner. The player who catches him will be the next *leader*. If the runner is not caught he will again be the *leader*.

Another version of the game is that the player receiving the pebble must let his identity be known by the time the *leader* reaches the last hand. The one having the pebble may even slip away and get a start before he is suspected by anyone. He may run wherever he sees fit.

Pebble Game

Ages: 9–12
Players: 2–6; single-group; informal
Place: home; schoolroom
Supplies: pebbles
Activity—pastime: catching
Appeal: skill

Two to six pebbles are placed on the back of the hand. The hand is turned over quickly and the object of the player is to catch the pebbles in the palm. This game is similar to "Jack Stones," which is played in many countries.

Schoenophilinda

Ages: 9–12
Players: 20 or more; group-and-one; circle
Place: gymnasium; out-of-doors

Supplies: rope
Activity—hunting: chasing, dodging, running, striking
Appeal: problem solving, skill

The players sit in a circle. One player, on the outside of the circle, has a rope that he tries to drop secretly beside one of the players. If he succeeds, he quickly picks up the rope and chases the circle player around the ring, flogging him as he goes. If he against whom the plot was laid detects it, he gains possession of the rope and flogs the first player around the circle.

Skaperda

Ages: teen
Players: 2; couple; informal
Place: out-of-doors

Supplies: post, rope
Activity—contest: grasping, pulling
Appeal: competition, self-testing

An eight-foot post is substantially placed in the ground. A rope is passed through a hole near the top of the post. Each player seizes an end of the rope and tries to draw his opponent up the beam. The player who lifts his opponent wins.

Surprise Ball

Ages: 9–12
Players: transition; informal
Place: gymnasium; playground
Supplies: playground ball

Activity—athletic: catching, dodging, throwing
Appeal: competition, skill

The players divide into two equal teams and stand facing each other on lines 30 to 40 feet apart. One side is given the ball. A player pretends to throw the ball to an opponent but throws it in the opposite direction and tries to hit another member of his opponents' team. When a player is hit he is out. The teams alternate in turns of throwing the ball. The game continues until all of one team are out.

Tree Toad

Ages: 9–12
Players: 12–20; group-and-one; informal
Place: out-of-doors

Supplies: not any
Activity—hunting: chasing, dodging, grasping, running
Appeal: skill

Greece—Skaperda.

This game is a form of "Hand Tag." The players escape *It* by jumping to clasp a tree trunk as a means of getting their feet off the ground. If the branches are low enough to reach, the players may grasp them and lift their feet. *It* may not remain near any player long enough to tire him out. Any player tagged while his feet are on the ground becomes *It*.

Triangle Ball

Ages: 9–12
Players: 2–6; single-group; informal
Place: gymnasium; out-of-doors

Supplies: small stones
Activity—pastime: pitching
Appeal: competition, skill

A triangle with a two-foot base is drawn on the ground. This distance from base to apex is 3 feet. The players stand 15 to 20 feet away. The triangle is divided into three parts with parallel lines equal distance apart and numbered from top to base—3, 2, 1. If a player pitches a stone in division 3, he scores 3; in 2, he scores 2; in 1, he scores 1. A stone that rolls outside does not count. Each player pitches three stones at a round. The first player scoring 50 points wins the game.

ITALY

Bimbo

Ages: 9–12
Players: 20 or more; two-group-and-one; line
Place: gymnasium; out-of-doors
Supplies: leaf

Activity—hunting: chasing, dodging, passing, running
Appeal: competition, dramatization, skill

One player is chosen to be the *bimbo* or captain and is given two small green leaves. The others stand in two lines facing each other about 15 feet apart. Each child holds his hand behind him, palm open. The *bimbo* walks slowly up and down behind the lines and quietly drops a leaf into one player's hands, then walks on. The player holds the leaf without indicating that he has it. The *bimbo* crosses to the other side, walks on, and then suddenly drops the other leaf into the hands of a player in that line. The *bimbo* walks on and then suddenly calls, "Stop! Thief! Lucky Leaf!" Then the two players who hold the leaves run as fast as possible across to the opposite side. Each of the two players tries to drop his leaf into the hands of some other player before the *bimbo* tags him. As the leaf goes to each player he passes it on to the next in line, for no player wants the *bimbo* to catch him holding a leaf. When a player is caught with a leaf in his hands, he becomes the new *bimbo* and the game is started again.

This game is very popular in Italy with both children and young people who play it during their outdoor festivals.

Cencio Mollo (SHEN-shio MOL-lho)

Ages: 9–12
Players: 20 or more; group-and-one; line
Place: home; schoolroom

Supplies: handkerchief
Activity—pastime: self-control
Appeal: dramatization

The players form a line, one behind the other. One player, chosen as *It*, holds a handkerchief in hand and goes to the first player in line saying, "The *Cencio Mollo* (wet handkerchief) has come to you."

The player replies, "Let it come. I shall not cry, laugh, nor kiss it." *It* tries to make the player laugh, but he can only touch the player's head and face, and only with the handkerchief. If he fails to make the player laugh, he must go to someone else in the line. The player who laughs must pay a penalty. A new *It* is then chosen.

Chicken Market

Ages: 5–8
Players: 20 or more; group-and-two; row
Place: gymnasium; out-of-doors

Supplies: not any
Activity—pastime: self-control
Appeal: dramatization

One child is the *market keeper*, another is the *buyer*. The other children are *chickens* and are arranged in a row. They stoop and either clasp their hands under their knees or place them on their knees. The buyer asks the *market keeper* if he has chickens to sell. "Yes, I have fine 'chickens.' Would you like to see them?" asks the *market keeper*. The *buyer* goes behind the row of chickens, places her hand upon the first chicken's head. "This one is too skinny," he

Italy—Chicken Market.

says. He tries the second. "This one is too tough." He tries the third. "This chicken is too old." At last he says, "This one is exactly what I want." Then the *market keeper* and the *buyer* take told of the little chicken's arms and swing it as they count, "One, two, three." The *chicken* tries to keep from smiling and to keep his hands clasped. If he is successful, the buyer takes him, otherwise he returns to his place among the other *chickens*. The game goes on until all the *chickens* are sold.

Dieci Passaggi (di-A-shi pa-SA-ghi)

Ages: 9–12; teen
Players: 12 or more; two-group; informal
Place: gymnasium; out-of-doors
Supplies: basketball
Activity—athletic: catching, throwing
Appeal: competition, skill

The players are divided into two equal teams, *A* and *B*. Each team draws to see which team will have the ball first. If *Team B* has the ball, it tries to pass the ball to each player on the team. Passes are counted aloud. When the ball touches the ground it is dead, points are lost, and the ball goes to the other team. Two players may not pass the ball back and forth to each other. Players on *Team A* run or stand anyplace. They may not touch an opponent with the hands. The team having *Dieci Passaggi* or ten passes first wins. A similar game is played in the United States of North America and is called "Keep Away" or "Ten Passes."

Filberta

Ages: 9–12
Players: 4–12; single-group; line
Place: out-of-doors
Supplies: filberts or stones
Activity—pastime: throwing
Appeal: competition, skill

Castles are made by placing three filberts (nuts), one on top of the other, on the ground. Several castles are made and placed a few inches apart in a row. The players stand about 3 feet from the castles and throw at them with a filbert. The player who knocks down the greatest number of castles wins the game.

Italian children think that a good ending for the game is to sit down and eat the filberts! A similar game is played in Colombia, South America, and is called *Casita* or little house.

Follow Chase

Ages: 9–12
Players: 30 or more; group-and-two; circle
Place: gymnasium; out-of-doors
Supplies: not any
Activity—hunting: chasing, dodging, running
Appeal: competition, problem solving, skill

The players stand in a circle with arms stretched sideways so as to put their hands on each others' shoulders. On one side of the circle under an arch is a chosen player called the *runner*. Opposite him is the *chaser*. At a given signal the *chaser* tries to catch the *runner* but must follow the same route as the runner. If the *runner* is caught he joins the circle; the *chaser* becomes the *runner* and chooses a *chaser* from the circle. If the *chaser* doesn't catch the *runner* after a long time, the leader may call "Time!" Then both join the circle and a new *chaser* and a new *runner* are chosen. This game is popular in many countries and is played with slight variations.

Hand Tag

Ages: 9–12
Players: 12 or more; group-and-one; informal
Place: out-of-doors

Supplies: not any
Activity—hunting: chasing, dodging, grasping, running
Appeal: competition, skill

The player who is *It* cannot tag the others when they are hanging onto a tree or piece of apparatus so that the feet do not touch the ground. In Greece the game is called "Tree Toad." A similar game, "Tiggy Touchwood," is played in England.

Painting Sand-Pictures

Ages: 9–12
Players: 8 or more; single-group; informal
Place: out-of-doors

Supplies: bags of colored sand
Activity—pastime: creating designs
Appeal: competition, skill

Each player has four bags of colored sand—red, black, yellow, and blue, and a bag of white. The white sand is scattered upon the ground in the form of a square. Then an outline of a bird, a man, or another animal is made by allowing the black sand to sift through the fingers. The other colors are used to finish the design. There is often competition between the young artists as to who can paint the best picture in a given time.

Pumpkin-Planter

Ages: teen
Players: 12 or more; group-and-one; circle
Place: home, schoolroom

Supplies: none
Activity—pastime: alertness, memory
Appeal: dramatization

One player is chosen to be the *pumpkin-planter* and the others are *pumpkins* and sit in a circle. The *planter* stands in the center and gives a number to each player. He starts the game by saying, "There are (for example) four pumpkins in my field." Pumpkin No.

4 asks, "Why four pumpkins?" The *planter* says, "If not, how many?" and No. 4 says (for example), "Eleven pumpkins." No. 11 replies in the same manner and the game continues faster and faster. If a *pumpkin* gets confused or fails to answer quickly to his number he is assigned some silly penalty.

Wolf and Lamb

Ages: 5–8
Players: 20 or more; group-and-two; circle
Place: gymnasium; out-of-doors
Supplies: not any

Activity—hunting: chasing, dodging, running, stretching, stooping
Appeal: competition, dramatization, problem solving, skill

This game is quite similar to the Chinese and the North American game, "Cat and Mouse." One player, the *wolf*, stands outside a circle formed by the other players. A second player, the *lamb*, stands in the center of the ring and cries, "I am the lamb." The wolf answers, "I am the wolf and I'll catch you!" The lamb declares, "Oh! no you won't." Whereupon the wolf tries to enter the ring. The circle players help the *lamb* by trying to keep the *wolf* outside. Should the *wolf* enter the circle, the players in the circle again help the *lamb* by raising their arms in order that he may run under them. If the *lamb* is caught he joins the circle players; the wolf becomes the lamb and then chooses a new wolf.

PORTUGAL

Berlinda

Ages: teen
Players: 10 or more; group-and-two; informal
Place: home; schoolroom

Supplies: not any
Activity—pastime: guessing
Appeal: problem solving

Berlinda is a difficult word to translate. It means "one in the attention of all others."

One player is chosen to be *It* and is told to leave the group. Another player, the *leader*, goes from one player to another gathering a secret from each. The secret should be something funny, the more exaggerated the better, about the person who is *It*. For example, a player may be "berlinda" because his shirt is too short, or because his hair is uncombed, or because his feet are too big, etc. *It* is recalled and the *leader* names over all the things said about him. *It* then chooses the description he prefers. The person who said that about *It* has to leave the group and be the next *It*. The players should agree to take the teasing in the attitude of friendliness or perhaps give compliments instead of criticisms.

Contraband

Ages: 9–12; teen
Players: 20 or more; two-group; rectangle
Place: out-of-doors (large area)

Supplies: coin, rock, or stick
Activity—hunting: chasing, running
Appeal: competition, skill

The playing field should be a large one. A chosen site, near the edge of the field, is agreed upon to be the boundary where the *contraband* must be placed. The players are divided equally into *police* and *contrabandistas* or *smugglers* who group themselves along three sides of a large rectangle, leaving one end open. The rectangle should be in the center of the playing area. The *police* are on the outside and the *smugglers* are on the inside of the rectangle. The *contraband* object, which may be a small coin, stick, or rock, is given to one of the players of the *smugglers'* team. He and his teammates try to keep the police from knowing who has the object. They also try to break through the police so that they can place the *contraband* article on or across the boundary line.

The game is finally won by either the *smugglers* as they are successfully able to get their contraband over to the agreed upon boundary or by the *police* for not letting them get through or catching them before they are able to reach the boundary.

Ghosts

Ages: teen
Players: 10 or more; group-and-one; row
Place: home; schoolroom

Supplies: not any
Activity—pastime: balance, coordination
Appeal: dramatization

This game is adaptable to a party or for a particular occasion. All players stand in a row. The *leader* begins a story about a *ghost* he saw once. He says, "He had his right hand on top of his head." All players then place their right hands on top of their heads and the *leader* continues, "He had his left hand behind his back," and all players follow instructions. "He had his left leg extended in front," all extend left leg, "and his right knee was bent and he was leaning to the left." When all of the players are in this amusing position, the *leader* then gives a little push on the first player and all begin to tumble like soldiers in a line. The game is over and the explanation is, "The ghost disappeared about this time!"

SPAIN

Hit the Pot

Ages: 9–12
Players: 4–12; single-group; infor-
   mal
Place: gymnasium; out-of-doors

Supplies: pot, stones
Activity—pastime: throwing
Appeal: competition, skill

This game is popular in England, Spain, Italy, and Germany. It comes from a cruel pastime of early days. It was a favorite game in ancient times to take a pot with a hole in the bottom, turn it bottom side up and place it over a chicken's neck. A blindfolded player then struck at the chicken's neck. Today the game is played by placing a pot or a pan over a stick that is placed in the ground. The blindfolded player is allowed three chances to hit the stick. If he misses, he must pay a forfeit by doing a song, dance, or stunt.

Moon and Morning Stars

Ages: 5–8; 9–12
Players: 20 or more; group-and-
   one; informal
Place: out-of-doors

Supplies: not any
Activity—hunting: chasing, dodg-
   ing, running
Appeal: dramatization, skill

One player is the *moon* and must stay within a large shadow, as that of a tree or a house. The other players are the *morning stars* and stay in the sunshine. The stars may go in the shadow but if the *moon* tags them, they become the *moon* and the *moon* becomes a *morning star*. While the *moon* is in the shadow, she is saying:

> Oh, moon and morning stars!
> Oh, moon and morning stars!
> Within your shadow,
> Who dares to tread, oh!

Pelota

Ages: teen
Players: 4; two-group; informal
Place: gymnasium; out-of-doors
Supplies: ball, wicker glove

Activity—pastime: catching, running, throwing
Appeal: competition, skill

In Spain the game of *Pelota* is, and probably always will be, the most popular sport in spite of the interest in bull-fighting. The *fronton*, a cement court with a wall at one end, is usually found in the villages.

There are two players on a side. Each player straps a scooplike wicker glove to his right wrist. The object of the game is to keep the ball in the air by catching and throwing it with the glove. This re-

Spain—Moon and Morning Stars.

quires alertness, agility, and unusual speed. This is similar to *Tack-raw*, a Malayan game.

Plantados (Plan-TA-dos)

Ages: 9–12
Players: 12 or more; group-and-one
Place: gymnasium; out-of-doors
Supplies: not any

Activity—hunting: chasing, dodging, running
Appeal: competition, skill

One player is *It* and tries to tag the other players who run from one designated base to another. When a player is tagged he is *plantados* or planted and must stand still. *It* may have one or more helpers who serve as protective guards to keep those who are planted, especially after two or more players have been tagged. As players are caught they, too, are *plantados* and hold hands with the others. An end player may be reinstated in the game by one of the runners pulling him out of line. Should more than one of the planted players break off during the pulling, he may also be reinstated. The game continues until all the runners have been *planted.*

Spanish Fly

Ages: teen
Players: 10 or more; group-and-one; informal
Place: gymnasium; out-of-doors

Supplies: not any
Activity—hunting: leaping, running
Appeal: competition, skill

This game is very similar to leapfrog, as played in the United States. While jumping the *leader* performs certain feats for the other players to follow. Many different stunts may be introduced. The *leader* may jump over and touch the back with one hand and wave a cap in the other, or jump without touching, or make a turn while jumping, or do as he desires. Any player who fails to follow the *leader* takes the place of the back to be jumped over. The game "*Dima*" from Iran is quite similar to "Spanish Fly."

Tintarella

Ages: 5–8
Players: any number; couples; informal
Place: gymnasium; out-of-doors

Supplies: not any
Activity—stunt: grasping, whirling
Appeal: rhythm, skill

This is a favorite activity with young Spanish girls. Partners stand toe to toe and grasp hands firmly and spin about as long as possible. This is the same as *Phugadi,* a favorite with the children of India.

Torero

Ages: 9–12
Players: 12 or more; group-and-one; informal
Place: gymnasium; out-of-doors

Supplies: cover for head
Activity—hunting: chasing, dodging, running
Appeal: dramatization

This game is a playground version of the national sport of Spain, bullfighting. It is a favorite amusement with the boys of Spain.

One player is chosen to be the *bull.* A basket-like covering, with a pair of bull's horns fastened to it, is placed on his head. He is then released and chased by others. The *bull* does his best to butt the players who chase and taunt him.

Another version of the game is that one of the players has a pair of toy banderillas, the sharp barbs that are stuck in bulls' hides in a real fight, and with these he taunts the mock *bull.* Finally a boy carrying a wooden sword advances and kills the *bull* with approved gestures that he has learned by watching the real bullfights on holiday occasions.

GAMES AND SPORTS—WESTERN EUROPE

BELGIUM

Tap the Line

Ages: 9–12
Players: 20 or more; transition
Place: gymnasium; out-of-doors
Supplies: pole

Activity—hunting: chasing, dodging, running
Appeal: competition, skill, problem solving

One player is chosen to be *tapper* and starts the game by chasing all of the other players until he succeeds in tapping one, who is called *bogey*. As soon as *tapper* has tagged *bogey*, they race for the pole that is in the center of the playing area.

If *bogey* succeeds in touching the pole first, he is free and may return to the group. If *tapper* reaches the pole first then *bogey* is a prisoner and must stay at the pole, touching it with one hand or one foot, while *tapper* is quite busy now for he not only chases the players but also keeps an eye on *bogey*, for if a player touches *bogey* this frees *bogey* and he may return to the group. If *tapper* tags a player before he frees *bogey*, then the player must join one hand with *bogey's* free hand. In this way the line at the pole becomes longer as the players are tapped.

If at any time one of the free players touches anyone in the line, the line players are then free and the game starts over. The same *tapper* must continue to serve until he has all of the players in the line at the pole.

This is a very popular game with boys and girls in Belgium. The game as it is played today is adapted from the Old Flemish Game of "Verlos."

FRANCE

Blow the Horn

Ages: teen (boys)
Players: 20 or more; two-groups; informal
Place: wooded area
Supplies: not any

Activity—hunting: hiding, running, searching
Appeal: competition, problem solving, skill

This is a very old boys' game, originating in France in the days of deer hunting.

Two players are chosen to be *deer,* and the others are *hunters* who are allowed four *hounds.* The hunters carry a horn and must go in a group. The hounds go in advance to scout the *deer.* A playing area is established within which the hunt must remain. The *deer* are allowed from 3 to 10 minutes to elude the *hunters* before the *hounds* are sent out from the starting point. The *hunters* must blow the horn every half-minute. The *deer* cannot return to the starting point before an hour or less time, unless they are previously overtaken by the hunting party. The *deer* are not considered caught until the *hunters* overtake them. The *hounds* aid the *hunters* by giving signals when they discover the *deer.*

To promote even play, the area over which the game is played should be neither too wooded nor too open. Boy Scouts enjoy this game very much when camping.

Exchange

Ages: 9–12
Players: 10 or more; group-and-one; circle
Place: gymnasium; out-of-doors
Supplies: large handkerchief, chairs

Activity—hunting: chasing, dodging, running
Appeal: competition, problem solving, skill

The players, numbered from one to the highest number playing, are seated in chairs in a circle around a center blindfolded player. The blindfolded player calls two numbers. The persons whose numbers are called must exchange places while the blindfolded player tries to catch one or secure either of their chairs. The player caught must exchange places with the center player. No player may go outside the circle.

My Lady's Toilet

(See England.)

French Dodgeball

Ages: teen
Players: 20 or more; two-group; line
Place: gymnasium; out-of-doors

Supplies: basketball
Activity—athletic: dodging, throwing
Appeal: competition, skill

The players are divided into two equal teams and play with a ball that is 6 or 8 inches in diameter. The playing area is divided by three parallel lines about 10 or more feet apart. The middle line is called *center,* the other two lines are the *back* lines. The teams, *A* and *B,* take their positions on either side of the *center* line. One team starts the game by throwing the ball at its opponents. If a player is hit (below the waist) he goes behind the *back* line that is behind his opponents. Play continues with each team throwing at its opponents. A player behind the *back* lines may throw the ball (if it goes his way), over the heads of his opponents, to his team, which tries to hit an opponent; or he may throw directly at an opponent from behind the *back* line. If he hits an opponent, he may return to his team. When all players of one team are behind a *back* line, that team loses; the game starts anew with the winners having the first throw at their opponents.

A similar game is played by children in the United States and is called "Three Court Dodgeball," wherein there are three equal teams instead of two. The teams are called A, B, and C. One team is in a center court and is the target of the two other teams who are on either side of lines that separate them from the center team. After a period of time the center players are counted, then one of the other team goes to the center and becomes the target for the other teams. In turn the third team goes to the center. The winning team is the one having the most players in the center after its time of play as target. The time limit is determined somewhat by the number of players on the teams.

Hopscotch

Ages: 9–12

Players: 2 or more; individual; see diagrams

Place: out-of-doors

Supplies: flat stone, diagram

Activity—pastime: hopping, tossing

Appeal: competition, skill

There are many varieties of hopscotch enjoyed by children in France, the United States of North America, and other parts of the world. Two favorites of the French children are "Double Line-Zig Zag" and "Heaven." Another is a circular one often called "Snail" by children in the United States of North America.

The players each have a flat stone, the *scotch,* which in turns they toss into the spot numbered "1." After each player tosses his *scotch* into the number "1" spot, he then hops (on one foot) into the spot and thence into each of the other numbered spots according to their consecutive numbers. When the player reaches the "return" area he lands on both feet, jumps, turns about, and lands again on both feet. He then hops back beginning in the area numbered "8," goes back down the numbers consecutively to number "1," picks up the stone, and hops out. If he has successfully followed the routine, without hopping on a line, he continues each time tossing the stone into a higher number, beginning with No. "2" and so on. If he loses

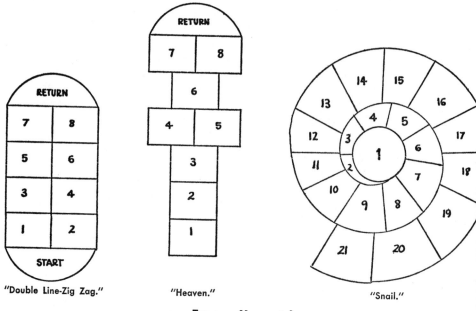

"Double Line-Zig Zag."   "Heaven."   "Snail."

France—Hopscotch.

by stepping on a line or failing to toss the stone within the boundary
of an area, he loses his place and another player begins his turn.
The winner is the one who first completes the procedure throughout
each of the numbers.

THE NETHERLANDS

Bag Race

Ages: 9–12   Supplies: potato bags
Players: 10 to 20; single-group; line   Activity—relay: jumping
Place: gymnasium; out-of-doors   Appeal: competition, skill

The players stand in potato bags or some other sack of cloth or
paper and jump forward to a goal. The activity may be used in
relay formation. It is often played by children in the United States
as "Sack Race."

Verlos

Ages: 9–12   Supplies: not any
Players: 20 or more; group-and-one;   Activity—hunting: chasing,
  circle   running
Place: gymnasium; out-of-doors   Appeal: competition, skill

A goal is established several feet away from the players who are
in a circle. *It* runs around the circle and tags a player on the

France—Hopscotch.

shoulder. The two then run for the goal. The player who reaches the goal first is *It* for the next time, and the other player must remain at the goal.

The Belgian game "Tap-the-Line" is similar to the Dutch game of "Verlos."

Windmill

Ages: 9–12
Players: 20 to 30; transition; line
Place: gymnasium; out-of-doors
Supplies: not any

Activity—hunting: balance, chasing, dodging, running
Appeal: dramatization, problem solving, skill

Two parallel lines are drawn 15 or more feet apart. The space between the lines is the neutral ground. At one end of the neutral space a square is drawn to represent a *canal*.

One player is chosen to be the *berger*. The others are divided into two sides and stand on the lines, facing the neutral ground. A leader called a *stork* is chosen for each line and he stands slightly in front of his line in the neutral ground. The *storks* start the game by imitating the movements of a windmill, or a stork. The players in each line do exactly what their *stork* leader does. The *berger* walks up anywhere between the lines and watches closely to see if each player is following his leader. As soon as he sees a player who is not following his *stork* leader he runs and tags the player, and calls, "Windmill!"

The player runs immediately for the *canal*. The *berger* and the children all chase him. If the runner reaches the *canal* before he is caught he is safe and returns to his place in line. If the *berger* tags the runner, the runner must go and stay in the *canal*. If one of the line players tags him, the runner must join the line that tagged him.

The game continues with the children in the lines trying to catch the runner before he is tagged by the *berger*. A player in the lines may rescue a prisoner from the *canal* whenever he can slip past the *berger* and tag the prisoner.

When all the players have been taken into one line or into the *canal*, the *berger* calls, "Windmill!" Then every player chases the *berger*. The player who catches him is the *berger* for the next game and may select the *stork* leaders for the two lines. This game is based on an old tale of early Dutch days.

GAMES AND SPORTS—THE UNITED KINGDOM

ENGLAND

Animals

Ages: 5–8	Supplies: not any
Players: 20 or more; single-group; informal	Activity—pastime: imitating animals, listening
Place: home; schoolroom	Appeal: dramatization

Each player chooses the name of an animal or bird whose cry they can imitate. The *leader* writes the names on the blackboard and then he begins to weave them into a story. When a player hears the name of the animal he chose, he stands and imitates the cry. If the *leader* calls "Menagerie" or "Zoo" all must jump up and cry.

Circle Thread the Needle

Ages: 9–12	Supplies: not any
Players: 6–12 in a circle; circle	Activity—stunt: running, turning
Place: gymnasium; out-of-doors	Appeal: competition, rhythm, skill

One player is chosen to be the *master*. The other players are divided into two or more groups. Each group consists of an equal number of players (6 to 12) who join hands and form a circle. Each player is given a number, and the *master* calls out two consecutive numbers, such as 5 and 6. The players having these numbers drop inside hands, continue to hold the hands of their neighbors, and run through the arch made by the two players under the arch and finally, the players forming the arch turn under their own arms and players 5 and 6 rejoin hands. The group to get in circle formation first wins. The players may be requested to finish sitting, kneeling, standing, or in some other position.

Disco

Ages: teen
Players: 2–4; two-group; informal
Place: gymnasium; out-of-doors
Supplies: tennis ball and net, 4
    wooden racquets

Activity—pastime: striking
Appeal: competition, problem
    solving, skill

This is a popular English game that requires agility and skill. The court is a rectangle, 14 by 40 feet. The net, which is 18 inches deep, is placed across the middle of the court at a height of 5 feet from the top to the ground. In each half of the court a service line is established parallel with and 6 feet from the base or back line. The service line is drawn between two posts that are 11 feet apart. The posts are 8½ feet high and support a disk 1¾ feet in diameter.

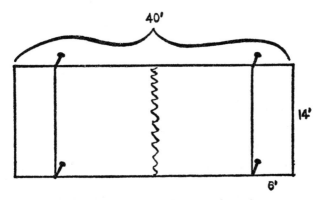

England—Diagram of Court for Disco.

The game may be in singles or doubles, that is, two or four players participating at one time. Each player has a wooden racquet 22 inches in diameter. A ball is served over the net. In doubles either opponent may return the ball to any part of the opposite court. The object of the game is to hit one of the discs with a return ball. The team that succeeds in hitting a disc first is the winning team. After the players have developed skill, it would be interesting to increase the number of hits a team must make before winning.

The ball is considered dead after it touches the ground. The service is like that in lawn tennis. One player serves until a game is completed.

Dodger Tag

Ages: 9–12
Players: 9 to 12; group-and-three; circle
Place: gymnasium; out-of-doors
Supplies: not any

Activity—hunting: chasing, dodging, running
Appeal: competition, problem solving

Six or eight players stand in a circle several feet apart. The *dodger* stands in the center; the *chasers* (two in number) stand outside on opposite sides of the circle. The *dodger* runs around any circle player or any number of circle players, scoring one point for each player whom he completely encircles. At the same time the *chasers* try to tag the *dodger*. If he is tagged, all players resume their starting positions and the game continues until the *dodger* has had three turns. After that he counts his total score and joins the circle players. One of the *chasers* becomes the *dodger;* one of the circle players becomes a *chaser*. The game continues until all players have had three turns as the *dodger*. The player having the highest score at the close of the game wins.

Exchange Race

Ages: 9–12
Players: 16 or more; file
Place: gymnasium; out-of-doors

Supplies: 2 beanbags or balls for each team
Activity—relay: passing, running
Appeal: competition, skill

Each team consists of eight or more players who are divided into two groups. The players of each group stand in files facing each other and about 30 feet apart. The *leader* of each group toes the starting line and holds a ball or beanbag.

At a given signal, the *leaders* of each file run forward to a center line, exchange balls or bags, run around each other, run back to their own half of the team, give the bag to the next player, and run to the end of their file. This continues until the original *leaders* hold the bags again. The *leaders* then run forward, join hands, and raise them above the head level. This last procedure proclaims the winning team.

Fielding Race

Ages: 9–12
Players: 10 or more; file
Place: gymnasium; out-of-doors

Supplies: a ball for each team
Activity—relay: bowling, running
Appeal: competition, skill

The players of each team stand in a file with their *leader* toeing a starting line. At a signal, the first player in each file bowls his ball forward with enough force to make it cross the goal line several feet away. As soon as he releases the ball each player runs after his own ball, picks it up beyond the goal line, turns and runs back to his file, gives the ball to the next player, and goes to the end of the file. The play continues until the *leader*, receiving the ball from the last runner, holds the ball high above his head.

Five and Ten

Ages: teen
Players: 2–6; two-group; informal
Place: gymnasium; out-of-doors
Supplies: tennis ball, tennis racquets, net with wooden frame

Activity—pastime: striking
Appeal: competition, problem solving, skill

A frame about 3 feet high extends across one end of the court. The upper part of the frame is made of wood, the lower part of net. In the center of the frame, the lower portion of the wood and all of the net is cut away. The space is filled with a *net pocket* or a box.

The court may be any size between the minimum of three by seven yards and the maximum of 7 by 12 yards. The back line is known as the *base line*. A *service line* is drawn parallel with and halfway between the frame and the *base line*. The section of the court nearest the frame is divided into halves and each half is called a *service court*. The object of the game is to serve the ball from the *base line* into the *pocket*. Should a player succeed in doing this he scores ten points. If his ball misses the *pocket* but rebounds from the wood into the opposite service court, he scores five points. Before starting the game the players should agree upon the number of points necessary for winning.

Grandmother Steps with Pat Bouncing

Ages: 9–12
Players: 10 or more; group-and-one; informal
Place: gymnasium; out-of-doors

Supplies: small ball for each player
Activity—hunting: pat bouncing a ball
Appeal: competition, skill

One player is selected to be the *grandmother*. She stands toeing a line at one end of the playing area with her back to the other players. The players stand in line and toe a mark at the far end of the court, each holding a small ball. At a signal, the players advance toward the *grandmother*, pat bouncing their balls. The *grandmother* quickly faces the group from time to time. If she sees a player move or drop her ball, that player must return to the starting line. The player who first bounces her ball over the *grandmother's* line becomes the *grandmother* and the game starts anew.

Human Skittles

Ages: teen
Players: any number; threes; line
Place: gymnasium; out-of-doors
Supplies: ball for each group of 3

Activity—athletic: catching, dodging, throwing
Appeal: skill

This game is dodge ball for three. The players are numbered 1, 2, and 3. In the middle of the playing area a circle 18 inches is drawn for each group of three. No. 1 stands in the circle. Nos. 2 and 3 are at opposite sides of the room, facing No. 1.

Nos. 2 and 3 are playing together and throw the ball at No. 1's feet. No. 1 may dodge by jumping with her feet together. She must remain inside the circle as she jumps. If her feet are hit, she exchanges places with the player who hit her. The circle player scores one point each time she successfully dodges the ball. The players who throw the ball score one point each time they hit the feet of the circle player. After a given period the scores are checked.

Recognition may be given to the individual with the highest score or to the group of three with the highest score.

Hunt the Fox

Ages: 9–12
Players: groups of 10; group-and-two; informal
Place: out-of-doors
Supplies: not any

Activity—hunting: chasing, dodging, running
Appeal: competition, problem solving, skill

This game has come down from the Middle Ages. The players are divided into groups of ten. Two players are chosen from each group to be the *foxes*. The other players stand behind a starting line until the *foxes* cross a line 20 feet away. As soon as the *foxes* cross the 20-foot line the players may chase them but must follow the same route as the *foxes*. If a player catches a *fox* before the *fox* crosses the starting line he becomes a *fox* for the next game.

Jingling Match

Ages: 9–12
Players: 10 to 30; group-and-one; informal
Place: gymnasium; out-of-doors

Supplies: large handkerchief
Activity—hunting: chasing, dodging, listening, running
Appeal: problem solving, skill

This game used to be very popular at the English country fairs. A circle, enclosed by a rope, was occupied by nine or ten people, and all except one were blindfolded. This player was called the *Jingler* because he carried in his hand a small bell, which he rang constantly. The blindfolded players, following the sound of the bell, tried to catch him. If he was not caught at the end of an allotted time, he received a prize, otherwise the prize went to the tagger.

King's Rebels

Ages: 9–12
Players: 20 or more; two-group-and-two; informal
Place: gymnasium; out-of-doors
Supplies: chair or box
Activity—hunting: chasing, dodging, reaching, running
Appeal: competition, dramatization, problem solving, skill

The playing area is a large square or rectangle. One player is chosen to be the *king* and stands on a chair in the center of the playing area. A circle with a three-foot radius is drawn around the chair. Four players are selected to be *guards* and stand outside the circle. The other players are *rebels* and station themselves about the playing area nearer the boundary lines than the *guards*.

The *rebels* try to pass the *guards*, gain entrance to the circle, and tag the *king*. If the *king* is tagged the game stops; the tagger becomes a *king* and the *king* becomes a *guard*. If a *guard* tags a *rebel*, the *rebel* must run to one boundary line, stand still, and count to 20 before he may continue to play.

The *guards* try to tag the *rebels* only when they are near the circle. Once a *rebel* enters the circle he is safe to tag the *king*.

Ladder Jump

Ages 9–12
Players: 24; 4 in a file, file
Place: gymnasium; out-of-doors
Supplies: not any
Activity—relay: jumping
Appeal: competition, skill

The players are divided into teams consisting of three or four members who are numbered 1, 2, 3, and 4. Each team stands in a file with No. 1 toeing the starting line. No. 1 jumps as far forward as possible keeping his feet together. No. 2 then jumps, his starting point is the heel marks of No. 1, and the race continues until all in the file have jumped. The team that covers the greatest distance wins.

If a player loses his balance and falls back in landing, the most backward mark is the starting point for the next player.

Loop Touch

Ages: teen
Players: any number; couples; line
Place: gymnasium; out-of-doors

Supplies: not any
Activity—relay: running, turning
Appeal: competition, skill

The players are in twos, partners facing, but standing 30 or more feet apart with the toes behind a *starting line*. A line known as the *center line* is drawn midway between the *starting line* of the two groups. At the signal, partners run forward to the *center line*, grasp right hands, and turn (run, skip, hop, etc.) in a complete circle on the spot. They then run back and touch their *starting line* (or the wall if played indoors); run forward again and turn with left hands joined. Once more they run and touch their *starting line* and finish at the *center line*, partners facing each other, with right or left hands joined and raised high above the head. The couple finishing the whole procedure first wins.

At the finish, each couple must join hands before raising them above the head.

My Lady's Toilet

Ages: 9–12
Players: 20 or more; group-and-one; circle
Place: gymnasium; home

Supplies: chairs
Activity—pastime: running, turning
Appeal: dramatization, repetition, skill

One player is chosen to be the lady's *maid* and stands in the center of a ring formed by the others who are seated in chairs. Each player chooses the name of an article of dress such as handkerchief, hat, jacket, comb, brush, mirror, watch, chain, or shoes. The lady's *maid* calls out, "My Lady is ready to make her toilet and wants her brush." The one who represents the brush stands and turns round quickly as she repeats her name. Should the word "toilet" be mentioned all players jump up and whirl around. As they turn, the lady's *maid* tries to get the chair of one of the players. If she is successful, the player who is without a chair becomes the next *maid*.

The French version of this game and the North American adaptation, known as "Spin the Plate," vary slightly from the above description. The *maid* crouches in the center and spins a plate or tray while she names the articles of toilet that My Lady wants. The player, representing the article named, runs to the center and catches the plate while it is spinning. If successful, she becomes the next *spinner*. If she does not succeed she pays her forfeit and returns to her place. Mention may be made of My Lady's preparation for a ball. At that time all players must change places. The *spinner* tries to secure a chair for herself.

Pell Mell (Pall Mall)

Ages: 9–12
Players: two-group; line
Place: gymnasium; playground
Supplies: two playground balls

Activity—hunting: chasing, bowling, dodging, running
Appeal: competition, problem solving, skill

This game is one of the oldest of English games that have come down through the years. It gets its unusual name from the famous street of London known throughout the world as Pell Mell. The game was derived from the old English holiday frolics on the Green when the people rushed away from the crowded street to the country.

The players are in two parallel lines, girls on one side, boys on the other, with a few feet between the lines. A *leader* is chosen for each side and stands at the head of his line, holding a large ball. Two lines, about 3 feet apart, are marked between the two rows of players. At a signal, the *leaders* bowl their balls down between the lines. If the balls do not cross a line, the *leaders* may bowl them again. If a ball rolls across one of the lines, the nearest player may run out of his place and grab the ball. He then runs around back of the lines of players and tries to return to his place before some player from the opposite side can catch him. If he is successful, he takes the place of the *leader* who lost his ball; otherwise the player who tags him becomes a *leader* and the tagged one drops out of the game.

The excitement of the game increases when the two balls roll over the lines. When only two players are left to bowl the balls down the lane, the game is at its peak. The others gather around the last two and urge them on.

The first ball now to cross the line is grabbed by the nearest player who flees while the whole group, shouting "Pell Mell," chases him. The player who tags the one with the ball is one *leader* of the next game. The other *leader* is determined in the same way and a new game is started.

Prisoner's Base

Ages: 9–12
Players: 10–30; transition
Place: gymnasium; out-of-doors
Supplies: not any

Activity—hunting: chasing, dodging, running
Appeal: competition, skill, problem solving

The players are divided into two equal teams and take their places in their assigned territory. The territory is marked into two equal parts with opposing corners as prison for that territory's side. A player may venture into the opponents' territory but if caught he must go to the opponents' prison. He may be freed by a free member of his own side tagging him. As the two try to return both may be tagged and returned to prison. A team may win by either taking all of its opponents as prisoners or getting one of its free men in the opponents' prison when no prisoners are there.

There are many variations of this game. The chief differences in the games are the positions of each side's territory and their prison. A detailed description of the different forms may be found in *Games* by J. H. Bancroft (New York: The Macmillan Company, 1937). There are different and interesting opinions as to the origin and history of this age-old game. *Compton's Pictured Encyclopedia* (Vol. XII, 1935) gives the origin to be in a game called "War is Declared" that was played during the ancient Olympic games. Bancroft's *Games* states that "Prisoner's Base" and similar games such as "Stealing Sticks" are thought to have originated during the days of border warfare.

Joseph Strutt in *Sports and Pastimes of the People of England* (London: T. T. and J. Tegg, Cheapside, 1833, p. 73) states that early in the reign of Edward the Third a proclamation at the beginning of the Parliamentary proceedings prohibited the playing of the game in the avenues of Westminster palace. The game, played by adults at that time, interfered with members of Parliament passing to and from the palace.

The game was once called "The Country Base" and is mentioned in Shakespeare's "Cymbeline." At one time it was called "Chivy," from Chevy Chase.

Red Rover

Ages: intermediate
Players: 20 or more; transition
Place: gymnasium; out-of-doors
Supplies: not any

Activity—hunting: chasing, dodging, running
Appeal: competition, problem solving, skill

Two lines are drawn about 60 feet apart. The players stand behind one line, while *It* stands in the center and calls:

Red Rover, Red Rover,
Come over, Come over!

The players run to the other side. Those caught go into the center to help *It*. The last player caught will start the next game.

Relievo

Ages: intermediate
Players: 30 or more; group-and-one
Place: gymnasium; out-of-doors
Supplies: not any

Activity—hunting: chasing, dodging, running
Appeal: competition, problem solving, skill

One child is chosen to be *It* and chases the others. When one player is tagged, the two join hands and try to tag the others with the free hand. As the players are caught, they join *It* with only the end persons being allowed to tag.

Sale of Honey Pots

Ages: 5–8
Players: 20 or more; group-and-two; line
Place: gymnasium; out-of-doors

Supplies: not any
Activity—hunting: grasping, not smiling, stooping, swinging
Appeal: dramatization

One player is the *market man* and another the *buyer*. The rest of the players are *honey pots*. They clasp their hands under their knees. The buyer asks, "Have you any honey pots for sale?" The *market man* replies, "Yes, plenty, will you walk around and look at them?" As the *buyer* examines them he places his hands on their head. Some he says are too small, or too deep, or too large, until at last he finds one to suit him. If any *honey pot* has laughed, he must pay a forfeit to be redeemed at the end of the game. The *market man* and *buyer* then take the selected *honey pot* by the arms. If he has not lost his grasp after swinging forward and backward three times, he is bought. The game continues until all are bought. In China the game is played as "Fruit Sale"; in Italy it is called "Chicken Market."

Shuttle Feather

Ages: teen
Players: 4 to 16; two-group; informal
Place: gymnasium; out-of-doors

Supplies: tennis racquet or wooden paddle, shuttlecock
Activity—pastime: striking
Appeal: competition, problem solving, skill

This game consists of batting the *shuttlecock* with the *battledore* back and forth between teams. A point is scored by the team opposite from where the *shuttlecock* drops to the ground.

The *shuttlecock* may be made by placing feathers of equal size at even distances into a cork. The *battledore* used to be a small hand bat but now it resembles a tennis racquet that may be used in the place of the *battledore*. This is a very old game, dating back to the fourteenth century.

As far back as 1710, young girls in England were known to have batted the shuttlecocks so that they would not lack exercise!

Smugglers

Ages: 9–12
Players: 20 or more; group-and-one; informal
Place: gymnasium; out-of-doors
Supplies: not any

Activity—hunting: chasing, dodging, running
Appeal: competition, dramatization, problem solving, skill

One player is chosen to be an *officer*. The others represent *smugglers* and stand in a corner of the field. The *smugglers* pretend that they are in a *harbor* and send one player out to keep watch. When he sees the *officer* approaching them, he cries, "Look out." The *smugglers* run and try to reach a designated goal before the *officer* catches them. The first player caught becomes the *officer*.

The game is often called "Police and Robbers" by town children.

Steering in Twos

Ages: teen
Players: any number; couples; informal
Place: gymnasium; out-of-doors

Supplies: not any
Activity—stunt: walking
Appeal: skill

Partners are facing and place both hands on each other's shoulders. At a signal one player walks forward and steers her partner backward. At a repetition of the signal, the players change directions and the one who walked backward becomes the *steerer*. The object of the stunt is for couples to move about without touching others. It is suggested that the activity with music could be used in teaching direction and timing, as well as sensory perceptiveness of others. This last skill is great fun if the *steerer* is blindfolded!

Stool Ball

Ages: teen
Players: 20 or more; group-and-one; circle
Place: gymnasium; out-of-doors
Supplies: ball, stones, or chairs

Activity—hunting: catching, dodging, running, throwing
Appeal: competition, problem solving, skill

This game was originally played with stools by the milkmaids in England.

It was very popular with the early colonists. On the second Christmas Day, the colonists in Salem, Massachusetts, expressed to Governor William Bradford that they felt it was wrong to work on Christmas. The Governor excused them from their tasks that Christmas morning but was greatly surprised to find them playing Stool Ball on the street later during the day. He demanded that they go back to their tasks for he felt that it was wrong to play on that day and when others worked. The game used to be played by ladies at Easter.

A certain number of *stools* (flat stones in the open air and cushions indoors) are set up in circular formation, at a considerable distance from each other. Each *stool* is occupied by a single player. When *It*, who stands in the center, throws a ball up in the air, every player must change his position, running in succession from *stool* to *stool*. If the center player can recover the ball in time to throw it and strike any one of the players before she reaches the *stool* to which she is running, that player becomes the *It* and the center player joins the circle. The game continues as before. Rising quickly from the stone or cushion requires considerable agility on the part of the players.

Tandem Tag

Ages: teen
Players: 20 or more; group-and-four; informal
Place: gymnasium; out-of-doors
Supplies: 4 balls or beanbags

Activity—hunting: catching, dodging, running, throwing
Appeal: competition, problem solving, skill

Four *couples* are selected and given different colored bands, such as red, green, blue, and yellow. One of each *couple* holds a beanbag or ball. The couples station themselves anywhere within the playing area. The other players stand singly and scattered about the field. Four bases are designated at one end of the playing area, one for each *couple*.

The *couples* run anywhere about the field, passing the ball between themselves. The object is to tag a *single player* with the ball. When a *single player* is tagged, he goes to the base belonging to the player who tagged him. The *couple* who tagged the greatest number of players wins the game.

Variations. One couple may wear the colored bands. When a single player is tagged, he wears a band and joins the couple in trying to tag the other players. The play continues until only one player is free; he is declared the winner. Bases are not necessary when played this way. No player may hold the ball longer than 3 seconds or run with it in his hands.

Tiggy Touchwood

Ages: 9–12
Players: 10–20; group-and-one; informal
Place: wooded area
Supplies: not any

Activity—hunting: chasing, dodging, running
Appeal: competition, problem solving, skill

The players are safe from the *It,* or *Tiggy* as long as they are touching wood. As they run from one piece of wood to another, *Tiggy* chases them and anyone caught must take his place. Children of Italy play a similar game, "Hand Tag." In Greece the game is "Tree Toad."

The common practice of "knocking on wood" to ward off ill luck is said to be derived from a custom of early Christians of touching wood, upon occasions of happiness or good cheer, as an expression of thanksgiving to Christ who died upon a wooden cross. The many varieties of the game "Wood Tag" in which the runners escape being tagged by touching wood may have their origin in this ancient custom.

Tip Cat

Ages: 9–12
Players: 6–12; group-and-one; informal
Place: out-of-doors
Supplies: baseball bat or long stick, broom handle 5 or 6 inches long

Activity—athletic: running, striking
Appeal: competition, problem solving, skill

The *cat* is a piece of broom handle 5 or 6 inches long that is sharpened at both ends.

One player stands within a small circle marked on the ground, and hits the end of the *cat* with a baseball bat or a long stick. As it flies into the air he hits it again with his bat and knocks it aside if he can. If it falls inside the circle the batter is out, and the first one who can touch the *cat* becomes batter. After a certain number of rounds, the one who has the highest score wins. Hitting the *cat* is called "tipping the cat." A similar game, "Hit the Stick," is played in the United States.

Trencher or Hoop Game

Ages: 9–12
Players: 20 or more; group-and-one; circle
Place: gymnasium; out-of-doors
Supplies: hoop

Activity—hunting: reaching, running
Appeal: competition, problem solving, skill

The players form a circle around a center player who holds a hoop in her hands. This player spins the hoop, calls the name of one of the circle players, and then rushes to that player's place. The circle player must rush to the center and try to catch the hoop before it has finished spinning. If she is successful, she then spins it and continues the game; otherwise the first spinner must resume her original place.

This game is much like "Spin the Plate" that is popular in both France and the United States.

SCOTLAND

Charlie Over the Water

Ages: 5–8
Players: 20 or more; group-and-one; circle
Place: gymnasium; out-of-doors

Supplies: yardstick
Activity—hunting: jumping, running
Appeal: rhythm, skill

The players form a circle. Charlie stands in the center, facing two players who hold a stick 12 inches above and parallel to the ground to represent a bridge. The circle players join hands and skip around, saying this rhyme:

> Charlie over the water,
> Charlie over the sea
> Charlie catch a blackbird.
> Can't catch me.

As the last line is said, Charlie jumps over the stick and runs to tag the circle players before they stoop. If he is successful, the tagged players become Charlie; otherwise Charlie must jump back and forth across the bridge as the words are repeated. The game goes back to the exile of Charles II of England in France. He was urged by the Scots to come back over the water.

Fire on the Mountains

Ages: 9–12
Players: 10–30; transition; circle
Place: gymnasium; out-of-doors; schoolroom

Supplies: chairs
Activity—hunting: running
Appeal: competition, dramatization

The players are seated in chairs in circle formation. One extra player is the *leader* and sits in the center of the circle to give signals. Another odd player stands any place in the circle between the chairs. The *leader* calls, "Fire on the mountain, run, boy, run!" At any time the *leader* may unexpectedly stop repeating the verse and say "chair" or "base." At this signal all circle players change places (running on the outside of the circle of chairs) and at the same time try to escape being the odd player. The player left without a chair takes another player's chair to sit outside the game. This makes one less chair. The *leader* repeats the verse and his signal. The object is to remain within the circle the longest. The leader repeats the verse until only two are left. The last two players circle the last chair and an object a few yards away. The last one in the game is the leader for the next game.

The reference to gun, red coats, and mountain fires suggests historical origin. The same game pattern is found in "Going to Jerusalem" from Germany and the United States of America.

Smuggling the Geg

Ages: 9–12

Players: 10 to 20; two-group; informal

Place: out-of-doors

Supplies: geg or treasure

Activity—hunting: chasing, dodging, hiding, running, seeking

Appeal: competition, skill

The players are divided into two equal teams. One is the *outs* or the *smugglers* and the other the *ins*. A den 4 feet by 6 feet is marked on the ground for a central or safe place for the *smugglers*. The *outs* have the *geg* or treasure and give it to one of their number in such a way that his identity is unknown in a group. The *outs* run to hide but first give the call, "Smugglers." The *ins* then begin the chase. If the player who has the *geg* returns to the den before being caught the *ins* become the *outs* for the next game. When one of the *ins* catches an *out* he must take off the *out's* cap and place the palm of his hand on the *out's* head before he may claim his prisoner and demand, "Deliver up the geg." At this point the *out* must cease to struggle. The player goes free if he does not have the *geg*.

Stealing Sticks

Ages: 9–12

Players: 20 or more; transition; informal

Place: gymnasium; out-of-doors

Supplies: 12 sticks

Activity—hunting: chasing, dodging, running

Appeal: competition, problem solving, skill

This game is similar to "Prisoner's Base" both in form and origin (see England). The playing area is marked into two equal parts. Six sticks are placed in a small goal at the end of each part. The players are divided into two equal groups and take their places, a group in each part of the field. The object of each player is to touch the opponents' goal without being tagged and bring one stick at a time to his own goal. No player may be tagged if he has secured a stick and is returning. If he is tagged while in the opponents' territory before reaching the goal, he must remain a prisoner in the goal until one of his group comes and touches him; neither may be tagged while returning to their territory. A stick may not be taken by a player if one of his men is a prisoner. The group gaining all the sticks first wins.

The game is sometimes known as "Scots and English." It is popular in the United States as "Stealing Sticks."

Wee Bologna Man

Ages: 5–8
Players: 20 or more; group-and-one; informal
Place: gymnasium; out-of-doors; schoolroom

Supplies: not any
Activity—pastime: imitation
Appeal: rhythm

A *leader* stands in front of the group. As he repeats the verse he imitates the members of a band. He may pantomime playing a fife, drum, fiddle, flute, triangle, or imitate the drum major. The *wee Bologna man* may use gestures of any kind. The group follows his movements. The activity will depend largely upon the initiative of the *leader* and the enthusiasm that is put into the movements.

GAMES AND SPORTS—REPUBLIC OF IRELAND

Blarney Stone

Ages: 9–12
Players: 20 or more; transition
Place: gymnasium; out-of-doors
Supplies: large stone

Activity—hunting: chasing, dodging, running
Appeal: dramatization, skill

In the wall of the famous old Blarney castle there is set a great, rugged stone known as the Blarney Stone. Each year thousands of tourists visit the castle and the story follows that if anyone kisses the stone, he will be blessed with a most polite and pleasing manner. Since the stone rests high in the wall, whoever kisses it must be held out to reach it and must almost stand on his head to touch the rock.

The game described here is adapted from the Blarney Stone legend that has great appeal to many tourists.

The children stand facing each other in two lines about 15 or 20 feet apart. A *stone* is placed in the center of the space between the lines. Each child shuts his eyes tightly and clasps his hands behind his back. A *leader* gives a signal for the game to begin whereupon the players walk forward slowly until the signal "Stop!" is given. They stop quickly, open their eyes, and run as fast as they can for the *Blarney Stone*. The first child to touch the *stone* stands still and holds one hand on it. Now that he has touched the *stone*, he can speak and is the *keeper* of the *stone*. The other players go back to their places in the lines, at the same time watching the child at the stone. Suddenly he cries:

Blarney—bum!!
Run—run—run!!

The players immediately start to run up and down past the child at the *stone*, going as close as they dare. The child tries to tag one of them, though he must keep one hand on the *stone*. If he touches a player, that player must stand at the *stone* and take hold of the free hand of the first one. The procedure is repeated until all the players except one are members of the chain at the center. When only one player is free to race past the *stone*, the child with his hand on the *stone* who first called "Blarney—bum!!" suddenly calls again:

Blarney—bum!!
Run—run—run!!

Then every player in the chain at the center drops hands and all chase the one player who is free. When he is tagged, he becomes the new Blarney Stone keeper and the game starts anew.

Chestnuts

Ages: 9–12
Players: 4 or more; individual; informal
Place: home; out-of-doors

Supplies: chestnuts
Activity—pastime: coordination
Appeal: competition, skill

Each player has a chestnut that has been pierced with a nail and is suspended on a string. Upon agreement one player swings and strikes his chestnut against that of another player. If the aggressor breaks his opponent's chestnut, he is declared *conqueror* and goes to another player and challenges him. If the aggressor's chestnut breaks, he is out of the game and the new *conqueror* continues the play, with the *conqueror* never having more than one swing at his opponent's chestnut. A champion is established and the play starts anew with the champion having the first swing at a chosen opponent. The Irish children often choose green chestnuts, which make the game more fun because the nuts do not break easily. Oak nuts are used sometimes.

Egg Game

Ages: 9–12
Players: 4–10; single-group; informal
Place: gymnasium; home; schoolroom

Supplies: cane, colored eggs, large handkerchief
Activity—pastime: guessing
Appeal: competition, problem solving

Six eggs are needed, one of each of the following colors: blue, black, red, green, white, and gold. When played outdoors, the eggs may be set up in sand; indoors, they may be propped up in cotton. The players take turns being blindfolded and trying to touch the different eggs with a rod or cane. The score of each player is based upon his accuracy in executing the action suggested in the rhyme that follows:

> Mike and Meg, Pat and Peg,
> Watch me tap this Easter egg;
> Blue and black, green, red and white
> Value at two, four, six, five, and one.
> Should I tap the egg of gold,
> That shall be mine to hold.

The player who scores 20 first wins the game.

6

Latin America

Although Mexico, Central America, and the West Indies are parts of the North American continent, their games are included in the games of Latin America. Thus these countries, and several countries of South America, are considered in their societal group rather than in their geographical classification.

The more than twenty Latin American countries cover a vast land area and are peopled by millions, yet they have less games than other continental or societal groups. One reason for the scarcity of games is that the Latins have through the years developed rhythmic patterns that combine song, dance, and gamelike activities, instead of game patterns as such. Another reason seems to be of geographical influence. Except for the people in the cities, the peoples of Latin America do not have opportunity to get together often in groups. When they do assemble it is usually for an annual few days of fiesta or for a political rally. Consequently there is not the close people-to-people relationship that promotes the passing on of play and its customs. Their folklore that lives in song, games, and dance is cherished and survives within family and village groups. Rarely does it extend from one society to another.

The fiestas are a combination of religion, fasting, feasting, and demonstrations of physical prowess. . . . often to the exhaustion of the participants. The game contests are of such a nature that only the men participate. The children, boys, and girls seldom do more than look on. Exceptions to this are the "Carnival Game" of Mexico and the *romper de pinata* of Guatemala. It is likely that other Latin societies have similar customs that provide for the children during the fiestas. There is need for more information about these peoples and their way of life. There is also need for more details of their play patterns.

An economic influence may have some bearing on the scarcity of games in this part of the world. A Latin friend recently said, "There are few games and play patterns in many parts of my homeland. There are many hungry people in my country. Children do not play games when they are hungry, nor do their parents dance and sing when there is sickness and no food for the family."

Books of Latin American games and sports are practically non-existent. The majority of games in the collection have come from United States personnel serving as teachers and missionaries in Latin America and from Latin nationals who are now in the States.

The people in the cities are becoming more interested in sports participation and this is through the influence of Great Britain and the United States of North America. As spectators the Latins have had great interest in the sports of Spain and Portugal. The once popular bullfights have been abandoned in most Latin American countries, although in Mexico, Colombia, Peru, and Venezuela the fights still draw large crowds. Sports in schools attract little attention. Large crowds do attend the professional games of baseball, basketball, and soccer.

The play of the children in the schools of the cities follow the adult pattern of rhythmic games and dances. The children of the farms and the interior often live far from schools or where there are no schools. There is little time for play, for the children must work to help make the living.

In this collection of games, play activities of the Latin children are dramatic, with the exception of the Araucanian Indian game from Chile and *Tejo* from Colombia. Kite flying is popular throughout Central and South America. The kite is called *El Cometa* or the comet. The sticks are bamboo, arranged in a hexagon, and covered with tissue paper. The players often show their artistic taste by decorating their kites with a fringe of tissue paper around the bottom. A musical effect is obtained by extending the sticks over the paper at the top and stretching strips of hide across them. In a strong breeze this gives a sound like an Aeolian harp. By loosening or tightening the strings a musical chord may be produced. The covering of the kite is sometimes painted to represent the face of a man, with the fringe around the sides being trimmed to give the appearance of a beard.

"Hide and Seek," "Pussy-wants-a-Corner," "Duck and Drake," varieties of tag games, and rope skipping are popular pastimes with the children of Latin American countries. Quoits, tennis, and baseball are beginning to be popular outdoor sports. Marbles is a favorite game. The players often prefer the hard, round nuts from a native tree to the marbles made of clay.

The indoor games are comparatively few, as the weather is mild and play in the patios is quite popular. Nevertheless, handball is played indoors to a great extent.

The Latin American game collection includes games from all areas mentioned except the countries of Central America:

CENTRAL AMERICA	WEST INDIES
MEXICO	Cuba Puerto Rico

SOUTH AMERICA

Brazil   Colombia
Chile   Paraguay

CENTRAL AMERICA

It was in Central America that rubber balls were first used in play activities. Their usage spread to other nearby peoples and became quite popular in Mexico.

Todos Santos, a village in the highlands of Guatemala, holds an annual Indian fiesta in October. The combined activities of religion, rockets, and rooster races are for the adults; finally an afternoon of *romper de pinata* or break the jar is given to the children. The *pinata* game is popular in Mexico and Colombia and is played in much milder form in these countries than in Guatemala. It is restricted almost entirely to the Christmas parties in Mexico.

MEXICO

The Spaniards who invaded Mexico were dumfounded by a strangely acting object, the rubber ball. One writer who sent a letter back to Spain declared that the Mexicans played with a ball inflated with some mysterious element said to be substance from the sap of a tree. The writer's reaction to the ball was that it seemed to be possessed of the devil, since it bounced vigorously upon the least blow from one of the players.

Although Spanish games are still favorites among the Mexican children, an interest in American sports is rapidly growing among the adults. Tennis, swimming, and baseball are becoming popular with the young people of Mexico. *Jai alai* is played enthusiastically throughout the cities; *Pelota,* a Spanish-Basque game, is popular in Mexico City.

The play of the Mexican children is quiet even when they are having a good time. They come of a quiet, self-contained race that shows little outward excitement in any of its activities. They are content to rely upon things that do not have to be bought for their happiness.

Most of the pastimes are those that lead into the occupations of the adults of this land. Wood carving is engaged in by the children to a large extent, and this pastime develops quite frequently into a paying vocation for many of the people there. Puppets are made by the children and puppet shows are a frequent sight in Mexico. Don Quixote is possibly the favorite of the many puppets made and used. Riding and playing with the burro entertains the younger children day in and day out. Physical education brought by the teacher is something new and exciting.

SOUTH AMERICA

BRAZIL AND CHILE

The children's play activities of Brazil, a country of superlatives, are suggestive of the play of the children in the United States of North America. The most popular activities are the singing games that are usually in circle formation. Adults of Brazil enjoy and participate in polo and horse racing.

The long coast line of Chile offers opportunity for water sports; the Andes Mountains provide the setting for skiing and mountain climbing. Many visitors go to Chile just to ski. Volley ball, soccer, and rugby are played by the children in the schools. Tennis is enjoyed by many Chileans.

COLOMBIA

Most of the pastimes, games, and sports of this progressive Latin American country had their beginnings either in Spanish or Indian customs. The bullfights are of national interest and are carried out with great color, seriousness, and Spanish tradition.

Colombia's national game of *Tejo* (te-HO) is of Indian origin, coming from the Chibchas (CHIB-chas) Indians, one of the most advanced of the South American Indian groups. It is played by boys and men of all ages and social levels. It is not uncommon to find it being played by laborers in the fields after a day's work; by friends in the patio of a home; by members of a sports club in special *tejo* courts; and by professionals in the National Olympics.

Other popular sports are *basquetbol* (basketball) and *beisbol* (baseball) of North American influence and *futbol* (football), which is much like European soccer.

Children's games, though scarce, are clever and in many ways resemble games of similar patterns played throughout the world. Educational opportunities and freedom to play may be said to go hand-in-hand. As more schools are built in this land and as more children are allowed time from work to attend the schools, it is hoped that the play-life of the children and youth, the girls especially, will expand proportionately.

PARAGUAY

The country of Paraguay is sports minded with *futbol* (football), which is really soccer, being the most popular sport. Each village has its soccer club and the small boys even play with balls made of socks stuffed with rags as they practice the game. *Tikichuela* (TIK-e-chew-A-la) or "jacks" is a favorite game with the girls. The games from Paraguay indicate that the children are especially fond of dramatization, puzzles, and riddles.

WEST INDIES

CUBA AND PUERTO RICO

The observations on Cuba relate to the play-life of the Cubans before the Castro regime. It is hoped that the nationals can preserve and finally maintain a way of life that fosters freedom, including the Cubans' interest and participation in games and sports. Before Castro there was great interest in baseball among the Cubans. They not only had their own leagues, but also participated in international tournaments. The swift ball game *jai alai* has been a very popular sport among the Cubans for years.

The recreational activities of the Cuban children were generally related to the sea and to rhythmic games. Swimming, surf-bathing, diving, and sailing were favorite pastimes; singing games and folk dances were enjoyed by the children and adults. The children's games in the collection are delightful and bear similarities to games popular in the United States.

The children of Puerto Rico, like their parents, enjoy playing games and dancing. Their favorite sports activities are sailing, fishing, swimming, horseback riding, and baseball. Tennis and golf are becoming popular among the young people. The children, like their parents, like to watch basketball, horse races, boxing matches, and baseball. The children spend much of their time after school working in the gardens. They enjoy the quiet evenings of playing the guitar, listening to others play, or joining some of the neighbors in musical games and dances.

GAMES AND SPORTS—MEXICO

Angel and the Devil

Ages: 5–8
Players: 20 or more; transition
Place: gymnasium; out-of-doors
Supplies: not any

Activity—hunting: conversation, walking
Appeal: dramatization, repetition

One player is chosen to be an *angel* and another is the *devil*. The others are secretly named different colors. The *angel* waves her arms like wings and pretends to knock on a door, then the following dialogue takes place:

Players: "Who is there?"
Angel: "A lonely angel with two wings."
Players: "What else can you want?"
Angel: "I seek a color."
Players: "What color, please."
Angel: "It is called blue."

The child named blue follows the *angel* and both fly about. The *devil* approaches with a forked stick on his head. He knocks and the dialogue follows:

Players: "Who is there?"
Devil: "A fearful devil with two horns."
Players: "What do you want?"
Devil: "I demand a color."
Players: "What color for you?"
Devil: "Green, I prefer."

Then the player named green has to be a little *devil*. The game continues until all players have been transferred into *angels* and *devils*. The side having the greatest number of players at the end of the game wins. This game is popular with young children in Colombia, South America.

Although the description does not suggest it, it seems that more fun could be added to the game if it were ended with a tug-of-war as in "London Bridge." This is done in "Angel and Imp" from Puerto Rico.

Carnival Game

Ages: 9–12
Players: large number; two-group; circle
Place: out-of-doors

Supplies: painted eggshells
Activity—pastime: walking
Appeal: dramatization, surprise

The name of this game could also be "Confetti Battle." During carnival time in Vera Cruz the boys and girls carry out a traditional confetti battle late one afternoon in the plaza. Confetti is sealed in painted eggshells. Hundreds of boys and girls walk in two endless processions near the edge of the square. The girls go in one direction, the boys in another. Every few steps the girls reach out and crush their eggshells on the boys' heads; the boys crush their eggshells on the heads of the passing girls.

Carpenteros, Carboneros, and Cardinales

Ages: 9–12
Players: 20 or more; two-group; line
Place: gymnasium; out-of-doors
Supplies: not any

Activity—hunting: chasing, running
Appeal: competition, dramatization

One player is chosen as *leader*. The other players form two parallel lines about 3 feet apart and facing each other. One team is the *carpenteros*, carpenters; the other is the *carboneros*, coal miners.

Play begins as the leader gives the calls. If he calls "Carpenteros!" that team turns and runs to a line about 30 feet away. The *carboneros* try to tag them before they cross the line. The players who are tagged are out of the game. If *carboneros* is called, they run to a line on their side, trying to reach it before the *carpenteros* tag them.

If *cardinales* is called neither team should move. If a player should move even a foot, he is eliminated from the game. The leader may add excitement to the game by pausing on the first syllable CAR so that the players do not know what to expect. The team with the most players at the end of playing time wins. Pronunciations: Carpenteros (car-pin-TĀ-ros), Carboneros (car-bo-NĀ-ros), Cardinales (car-di-NĀ-les).

Colorinas

Ages: 9–12
Players: 4–6; individual; informal
Place: gymnasium; out-of-doors
Supplies: small beans

Activity—pastime: catching, tossing
Appeal: skill

A small hole is dug in the ground if played out-of-doors, or a bowl placed on the floor if played indoors. A line is drawn about 8 feet away from the hole. The players take a handful of little red beans called *colorinas* and stand on the line. One at a time the players see how many beans they can throw into the hole. The whole handful of beans must be released at one time. If any fall into the hole, the player picks them up and puts them in the palm of one hand. Then with a jerk he throws the beans into the air and tries to catch them on the back of the hand; once again he throws them and catches them in the palm. The player who has the greatest number of beans in the palm after the last person throws is the winner. The players must each have an equal number of beans to start the game.

Early Ball Game

Ages: teen
Players: 20 or more; two-group; informal
Place: out-of-doors

Supplies: playground ball
Activity—athletic: kicking, running, striking
Appeal: competition, skill

This ancient game may be classed as a strenuous type of soccer. The playing area was about the size of a football field. A very large stone, which served as a goal post, was set up at each end of the field. A hole or pocket had been cut in the center of the stone.

The players were divided into two teams and each team claimed one of the goals. The object of the game was for a team to send the ball into its own goal. The ball was not thrown or kicked as it is played today. It was passed or hit with the hip. As a means of protection, the players wore a leather pad on the hips. Each goal scored one point. A final score was decided upon before the game started. The games often lasted 4 hours.

Today's adaptation of this game is to use standard football or soccer goals with the height much lower and to set a time limit for the game.

Figures of Clay

Ages: 9–12
Players: 8 or more; two-group; line
Place: out-of-doors

Supplies: small clay figures (hard)
Activity—pastime: throwing
Appeal: skill

Small figures of clay are needed for this game. The players are divided into two teams, *red soldiers* versus *blue soldiers,* or dogs versus cats, according to whatever figures are used. Two lines are marked on the floor or ground. The first, the *goal line,* is 6 inches from the wall and the second, the *starting line,* is 12 feet from the wall. The teams are lined upon the starting line, and each side throws alternately. The play is as follows: Throw a small figure so that it strikes the wall; if it falls between the wall and the *goal line,* it scores; if it falls outside the *goal line,* it is forfeited to the opposite team. Each player throws one figure. This constitutes a round; three rounds make a game. At the end of each round, the captains of the two teams collect the figures lost by the opposing team. A throw that does not strike the wall is foul, and must be tried again. The team with the greatest number of figures wins.

If there are more than six players to a team it is best to have two games, using opposite walls.

Little Parrot

Ages: 9–12   Supplies: small object
Players: 10–20; single-group; circle   Activity—pastime: alertness
Place: home; schoolroom   Appeal: dramatization

A *leader* is chosen and given a small object or *little parrot* to hold in his hands; he and the other players sit in a circle. The leader starts the play as he turns to the player on his left and asks quite seriously, "Would you like to buy this pretty little parrot?" The player asks just as seriously, "Will it bite?" The *leader* answers, "Why, no, it will not bite," and then passes the small object or *little parrot* to the player on his left. This player turns to the player on his left (or the third player) and asks, "Would you like to buy this parrot?" The third player asks, "Will it bite?" When the second player is asked the question about the parrot biting, he must not reply. He must turn to the *leader* and ask, "Will it bite?" The *leader* answers, "Why, no, it will not bite," whereupon the second player turns to the third player and repeats, "Why, no, it will not bite," and passes the *little parrot* to him.

The play continues with questioning always going back from player to player until it reaches the *leader*. The answer, "Why, no, it will not bite," is repeated to the player holding the *little parrot*. Should a player laugh or forget to pass the *little parrot*, he must pay a penalty.

Moon and Stars

(See Spain.)

Pilma

Ages: 9–12   Supplies: playground ball
Players: any number; couples; in-   Activity—pastime: dodging, leap-
   formal   ing, throwing
Place: gymnasium; out-of-doors   Appeal: competition, skill

Two players stand 12 feet apart. One of them has a light fiber ball that he strikes with his hand. He tries to hit the body of his opponent. The opponent tries to avoid the ball by dodging, leaping into the air, or falling on the ground. After five attempts, the players change places. The one scoring 20 hits first wins. The same game is played in Colombia, South America, with a hard ball that is thrown at the opponents. The game is called *Envenenada* (En-

Mexico—Pilma.

ven-e-NAH-da) or *poison ball,* the "sting" from the ball suggesting
poison.

Piñata

Ages: 9–12   Supplies: clay jar, trinkets, large
Players: 10–30; transition; informal   handkerchief
Place: home; schoolroom; out-of-   Activity—pastime: running, striking
  doors   Appeal: problem solving, skill

This game is played by the Mexican children during *Pasada*
(Pah-SAH-dah) parties at Christmas time. These parties are similar to American Christmas tree parties. A big clay jar, the *Piñata,*
is colorfully decorated and filled with trinkets, confections, and
precious trifles dear to the heart of any child. The *Piñata* is swung
from the ceiling and may be adjustable so that it can be quickly
lowered or raised. When the guests have arrived and have chanted

prayer and songs of rejoicing, the party turns from ceremony to fun.

One child is blindfolded and holds a long stick with which he strikes at the jar. The others turn him around, sending him in wrong directions, and swing the jar away from him, as they shout, "*Que viva Piñata!*" The children take turns at trying to hit the jar before someone is lucky enough to hit it hard enough to break it and send the contents scattering to the floor. Then a scramble for the trinkets begins. Supper, games, and dancing follow and on the following night all will go to the house of a friend who gives the next *Pasada* party in just the same manner.

Sick Man

Ages: 9–12
Players: 10 to 20; group-and-one; line
Place: gymnasium; out-of-doors; schoolroom

Supplies: not any
Activity—pastime: conversation
Appeal: dramatization

The players sit in a line. One player, the *doctor*, names each player something that may be given a sick person, such as food or medicine. He then begins a dialogue that runs like this:

Doctor: "What do you prescribe for the sick man at three o'clock?"
First Player: "Quinine, sir."
Doctor: "Quinine at three o'clock?"
First Player: "Yes sir, quinine at three o'clock."
Doctor: "At three o'clock, quinine?"
First Player: "Quinine at three o'clock, I say."

The *doctor* continues down the line asking each player similar questions except for a change in the time of day. The object of the game is for the player to answer in the opposite order to that of the question. If he fails, he must pay a forfeit.

GAMES AND SPORTS—SOUTH AMERICA

BRAZIL

Coelho Na Toca (Co-EL-yo na-TO-ca)

Ages: 5–8
Players: 22 or more; three-and-one; circles
Place: gymnasium; out-of-doors

Supplies: not any
Activity—hunting: running
Appeal: dramatization

One player is chosen to be *It* or the *rabbit-without-a-house*. The other players are in groups of three and form a *house* by two of them holding hands. The third player is inside the *house* and is also called a *rabbit*.

At a signal all *rabbits* must run to another *house*. The *rabbit-without-a-house* tries to find a home. The *rabbit* left outside awaits or gives the signal and then tries to become a *coelho na toca,* or a *rabbit in his house.*

Gato Doente (Ga-TO Do-EN-te)

Ages: 5–8   Supplies: not any
Players: 10–20; group-and-one; in-   Activity—hunting: chasing, dodg-
 formal   ing, running
Place: gymnasium; out-of-doors   Appeal: dramatization

A player is chosen to be the *gato* or cat. The other players scatter about the playing area. When a signal is given the *gato* chases the other players who become *gato doente* or *sick cats* and must hold the left hand on the part touched.

The *sick cats* help catch the untouched players. Play continues until only one player remains untouched. That player is the winner and starts the new game.

Luta de Galo (LU-ta de GA-lo)

Ages: 9–12   Supplies: handkerchiefs
Players: any number; couple; in-   Activity—contest: pushing, reach-
 formal   ing
Place: gymnasium; out-of-doors   Appeal: competition, skill

Several couples may play at a time. Each player tucks a handkerchief in his belt, places his right arm over his chest, and hops about on his right foot. The free left arm is used to reach for the opponent's handkerchief. Each contestant, while trying to defend his own handkerchief, pushes, and bumps his opponent and tries to snatch his handkerchief. The winner is the player who succeeds in getting the handkerchief. Winners of each couple may challenge each other until a final champion is established. A player whose left foot touches the ground or whose right arm unbends is disqualified. *Luta de galo* means a "fight of roosters."

Neighbors

Ages: 5–8   Supplies: not any
Players: 10 or more; single-group;   Activity—pastime: pulling, stoop-
 line   ing
Place: gymnasium; out-of-doors   Appeal: dramatization

The players stand in a line holding hands. The head player is the *farmer,* the foot, the *neighbor.* The *farmer* calls out, "Neighbor, I'll find the thief," then ducks under the arms somewhere in the line, pulling the other players with him. The player who is not able to go under because his arms are crossed becomes a *prisoner* and is put in *jail*. The play continues until all players except the *farmer* and the *neighbor* are *prisoners*. Then the *farmer* and *neighbor* judge the *prisoners*.

Peteca (Pe-TA-ca)

Ages: teen
Players: 10 or more; single-group; informal
Place: out-of-doors

Supplies: *peteca* or badminton birdie
Activity—pastime: batting, striking
Appeal: competition, skill

The *peteca*, meaning basket, is made by sewing a piece of leather into a cone shape and filling it with sand until it is about the size of a tennis ball. Several long feathers are stuck into the upper end of the sand and tied firmly. A badminton birdie may be used though it is smaller than the usual *peteca*.

One player tosses the *peteca* into the air. Each player then tries to keep it there by striking it upward with the palm of his hand. The *peteca* may be hit only once at a time and always upward. When the *peteca* falls, the game is started over. The winning player is the one who hits the *peteca* the greatest number of times. Sometimes players repeat the letters of the alphabet as they strike, using one letter for each upward strike.

CHILE

Chueca (Chu-A-ca)

Ages: teen
Players: 20 or more; two-group; informal
Place: out-of-doors

Supplies: hockey or curved sticks; ball
Activity—athletic: running, striking
Appeal: competition, skill

This game has the skills of hockey, although the Araucanian Indians played it long before a European landed on their shores. Chueca means curved stick. The Araucanians played with a natural club of hazelwood that was curved at one end. They regarded the game as a serious contest. Players were influenced by their dreams the night preceding a game. If a player should dream and it were a good one, he took it as a sign of victory. If the dream were a bad one, it forecast defeat and no amount of persuasion could induce him to play.

Players today use a cane, a curved umbrella handle, or a hockey stick. Two teams of equal number and skill stand in two lines several feet apart and facing each other. A goal line is marked across one end of the field. A hole is marked between the two lines of players and the ball is placed in the hole.

One player from each team steps forward, at a given signal, and tries to knock the ball from the hole. The player who succeeds starts driving the ball toward the goal. His teammates join him, while the opponents try to hit the ball away from them and score the goal. When the ball crosses the goal line, one point is scored and the play starts from the hole.

Teams change positions when one side has scored two points. If the losing team makes a point, it is subtracted from the two scored by the opposing team; thus the score is one-one. Should the losers make another point, the score of both teams is canceled and the game starts all over again. The winning team is the one making four points.

Who Is It?

Ages: teen
Players: 20 or more; group-and-one; line
Place: home; schoolroom

Supplies: not any
Activity—pastime: guessing
Appeal: dramatization

One player is chosen to be *leader* and to head a line formed by the other players standing directly behind him. The game starts as the *leader* asks the question, "Have you seen my friend?" The players answer, "No, sir." The *leader* then asks, "Do you know where he is?" The answer is, "Yes, sir."

After this conversation the *leader* slowly walks forward nine steps. During this time, the players quietly and quickly shift places in the line as they wish. One player moves directly behind the *leader*. The others call, "Who is it?" The *leader* may ask three questions of the players before he answers. The questions may be, "Is it boy or girl? Is he fair or dark? Is he short or tall?" After asking the three questions the *leader* must guess who stands behind him. Should he guess correctly, he is *leader* again; otherwise another player takes his place.

COLOMBIA

Casita (ca-SI-ta)

Ages: 9–12
Players: any number; couple; line
Place: out-of-doors

Supplies: palm nuts
Activity—pastime: throwing
Appeal: competition, skill

Each player has a palm nut that in turn he throws at the *casita* or *little house*. The *casita* is made by placing three palm nuts close together in a circle; another nut is placed in the center of and atop the three. One player, standing about 15 feet from the *casita,* throws his palm nut at the *little house.* If he succeeds in hitting the *house,* he wins the game and the nuts. If he fails, the other player then builds another *little house* and starts a new game. In Italy the game is called *Filberta.*

De La Habana Vino un Barco (de la A-BAN-a B-no un BAR-co)

Ages: teen
Players: 10 to 20; group-and-one; circle
Place: home; schoolroom

Supplies: handkerchief
Activity—pastime: alertness
Appeal: intellectual challenge

Players are seated in a circle. One player throws a handkerchief to another player and says, "From Havana came a boat loaded with . . . . ," whereupon the player who caught the handkerchief quickly names an article beginning with the letter "a." This continues with the handkerchief being thrown to another player and so on until a player fails to name an article beginning with "a." The player who fails must do a stunt, sing, or pay a forfeit. Play starts where it left off with the handkerchief being thrown to the next player who names an article starting with the letter "b." The game continues until each letter of the alphabet has been used.

La Cachanga (La Ca-CHAN-ga)

Ages: 9–12
Players: 15–30; group-and-one; circle
Place: gymnasium; out-of-doors

Supplies: shoe
Activity—hunting: kneeling, passing
Appeal: rhythm, skill

The term *la cachanga* is Spanish for a sandal made of cotton. The sole of the shoe is flat and the shoe is held on by a strap. The players are in a close circle, kneeling on one knee, the other is at right angles. A shoe is passed quickly under the knee of each player. One player on the outside of the circle moves around the group in the direction in which the shoe is sent and tries to locate the shoe. The circle players say together repeatedly,

Que corra la cachanga
Que corra la cachanga.

The sandal that runs
The sandal that runs.

If the outside player locates the shoe, he taps the shoulder of the player holding it and then exchanges places with that player.

Piñata (Pin-YAT-a)

Ages: all
Players: 10–30; single-group; circle
Place: home; out-of-doors
Supplies: *piñata*

Activity—pastime: striking, walking
Appeal: surprise

A detailed description of the game, *Piñata,* is given in the games from Mexico. There is a variation in the pattern of the game as it is played in Colombia.

In the first place, the Colombian game is played at birthday parties and often following the breakfast of the First Communion of boys and girls, rather than during the *Posada* parties at Christmas as in Mexico. The Colombian children enjoy the game because of surprise elements often introduced. Three *piñatas* are suspended in the inside patio or in the yard. One *piñata* is filled with candy and trinkets; one is filled with water; the third contains sand. The players do not know the contents of each specific jar, although they anticipate the surprises. Great excitement and fun are part of the game from beginning to end.

Romana (Ro-MAN-a)

Ages: teen
Players: any number; couples; informal
Place: gymnasium; out-of-doors

Supplies: not any
Activity—stunt: lifting, balance
Appeal: strength

Players stand back to back with a partner about the same size. Partners link arms at elbows and steadily lift each other alternately in a rocking position. The same stunt is called "Churn the Butter" by children in North America. *Romana* in Spanish means a measure or to weigh.

Tejo (TE-jo)

Ages: 9–12; teen
Players: 2–12; individual or couples; informal
Place: out-of-doors

Supplies: disks, flares
Activity—pastime: throwing
Appeal: competition, skill

The playing court consists of two scoring areas that are from 40 to 75 feet apart, depending on the age of the players. The scoring areas are terraced about a foot high at the back and slope downward to ground level toward the center of the court. In the center of each terrace a hole is dug from 3 to 6 inches in diameter and several inches deep. An iron cup is sunk into each hole. During play the ground around the cup and for several feet thereabout is kept moist. Four small flares containing a mild and harmless explosive are placed in a squarelike arrangement around each cup. The flares are lighted just before play starts.

Each player has a *tejo* or flat, round iron disk that is from 2 to 5 inches in diameter. All players, either as individual participants or couples, stand at one end of the court. Play begins by a player throwing his disk (underhand) to score in the distant cup. Players have one turn each, then walk to the opposite end of the court and determine the score, which is counted as follows:

3 points for a disk in the hole.
1 point for the disk or disks nearest the hole.
3 points if a disk hits and explodes a flare.
6 points if a disk hits, explodes a flare, and then lands in the hole.

The game consists of 9 points. Several games may be decided upon as a set, the winning player or team being determined by the winner of the greatest number of sets.

Tunel (TU-nel)

Ages: 9–12
Players: 10 to 20; single-group; line
Place: gymnasium; out-of-doors

Supplies: not any
Activity—stunt: stooping, walking
Appeal: dramatization, skill

The players stand in line one behind the other. Bending over at the waist, each player extends his right hand between his own knee and joins it with the extended left hand of the player just in front of him. The action begins by the last player in the line starting through, between the legs of the players. The next player follows, keeping his hands joined, and so on until all players have gone through the tunnel.

Un Burro (un BOO-ro)

Ages: teen
Players: any number; threes; informal
Place: gymnasium; out-of-doors

Supplies: not any
Activity—stunt: balance, grasping
Appeal: dramatization, strength

One player is on his hands and knees. The two other players sit one on each side of the kneeling player and place their feet over his back with the soles of their shoes touching. They grasp hands, pull their hips up; the boy supporting them shifts his weight to his hands and feet and walks with his *burden.*

PARAGUAY

Define, Define, What Is It?

Ages: teen
Players: 10 or more; group-and-one; informal
Place: home; schoolroom

Supplies: not any
Activity—pastime: alertness, guessing
Appeal: dramatization

One player starts the game by presenting the group with a situation or a problem. For example, he says: "What has six legs, four arms, and a woman's head on it and it moves like this . . . . . ?" Then he moves forward and backward. "It also has many colors, etc." Players may make guesses as the description goes on. The person who guesses correctly starts the next game. (Answer: a chair with a lady in it.) This game is somewhat like the game of charades in which several players present the problem, usually in pantomime.

Hiding the Belt

Ages: 9–12
Players: 20 or more; group-and-one; informal
Place: home; schoolroom

Supplies: belt
Activity—pastime: alertness, observation
Appeal: suspense

A player is chosen to be *It*. All other players leave the room while *It* hides his belt. He calls the players back and as they search for the belt, *It* may give clues such as "very cold, cold, warm, warmer, hot, very hot." He does not, however, indicate which players are close to the belt because the finder may thrash those around him. Safety is a factor to be considered when playing this game.

The Lost Ring

Ages: teen
Players: 10–20; group-and-two; circle
Place: home; schoolroom

Supplies: ring
Activity—pastime: alertness, observation
Appeal: dramatization, suspense

One player is chosen the *leader* and is given a ring. Another player is *It* and leaves the group. All other players sit in a circle with hands in a prayer position. The *leader* passes his hands over the hands of each player pretending to drop the ring. He may go around the circle twice. When he does drop the ring, neither he nor the receiving player should indicate who has the ring.

It is recalled and the leader asks, "Who has the ring?" *It* has only one guess. He may try to make a player laugh or indicate in some way that he has the ring. If *It* guesses the person with the ring, he may give either a punishment or a prize to the player. In Paraguay a boy would ask another boy to do a stunt and would usually kiss a girl. Should *It* guess the wrong person the group decides on the stunt for *It* to perform. This game is similar to "Hide the Thimble," popular with the children of the United States from Colonial days.

GAMES AND SPORTS—WEST INDIES

CUBA

Angel and Imp

Ages: 5–8
Players: 20 or more; transition
Place: gymnasium; out-of-doors

Supplies: not any
Activity—hunting: conversation
Appeal: dramatization, repetition

Three players are chosen from the group: one is a *saleswoman*, another is the *angel*, and the third is the *imp*. All of the other players are *ribbons* and secretly choose a color. The *angel* knocks on the door of the *saleswoman* and this dialogue follows:

The saleswoman asks, "Who knocks?"
The angel replies, "The Angel."
The saleswoman inquires, "What can I do for you?"
The angel says, "I want ribbons."
The saleswoman asks, "What color do you prefer?"

The *angel* states a color and the player of that color joins the *angel's* side. If the *angel* fails to name a color of one of the players, she must go away alone.

The *imp* follows the same procedure. The side having the greatest number of *ribbons* at the close of the game wins.

This game is played in Puerto Rico. The winning side is determined by a tug-of-war after all ribbons have been sold.

Chocolonga (cho-co-LONG-a)

Ages: 9–12
Players: 10 or more; group-and-one; informal
Place: home; schoolroom

Supplies: blindfold
Activity—pastime: balance
Appeal: chance

A circle is marked on the blackboard or on a piece of paper attached to the wall. One player is selected to be *It* and stands at arms length in front of the circle. He is blindfolded and told to touch as near as possible the center of the circle. Before he tries to touch the circle, he is turned around three times. Meanwhile another player stands in front of the circle so that the fingers of *It* are grasped (pinched) by those of the players. Fun may be added by having *It* guess the name of the player pinching his hand. "Chocolonga" is Cuban slang for "to put into."

Dog and Chickens

Ages: teen
Players: 10 or more; group-and-one; circle
Place: home; schoolroom

Supplies: not any
Activity—pastime: alertness, memory
Appeal: dramatization

The players and their *leader* are seated in a circle. Each player is named a city or town. The *leader* says, "In _____ the chickens bark and the dogs crow." The player with the name called by the *leader* must answer quickly, "No, sir, in _____ the chickens do not bark and the dogs do not crow. Where the chickens bark and the dogs crow is in _____." The game continues with the *leader* then calling the name of another city as in his first statement. If a player makes a mistake or fails to speak, he must pay a forfeit.

Flower Garden

Ages: all
Players: 10–20; group-and-one; circle
Place: home; schoolroom

Supplies: not any
Activity—pastime: alertness
Appeal: dramatization

One player, *It*, gives the name of a flower to each of the other players who are seated in a circle. The play begins as *It* says, "I saw a garden of flowers, but the violet was missing." The violet must reply, "The violet was not missing, because I saw it in the garden." The *leader* then asks, "What was missing?" The violet answers, "The rose was missing." The rose must respond with, "The rose was there because I saw it. It was the daisy that was missing." The game continues in quick sequence until a flower fails to respond. This player must pay a forfeit or fine. The game is excellent for teaching names of flowers to young children. Variations: the "Zoo," the "Vegetable Garden," or even the "Countries," and similar ideas may be used.

Policemen and Pirates

Ages: 9–12
Players: 20 or more; two-group; informal
Place: gymnasium; out-of-doors

Supplies: not any
Activity—hunting: chasing, dodging, running
Appeal: competition, skill

The players are in two bands that are chosen as follows: All stand in one line while one of the group, covering his eyes with his hands, walks in front of the line saying, "Policeman, pirate; policeman, pirate, etc." The players touch him as he walks in front of them and thus receive their assignment to a band.

A *leader* is selected for each band. The *pirates* band together while the Chief of Police calls his men to Headquarters. The play begins when the Chief of Police blows his whistle. The *policemen* chase the *pirates* until the leader and three of the *pirates* have been caught.

The Priest's Hat

Ages: teen
Players: 10–20; group-and-one; circle
Place: home; schoolroom

Supplies: not any
Activity—pastime: self-control
Appeal: dramatization

One player, the *leader*, stands in the center of a circle formed by the other players who are seated. The *leader* says, "The priest has lost his hat, and they tell me that someone in this room found it and hid it." (A clever *leader* may elaborate on this.) "I do not know who it is, but I think it is ―――." Whereupon he points to a circle player. The player must not smile or speak, but must deny the charges with vigorous motions of the head and point to someone else, who in turn denies and points to another player. The object of the game is to make a player smile, laugh, or speak. A player who is guilty of any of the offenses must pay a forfeit. After the forfeit is paid, the *leader* may start the game again and finally choose someone to take his place. This game is the Cuban version of "The Prince of Paris Lost His Hat."

PUERTO RICO

Angel and Imp

(See Cuba.)

La Candelita

Ages: 5–8	Supplies: not any
Players: 15 or more; group-and-one; circle	Activity—hunting: running
	Appeal: dramatization, problem
Place: gymnasium; out-of-doors	solving, skill

The players stand in a circle about 3 feet apart. The one chosen to be the *It* is in the center of the circle. He goes to one of the circle players, extends his hand, and says, "Give me a *candelita*" (little candle). The circle player then points to another across the circle and says, "There is a candle smoking over there." *It* goes to the player designated and repeats his request. At the same time the first circle player questioned changes places with another. *It* tries to get the place of one of them. If he is successful, the odd player becomes *It* and goes about asking for a little candle. The same game pattern is found in the Lebanese game, "Oh! Neighbor, Have You Fire?"

La Cebollita

Ages: 5–8	Activity—hunting: chasing, dodging, running
Players: 20 or more, transition	
Place: gymnasium; out-of-doors	Appeal: dramatization, skill
Supplies: not any	

One player is chosen to be the *seller*, another is the *buyer*. These players stand in a circle formed by the others who are *cebollitas* or *little onions*.

The *buyer* begins a conversation with the *seller* by saying, "Sir, my mother wants an *onion*." The *buyer* answers with, "Where is the one you bought last night?" The following dialogue is held:

Buyer: "The rats ate it, sir."
Seller: "Where was your mother?"
Buyer: "Attending a dance, sir."
Seller: "Show me how she danced."

The *buyer* executes a comical motion. Then the *seller* tells him to select a ripe *onion*. The buyer taps several *onions* on the head, smells his hands, and finally says, "This is a good one. I will buy it." He then takes the *onion* home to his mother. The conversation is repeated until all *onions* have been bought. The *buyer* then invites the *seller* to have supper with him. As the two approach the *onions* they find them all squatting on the ground. The *seller* joins them and begins to eat. Suddenly all of the onions begin to imitate a dog's bark and chase the *seller,* who tries to reach his home before being tagged. The *onion* who tags him becomes the new *seller.* Another *buyer* is selected and the game starts anew.

7

North America

The geographic boundaries of North America are expansive and far flung. Most of her societal groups are composites of varied and intermingled peoples, yet some are singularly unique in their cultural patterns. The play and games heritage of North America is more extensive and more far reaching than the boundaries. It is equally as varied and entwined as are many of the peoples, and it parallels some in unique cultural patterns.

The areas included in the North American games collection are Canada and the United States. Mexico and Central America are in their societal groups within Latin America. There are generalizations on the games and sports from Canada and the United States with the exception of the games of the North American Indian, the Alaskans, and the Hawaiians. The omission of descriptions of games from Canada and the United States is to avoid repetition. The children's games and the sports played in Canada and the States are adaptations, variations, and medleys of play patterns from all parts of the world.

The games of the children in Alaska and Hawaii are given in detail because of the unique societal patterns of the peoples in these states. The overview of North American games and sports within this collection is:

CANADA   NORTH AMERICAN INDIAN

               UNITED STATES
               Alaska
               Hawaii

CANADA

The people of Canada are from many countries. Their sports and games are more similar within the entire country than are the games and play patterns of the United States. This is due in part to the fact that most of the Canadian sports and games had their beginnings in England, Scotland, and France, whereas the games of the United States may be traced to many lands.

Hockey is the national game of Canada. Young boys play hockey in organized leagues each winter much like the boys in the United States play baseball in the summer. Both Canada and the United States enter professional teams in the world's leading hockey matches, the National Hockey League.

Lacrosse was adopted from the Indians in the early 1800's and has been popular in Canada since that time. From Scotland the ancient game of curling made its way into Canada and today it is played throughout most of the country during the winter. It is a kind of "shuffleboard on ice," using brooms and heavy circular stones as equipment. It compares in popularity to bowling in the United States. *Bonspeils* or national tournaments in curling are often held in the province of Alberta.

Another event of renown which delights both young and old is held in Alberta. It is the Calgary Stampede, and annual rodeo, which attracts the championship cowboys of North America. The steer throwing, calf roping, and chuck wagon racing events start many young boys dreaming and planning for their future and fame in similar situations.

The sports of baseball, football, and soccer, along with fishing, swimming, canoe riding and racing, hiking, tennis, golf, and horseback riding, are known as summer activities in Canada. A summer event in northeastern Nova Scotia, the *Gaelic Mod*, a festival of Scottish dances, games, and songs, is enjoyed by many Canadians and visitors.

Boys in the Northwest Territories and the Yukon spend their short summer developing the skills of rowing kayaks in order to be ready for the seal hunts, when they are old enough to accompany their fathers.

Long Canadian winters restrict play activities, especially among the children. Nevertheless, the Canadian boys and girls get to do some sports and games that children of many other lands rarely ever experience. Canadian children start learning their sports quite early in life. Skating is learned as soon as one can walk. Skiing is learned at an early age and among all peoples in Canada. The children of the poor often learn on barrel stakes. The activities of tobogganing and dog sled racing are also popular in most all provinces.

The children in the Canadian schoolrooms and on the playground enjoy many universally popular play patterns, including hopscotch, follow-the-leader, tag games, hide the object, spin the plate, and other similar games. Canadian boys and girls would feel quite at home in game groups from England, France, Scotland, and the United States.

NORTH AMERICAN INDIAN

The skill and daring of the Indian, the variety and individuality of his play patterns, the devotion and loyalty of each tribal group to its games and sports, and the contribution each tribe has made to the play heritage of North America (and Latin America) can be touched upon only briefly in this collection of games. The monumental work of Stewart Culin, *Games of the North American Indians* (extract from the Twenty-fourth Annual Report of the Bureau of American Ethnology, 1907) is an authentic and complete record of North American Indian games including variations of Cat's Cradle, a universal string game. It is hoped that before time is too nearly spent, a similar contribution will be made to global games literature through a compilation of the games of the Latin American Indians.

North American Indian games may be generally divided into two groups. One is games of chance; the other is games of dexterity. The guessing games in this collection fall in the former group. The games of physical skill are in the latter. They far outnumber and outclass the games of any other peoples throughout the ages in the strength and endurance demanded of the participants. The Greek and Roman games may be considered as parallels, although they lack the variety and ingenuity found in North American Indian games. Another distinctive and pleasing quality found in the Indian games is that they appear to be direct and natural outgrowths of the original societal or tribal groups in America. The two exceptions to this are the simple card games and the board games of "Nine Men's Morris," so typically English. On the other hand, *lacrosse*, a favorite game of Canadians; the racket games of the States; and many Indian games played under Spanish names in Mexico have all been borrowed from the North American Indians.

The Indians spent much of their time in amusements and athletics. Their diversions ranged all the way from the simplest forms of child's play to great intertribal ball games during which several hundred players occupied the field. Some of the activities, like "Snow-Snake" and "Saddlebags," deserve a place among the leading games of the world.

Since the pony and the canoe were the only modes of travel

known to the American Indian, naturally he was on his feet most of his time. With this in view it is easy to believe that games of running would be quite popular with this people. Footraces were very common, and the young Indian early acquired an elasticity and swiftness of limb that usually proved valuable to him in later life.

The races were usually between young braves from different villages. The villages picked the best runners, of course, to run against their rivals, and both teams were given the same length of time in preparation for the race—usually four or five days. A great amount of superstition entered into the races, and the losers always attributed their results to the influence of some herb or to some other form of nature. An attitude of superstition also prevailed among the Indian of Latin America. They often interpreted their dreams as forecasts of their winning or losing a game.

The Indian women played a unique game that consisted of throwing plum or peach stones into a basket or bowl. They enjoyed shinny, too, using a soft ball made of moss or buffalo hair covered with buckskin.

UNITED STATES

The games brought to the New World have followed the ways of the peoples who "brought" them here. Some games have remained virtually the same in behavior patterns and in names; some have maintained their original behavior patterns though they have acquired new names; some can scarcely be identified as having roots in old world beginnings. They have intermingled with others to the degree that their behavior patterns along with their names have been completely changed.

Among the game descriptions in this book there is often a reference to an identical or a similar game pattern popular in the United States today. Reference is made in Appendix C to books that have detailed descriptions of games and sports commonly played throughout the States today.

Although the United States is credited with having evolved the "most productive society that man has ever known," she can claim credit for having created only two sports, basketball and volleyball. Little did James Naismith realize that the game basketball, which he invented in 1891 to play indoors on winter evenings, would be so widely accepted and played by boys, girls, men, and women the world over. Volleyball, invented in 1895 by William G. Morgan, has become universally popular. In England a variation, water volleyball, is a favorite activity.

It is from an old English sport called *rounders* and the game of cricket that the game of baseball was developed in the States. Colonial children enjoyed "one old cat" and "two old cat." Later "town ball" was played enthusiastically. Cricket devotees developed a game called "the New York game." All of these games are related to cricket and rounders and had influence on the evolution of baseball. However, baseball as played today is considered a North American game.

Football was developed from the English game rugby. Today American football is played everywhere in the States; from sand lot to the Rose Bowl in California; from rural school to major college and university; and from "charity bowls" to spectacular professional stadiums. Football was first played in the States by rules much like soccer, with kicking skills only. Later the passing and catching skills were added.

Sports and games in the United States today are not only fun for all ages, they are also big entertainment and big business for millions of people. The tournaments and contests held in the arena-type stadiums and ball parks, the television and radio have engulfed the leisure time of more millions of people. In the States "more persons spectate than participate" in sports. Nevertheless, the discipline demanded of the participants and the teamwork expected of them are potent factors in developing an overall pattern of national cooperation, perseverance, and rallying to meet a crisis when necessary.

Children's play and games have suffered somewhat in the States in recent years because of the national fever of major sports. The lead-up games of sports are neglected by leaders and teachers who often try to quickly meet the challenge of the youngster who wants to bypass progressive learning and try to play the game as it is done by the professionals. Traditional games, too, are sidetracked as both children and adults try to keep up with the momentum of big-time athletics. It is hoped that the persons in the States who have the responsibility of planning and executing recreational and physical fitness programs in schools, camps, clubs, and similar situations will emphasize more specifically lead-up games, traditional contest, games, and relays as foundations for physical skill, strength, and endurance. If the United States is to maintain her role of world leadership, she must strengthen her human resources physically, morally, and spiritually.

It is a recognized fact that the children and youth of the United States have more leisure time than children in any other part of the world. It is encouraging that much is being done today to strengthen the physical status of American children and youth. Emphasis on purposeful and meaningful programs of physical fitness is being fostered from the national level throughout the entire country. Results are gratifying, yet much remains to be accomplished.

Along with their increasing interest in games, sports, and physical fitness it is reassuring to realize that children and youth in the States are more ready now to grasp the significance of global relationships than ever before. This is due to intelligent and effective adult leadership. There is need for more leaders of this caliber. World empathy is essential for fulfillment of the role of world leadership. It is also essential for survival. Play, games, and sports are forceful media through which national and international horizons may be expanded.

ALASKA

In Alaska, as in many parts of Canada, it is generally understood that the long winters are busy times for both children and adults. Boats are repaired, tools are made, clothes are mended, all of this in preparation for the even busier short summers of hunting and fishing. Winter is also the season for sports and amusements. Playing with the bow and arrow, sled coasting, dog sled racing, and football (on ice) are favorite activities among all Alaskan children.

The unique winter recreational activities of the Eskimos in Alaska are worthy of mention. It is during this time that several families live together. The monotony of long periods of staying indoors is broken by ceremonies called *drum dances*. These occasions include dancing and telling stories that have been handed down from father to son for generations. Tag games, sled races, and the building of small snow houses are outside activities of short duration enjoyed by the Eskimo children during the long winters.

Other play patterns of the Alaskan boys and girls may be generally classified as stunts and active games that are strenuous and call for much endurance, using either small or large numbers of participants. There are some inactive guessing games that are similar in pattern to the numerous guessing games of the Indians throughout Canada and the United States. There are scarcely any singing games among the Alaskans, which may be explained by the fact that singing is primarily a group activity, and the Alaskans do not get together often in groups.

HAWAII

This state, part of an island group in the Pacific, consists of eight beautiful islands. Today the play life of Hawaii follows the habits and customs of North Americans. In the past there was an old and favorite sport of the early ruling class of "the Big Island." This sport, *holua* (ho-LOO-ah), meaning sledding, consisted of coasting down the sides of a mountain on sleds with runners. The runways were grass-covered and slanted steeply downward. Even today traces of the old *holua* courses may be seen.

Another interesting and ancient custom among Hawaiians was the honor to the god Lono by declaring a four-month vacation. During that time work was suspended and anyone caught in a task of actual labor was punished. One outstanding celebration enjoyed during this time was the *Makahiki* (MAH-kah-HEE-kee), a festival of games. Boxing, foot racing, holva sledding, surf-riding, and canoe racing were some of the principal sports of the festival. The members of the king's court engaged in wrestling, spear throwing, and sham battles. It is interesting to find that no reward was given the winner of the competitive activities despite the fact that the contestants often spent several days and sometimes weeks training and conditioning for the events. It is recorded that some of the contests and games were staged without an audience. And that is quite unusual in view of the development of "Spectatoritis" in the United States.

Today enthusiasm for baseball is increasing in Hawaii. The boys enjoy playing football whereas the girls are enthusiastic about soccer. The boys and girls prefer to play these games barefoot. Other favorite play activities of the children are skipping rope, flying kites, spinning tops, throwing darts, and walking on stilts. Contests of jumping, footracing, swimming, boating, and surf-riding are popular. Swimming and surf-riding, however, come above all others in the sports enjoyed by the Islanders of all ages. Every Hawaiian child becomes expert in these activities at an early age.

A pamphlet by Donald Mitchell, Kamehameka schools, Kapalama Heights, Honolulu, is a source of Hawaiian games for children and youth.

GAMES AND SPORTS—NORTH AMERICA

NORTH AMERICAN INDIAN

Archery Game

Ages: teen
Players: 2–10; single-group; informal
Place: out-of-doors

Supplies: arrows
Activity—pastime: throwing
Appeal: competition, skill

Each player is equipped with several arrows made out of twigs about two inches long with three feathers fastened to each arrow. The arrow is held between the forefinger and thumb (as one holds a pencil). The game is started by one player throwing an arrow a distance of about 12 feet. A second player throws, aiming so that the feathers of his arrow touch those of the arrow on the ground. If he succeeds, he takes both arrows and makes a throw with one of them. The third player aims at the arrow on the ground; if he fails, his arrow remains in place and another player takes his turn. The game continues, and each player claims the arrows that are touched by his arrow. The player first claiming all of the arrows wins.

Ball and Darts Game

Ages: 9–12
Players: 6 or more; single-group; informal
Place: out-of-doors

Supplies: ball or yucca leaves; corn-cob darts
Activity—pastime: throwing
Appeal: competition, skill

The Indian children make a ball out of yucca leaves. Any material that can be easily pierced may be used. The body of the dart is a corncob. At one end of the cob two feathers are attached; at the other end there is a slender sharp-pointed stick.

The players stand some distance from the ball, which is placed on the ground. The first player throws; if his dart pierces the ball it remains in place. The second player throws. If he succeeds, it is a tie; if he fails, the next player throws and so on until all have had their turn. The player who pierces the ball most often wins.

Ball Game

Ages: 9–12
Players: 10 or more; two-group; informal
Place: gymnasium; out-of-doors

Supplies: Indian clubs, playground ball
Activity—athletic: running, striking
Appeal: competition, problem solving, skill

The size of the court may vary according to the grade level. A square court 30 × 30 feet is suggested for grades three and four. A larger one for grades five and six. The players are divided into two teams. Each player has a stick or club. The two teams advance toward each other and a ball that is placed in the center of the court. The object of the game is to knock the ball over the opponents' goal line. Every time this is done, one point is scored for the team. The team having the highest score at the end of a 10-minute period wins the game.

Ball Kick Game

Ages: 9–12
Players: 8–12; two-group; file
Place: gymnasium; out-of-doors

Supplies: playground ball
Activity—athletic: kicking, running
Appeal: problem solving, skill

The winning of the game depends upon accuracy in kicking rather than speed in playing.

The players line up behind the starting line that is 60 to 70 feet from the goal. The first player on each team kicks a ball forward to a halfway line and from there he tries to kick it between two goal posts that are about 10 feet apart. One point is scored each time a ball goes between the goal posts. The ball is returned to the starting line and the second player kicks. The team having the highest score after all have kicked wins.

Ball Play

Age: This game is offered as background material rather than for actual teaching
Players: 20 or more; two-group; informal
Place: out-of-doors

Supplies: playground ball
Activity—athletic: catching, running, throwing
Appeal: competition, problem solving, skill

It was a strenuous game when played by the Indian braves, because of the large playing area and the absence of rest periods throughout the game. Each side had its goal, 250 paces from the middle of the field. The goal posts were 6 feet apart and about 6 feet high, with a crossbar at the top.

The Indians had *umpires* who were usually the old men of the tribe, and their chief duty seemed to be to watch the articles that were wagered by the enthusiastic spectators.

The players were divided into two sides with one on each side acting as *captain*. One of the *umpires* started the game by tossing the ball into the air, and the players of both sides rushed to catch it. As soon as a player caught the ball, he threw it toward the opponents' goal. An alert opponent rushed to catch it and send it back. The players were allowed to snatch or knock the ball from another's hands. The game continued until one side had thrown the ball through the opponents' goal. After a goal, the ball was immediately thrown back by the side that did not score, instead of being carried to the center as in most ball games of this type. The team that threw the ball between the opponents' goal one hundred times was the winner. The Indians were so skillful and alert that they played a very fast game.

It was a ball game of this type that was used as a disguise before the terrible massacre at Fort Mackinaw, which took place after the French and Indian War, during the Pontiac conspiracy.

Bas-Quoits

Ages: 9–12
Players: 2–6; two-group; informal
Place: gymnasium; out-of-doors; schoolroom

Supplies: pegs, rope rings
Activity—pastime: pitching
Appeal: competition, skill

Two pegs, about 12 inches high, are set up as far apart as one can pitch. Rope rings about 4 inches in diameter are bound half with green and half with white cord.

The players on opposite sides take turns pitching and trying to ring the peg at the opposite edge. A ringer counts three. In case of a leaner with the green part of the ring touching the peg, the count is two; if the white touches, the count is one. Today's popular game of Quoits is played much like Bas-Quoits.

Battledore and Shuttlecock

Ages: teen
Players: 4–12; single-group; circle
Place: gymnasium; out-of-doors

Supplies: shuttlecocks, wooden paddles
Activity—pastime: striking
Appeal: competition, skill

The players stand in a ring and each bats the shuttlecock to his neighbor on his right. If the one batting the shuttlecock sends it behind his neighbor, he must drop out of the ring. If the one to whom the shuttlecock is batted fails to bat it on properly to his neighbor, he must drop out of the ring. In this way the circle contracts and the last one in is the winner.

The shuttlecock is made of a stout twig to which three feathers are tied securely. The battledore is made of a circular board, 9 inches in diameter, attached to a wooden handle.

Bead Guessing Game

Ages: 9–12
Players: 20 or more; group-and-two; informal
Place: home; schoolroom

Supplies: a bead
Activity—hunting: guessing, running
Appeal: problem solving, skill

Two players, one holding a bead behind him and the other, a *guesser*, stand in front of the seated players. The player holding the bead changes it from hand to hand until the *guesser* points to one hand. At this time he must put his hands in front of the *guesser* and open them. This is done until the *guesser* has correctly guessed three times. On the third correct guess the one holding the bead runs to his seat. If the *guesser* catches him, the *guesser* holds the bead and chooses a new *guesser*.

California Relay

Ages: teen
Players: 20 or more; two-group; file
Place: out-of-doors
Supplies: playground balls, hockey
sticks

Activity—relay: running, striking
Appeal: competition, problem solving, skill

A starting line is drawn on the ground on which are placed two balls eight feet apart. The *captains* take their positions beside the balls. Behind each *captain*, down the field in a file, is stationed his team. Each man stands 100 feet from his neighbor, and the goal is 100 feet beyond the last player. (Shorter distances may be used although the Indians used distances of 500 feet.) Each player is responsible for the section of the track directly ahead of him.

A cry of "Hi!" is the signal for the *captains* to strike their balls down the course using a hockey stick or something similar. If the ball does not go the allotted distance in one stroke, the *captain* runs forward to give the ball another stroke. He counts in a loud voice each drive as he makes it. When the ball passes into the territory of the second man, this player waits while it rolls as far as possible and has fully stopped before striking. The object of the game is not speed but few strokes. The second man, counting the score out loud, sends it down the track to the third player and so on. The team that drives the ball over the line in the fewest number of strokes wins.

This game may be played on ice and the teams play on skates. It also is adaptable to soccer skills of kicking and passing.

California Relay Football

Ages: teen (boys)
Players: 8–12; two-group; line
Place: out-of-doors
Supplies: football, goal stakes

Activity—relay: kicking, running
Appeal: competition, problem solving, skill

The field may be any straight level stretch of ground. At one end of the field two goals are placed, each of which is made by driving two stakes into the ground, 3 feet apart. The goals resemble gate posts.

The teams line up in two parallel lines, each team facing its own goal. The players in each line are 20 yards apart and the last player is 20 yards from his goal. Twenty yards beyond the last player in each line, a ball is placed, and 50 feet beyond the balls stand two men who act as *starters*.

At a signal, the *starters* dash forward and kick their respective balls down the field toward the first teamman, following the ball to give another kick in case the first does not send it across the entire distance. As soon as the ball rolls near the first teamman, he kicks it farther down the line after which he joins the *starter* in running down the field, ready to be of assistance. The second man does likewise and thus the teams follow their ball down the field in two groups until all are gathered around the goals. The first team to send the ball through its goal wins the game. No handling of the ball or interference is permitted.

Clown Game

Ages: teen (boys)
Players: 20 or more; single-group; informal
Place: out-of-doors
Supplies: cord, playground balls
Activity—relay: kicking, running
Appeal: competition, skill

The Indians have clowns, and like all clowns, they often imitate events that take place about them. This century-old game was a great feature of the Zuni holiday activities. Although it is not played in definite relay formation, it is classed as a relay because it is based on "Kicking the Stick," a popular relay with Indian boys and men.

In the place of a stick the clowns use a soft ball, known as a slinging-ball, to which a loop of cord is fastened. The ball, about 4 inches in diameter, is usually made of buckskin stuffed with hair. However, in the Free Museum of Science and Art of the University of Pennsylvania, there is a slinging ball made of an old stocking to which is attached a braided cord 10 inches long.

The players divide and stand on the starting line with their backs to the goal. Upon signal all contestants lie on their backs and then lightly place the cord around the toes of the right foot. At a second signal, the players give a vigorous kick to send the ball over their heads down the field. Each player then runs to recover his ball and assumes the same position to send the ball toward the goal again. The first player to send his ball backward over his head through the two goal posts wins the game. There is often a great scramble at the end.

Dodge Ball

Ages: 9–12
Players: 12 or more; two-group; line
Place: gymnasium; out-of-doors
Supplies: playground ball
Activity—athletic: dodging, throwing
Appeal: competition, problem solving, skill

Team I stands 12 feet from Team II. The first player at the head of Team I steps forward, and the opposite player of Team II tries to hit him with a soft ball. The player of Team I may dodge in any way as long as he does not move his feet. If the player of Team II succeeds in hitting him, he must become a member of Team II. If the player of Team II fails, he becomes a member of Team I. This continues until all of Team II have thrown at Team I. Team I throws at Team II in like manner. The winner is the team having won the greatest number of players from the opposing side.

Guessing Game

Ages: 9–12
Players: 10 or more; group-and-one; informal
Place: home; schoolroom

Supplies: two bundles of sticks
Activity—pastime: guessing
Appeal: problem solving

One player has two bundles of sticks. One bundle contains an even number of sticks and the other an odd number. The other players guess which bundle has the odd or the even number. This was a popular game among the Indians of the North and West.

Another guessing game was played with a ball and four cups. One player hides the ball under one of the cups and the others must guess which cup is the hiding place for the ball. The player who guesses correctly becomes the leader.

These games and many similar ones were great time-passers for the Indians.

Indian Wrestling

Ages: 9–12
Players: any number; couple; informal
Place: gymnasium; out-of-doors

Supplies: not any
Activity—stunt: balance, pulling, pushing
Appeal: competition, skill

Two players stand face to face with right foot forward and touching that of the opponent; the right hands are clasped and are directly over the center of the feet. The umpire says, "Go," or slaps the hands lightly and the wrestlers try to throw each other off balance by pushing, pulling, or swinging the hands. A player loses the match as soon as either foot moves from its place.

Kicking the Stick Relay

Ages: 9–12
Players: any number; 4–6 in a file; file
Place: out-of-doors

Supplies: 4-inch pegs
Activity—relay: kicking, running
Appeal: competition, skill

North American Indian—Wrestling.

This game was played by the Indians in the spring of the year.
The players are divided into equal teams and stand behind a
smooth round stick 4 inches long that has been driven in the ground
2 inches. The first player of each team pulls his stick out of the
ground with his feet and kicks it forward around a goal, and back
to the starting line. The second player then kicks the stick forward.
The team finishing the race first is the winner.

Kinxe

Ages: teen
Players: 6–20; two-group; line
Place: gymnasium; out-of-doors
Supplies: willow rings and spears

Activity—athletic: catching, throwing
Appeal: competition, skill

A willow ring and a willow spear three to six feet long are needed
for each player. (Yardsticks and quoit rings may be substituted.)
The players divide into two teams and line up in parallel lines. The
lines are about 15 feet apart and the teams are facing.

The *captain* of one team signals his men to start and the players cast their rings in the direction of their opponents. They try to confuse the opponents by the irregularity with which they throw the rings. They may throw them in a number of ways; all at one time; one or two at a time; or fling them in quick succession. The rings may be rolled along the ground or they may be cast flat through the air.

As soon as the rings have been cast, the opposing team breaks forward from its line and tries to catch the rings, while they are still flying through the air or rolling along the ground, by thrusting their spears through the rings. The game is won if all the rings are captured. Each player is allowed to catch any number of rings on his spear. If the entire number is not captured, the rings are returned to the owners and the game continues, alternating from one side to the other until one team succeeds in capturing all the rings in a single flight.

A simplified version of the game for unskilled players is to score one point for each ring that is captured. Allow each team the same number of rounds (a round is the casting of the rings by the players on one team). The team holding the highest score at the end of the game wins.

Kwai-Indao

Ages: teen
Players: 4 or more; single-group; informal
Place: gymnasium; out-of-doors

Supplies: 40–50 short sticks: large handkerchief
Activity—pastime: memory
Appeal: problem solving

A set of forty or fifty sticks is divided into ten groups, representing the different numbers from 1 through 10. The number of chalk marks on any stick indicates the number represented by the stick. Sticks representing the same number are grouped together and all are placed in a row. The players take turns repeating from memory, blindfolded, the order in which the ten groups are arranged.

Making the Wood Jump

Ages: 9–12
Players: 6 to 8; individual; informal
Place: gymnasium; out-of-doors

Supplies: pieces of wood
Activity—pastime: throwing
Appeal: skill

An imaginary *stream* is marked off on the ground and a piece of wood is placed in the *stream*. The players pretend that they are standing on the icy banks of the *stream* and take turns hitting at the piece of wood, trying to send it flying into the air. The winner is the first player who makes the wood jump above the head level.

Ring and Arrow Game

Ages: teen
Players: any number; groups of four; line
Place: gymnasium; out-of-doors

Supplies: corncob arrow, cornhusk hoop
Activity—pastime: throwing
Appeal: competition, skill

This is a game for four people. Each player has an arrow about 10 inches long made of a corncob with two feathers attached to one end and a wooden point to the other. A ring is made out of dry cornhusks. It is 7 inches in diameter and is wrapped half with red and half with white yarn.

Two players face each other and roll the ring between them. The other two throw at it with darts. The middle finger is placed between the two feathers, the arrow being thrown with force. A round consists of ten rolls. The player who throws through the ring or hits it the greatest number of times during a round wins.

This game is similar to "Rolling Target."

Ring and Pin Game

Ages: 9–12
Players: 6 or more; single-group; informal
Place: schoolroom; gymnasium

Supplies: bone or wooden ring; stick; string
Activity—pastime: ringing the pin
Appeal: skill

A small ring, about five inches in diameter, is made out of bone, a piece of wood, or a twig wrapped in yarn. The ring is attached to one end of a 21-inch stick by means of a string 4 to 7 feet long. The stick is held in one hand and with a quick movement the ring is tossed up into the air. The object is to catch the ring while it is in the air on the end of the stick. This type of game was popular among many tribes of Indians.

Rolling Target Relay

Ages: 9–12
Players: 12 or more; two-group; line
Place: gymnasium; out-of-doors

Supplies: beanbags, hoop
Activity—relay: throwing
Appeal: competition, skill

The players are equally divided into two groups. The players of each team take their places about 5 feet apart with a stick or beanbag in their hands. A *leader* stands at the head of each team and about 10 to 20 feet in front. He rolls a hoop 6 inches to 2 feet in diameter the entire length of his line. The players who are successful in hurling the object through the rolling hoop score one point for their team. The hoop is rolled three times for the members of each team, and so on, until one team reaches a score of 100 points.

Each player may score independently if there are only a few players. The player scoring 21 points first wins.

Saddlebags

Ages: teen (boys)
Players: 20 or more; two-group; informal
Place: out-of-doors

Supplies: 2 beanbags attached by a strap; sticks
Activity—athletic: catching, running, throwing
Appeal: competition, skill

This game is sometimes called "Squares" or "Sky Shinny." It is like lacrosse, the national game of Canada, but does not require expensive equipment. In the place of a lacrosse ball, two beanbags, 4 by 7 inches, are used. The bags are fastened together with a band of cloth about 2 feet long. A strong stick that resembles a hockey stick is carried by each player. The bags are handled with the stick since it is against the rules of the game to touch the bags with hands or feet. Rough play of any sort is not allowed. The bags may be caught in the air, picked from the ground, or carried toward the goal. Also the bags may be thrown from the stick high in the air toward the goal.

The playing areas are called *prairies* and are about the size of a football field. The goals at each end of the field are made of two upright posts and a cross-bar 10 feet from the ground. The players are divided into *tribes* called the *braves* or *backs*, and the *goalkeepers* or *bucks*. The captain of each team is known as the *chief*.

The *chiefs* toss for choice of goal or first cast and then place their men in their respective places. The play is started by the *chief* of one of the *tribes* taking the bags on his stick and casting them as far as he can toward his opponents' goal. One of the opposing *braves* tries to catch the bags on his stick. If he succeeds he then runs for the goal or passes the bags on to a teammate, as in American football. The opposing team may lift the bags from the stick of the runner or catch them as they are in the air, provided the runner's stick or person is not touched. The fair method of securing the bags from the runner is to slip the end of the stick under the bags and lift them off.

The scoring of the game is as follows:

One "*scalp*" for running over the goal line with the bags; three *scalps* for throwing the bags under the cross-bar and between the space indicated by the upright posts; ten *scalps* for throwing the bags over the goal posts. Eight *scalps* are scored if the bags catch or hang on the cross-bar or the goal posts. When a score is made, play is started from the center with the side that did not score having the cast. When the bags are thrown out of bounds, the *umpire* throws them in where they went out, and the players on both teams stand in the places where they were when the bags crossed the line.

Seashore Football

Ages: teen (boys)
Players: 20 or more; two-group; informal
Place: out-of-doors

Supplies: football, four long sticks
Activity—athletic: kicking, running
Appeal: competition, skill

Football was known to only a few Indian tribes, chiefly to the Algonquins of the New England seacoast and a few tribes of California. It is thought that a red-skinned athlete must have conceived and taught the game to his own people for these Indians lived so far apart, they could not have learned the game from one another.

The field was a smooth level stretch of seashore. At each end of this a goal was set up. Two sticks thrust into the sand, leaning across each other like poles in a wigwam, served as a goal. A line was scratched on the ground, halfway between the goals. The players lined up 20 paces back of this dividing line, one team on either side, and each team faced his goal. The individual players were about 2 feet apart. The ball was placed on the center of the dividing line.

Before beginning the game the players shook hands with their opponents, then took their places on the field. A sharp cry, the signal to begin, was given by an old man on the sidelines. The players rushed forward and tried to kick the ball through the opposing line to their home goal. If the ball was kicked into the water, the nearest players followed it.

No player was allowed to kick a man's heels out from under him but he could catch his opponent around the neck as a holdback until he, himself, could kick the ball.

If dusk fell before a game was finished, the ground was marked where the ball was last in play and the game continued the following day.

The Indians removed their moccasins and played barefooted. In order to disguise themselves they bedecked in all the glory of war paints. This was done so that if during the game any accident should occur to anger a player, it would be difficult to identify his opponent and later repay the grudge.

One unique feature of football among the Indians of various tribes was that in the game the players were not allowed to throw the ball. They were skilled in controlling the ball by kicking it. The pleasure of the game consisted of kicking the ball and racing after it to kick it again and again.

Shinny (Circle)

Ages: teen
Players: 8–12; two-group; informal
Place: out-of-doors
Supplies: ball, sticks

Activity—pastime: running, striking
Appeal: competition, skill

The game is played by two players or two teams, usually four or six on a side. Two circles or goals are drawn on the ground about 250 yards apart. Midway between the goals a hole about a foot in diameter is dug. The shinny ball is laid in the hole and covered with sand. An outsider hides the ball, so that the players will not know where to dig for it with their sticks.

When only two players participate in the game, each stands with his back to his own goal and faces his opponent. If two teams play, the captains stand by the sand mound, and each team stands in parallel lines 8 feet back of its captain.

An umpire starts the game with a loud cry. The two players or two captains begin to dig to uncover the ball, after which the object is to drive it into the opponents' circle.

No stroke is given the ball while it is inside a goal circle; that is, when it has rolled inside a ring, the player must wait to see if it will cross it and come out again, or whether it will stop either inside or on the line of the circle, thus ending the game. If a player sends the ball into his own circle, it scores the same as though his opponent had done this.

Shinny (Wood)

Ages: teen
Players: any number; couple; informal
Place: out-of-doors

Supplies: sticks, wood block
Activity—pastime: running, striking
Appeal: competition, skill

This is a game for two players. A block of wood about 5 inches long and 2 or 3 inches in diameter is laid on the ground. Starting from this point the players take fifty steps in opposite directions, and scratch a long line on the ground which serves as the opponent's goal. Standing on this line the players face each other and count together in a loud voice, "One, two, three!" On "three" they rush toward the wooden block. The one who succeeds in first putting his foot on it has the right to take aim with his stick and strike the block toward the goal that was marked for him. As soon as he hits, the two players stand shoulder to shoulder, count "One, two, three," and again race forward. The one that first sets his foot on the block has the right of the next stroke. Thus the game is played back and forth between the players until one of them sends the block across his line.

Snow Dart

Ages: 9–12   Supplies: rounded stick
Players: 4 or more; single-group   Activity—pastime: running
Place: out-of-doors   Appeal: competition, skill

This game is an adaptation from one that was once very popular among the Cree Indians. Each player has four darts about 8 inches long, made of a rounded stick with a blunt end and tapering toward the back end. A groove about 60 feet long is made down a steep hill of snow, and at intervals hazards of little rises or hollows are made in the surface that is otherwise very hard and smooth. The object of the game is to slide the darts down the hill. One point is made for each obstacle crossed. The player with the highest score wins. The darts are not thrown, but simply loosed from the hand. The running up and down the hill after the darts affords exercise that keeps the players warm even in very cold weather.

The Crees called this game "Puckitseeman" or "Puck" for short. They established four hazards and had two ways of scoring. The one was that one point was scored for two hazards; two points for three hazards and five for four barriers; the final score being 20. The other was that the players must send the "puck" through all four hazards four times to win.

Snow Snake

Ages: teen   Supplies: notched sticks
Players: 4 or more; single-group;   Activity—pastime: throwing
  informal   Appeal: competition, skill
Place: out-of-doors

The players stand at a given line with three to five smooth but somewhat heavy sticks each. The sticks are marked, the first stick has one notch, the second has two, the third has three, and so on. The sticks are thrown one at a time so as to skim over the hard surface of the ice. When each player has thrown one stick the score is counted. The stick thrown farthest wins for its owner the number of points or the number of notches on the stick. These sticks are put to one side and others are thrown and scored in the same manner, and so on until all sticks have been thrown. The winner may be the one with the highest score at the end or a certain number may be set for the winner, usually some number from 7 to 10.

When played in the soft snow the game is not unlike bowling. A long groove from 10 to 18 inches deep is cut in the snow and serves as the *alley*, the *snow snake* being thrown down the groove.

This game may well be considered the national game of the Iroquois. Its popularity through the centuries is due to the amount of skill that can be put into throwing the *snow snake*.

Stone Throwing Game

Ages: 9–12   Supplies: stones
Players: any number; couple; in-   Activity—pastime: pitch
   formal   Appeal: competition, skill
Place: out-of-doors

Two persons play against each other. The players stand 30 feet away from a hole in the ground and pitch three stones each. The nearest stone of either player to the hole scores one point. If a stone falls in the hole, it scores four points. But if the second player's stone falls on top of the stone of the first, it *kills* the stone and there is no score. The winner is the player scoring 12 points first.

Toss Ball

Ages: teen   Supplies: playground ball
Players: 20 or more; two-group; in-   Activity—hunting: catching, run-
   formal   ning, throwing
Place: gymnasium; out-of-doors   Appeal: competition, skill

The players are in two teams. The game is started by one team throwing the ball into the opponents' territory. The object of the game is to keep the ball in the air by batting it back and forth. When the ball touches the ground on one side, the opponents score one point. The ball is put in play again and the game continues.

Turn Around Game

Ages: teen   Supplies: sticks 6 inches long
Players: any number; couple; in-   Activity—pastime: catching, throw-
   formal   ing
Place: out-of-doors; schoolroom   Appeal: competition, skill

Between 20 and 40 sticks 6 inches long are thrown from the palm up in the air, and as many as possible are caught on the back of the hand. Those that fall to the ground are thrown up again and the player tries to catch an odd number in the palm. If he is successful, one stick is kept, and he tries again. If he catches none or an even number, the other player takes his turn. The player who catches the last stick wins all of his opponent's sticks and the game is started again.

Wela

Ages: 9–12   Supplies: darts, hoop
Players: 4–10; group-and-one; in-   Activity—pastime: running, throw-
   formal   ing
Place: out-of-doors   Appeal: skill

Each player has a dart about 1 foot long. One end of the dart is pointed and a bright-colored feather is fastened to the other end. The feathers usually vary in color. The *wela*, about 15 inches in diameter, is made of broom corn or cornhusks bound together to form a hoop, the rim of which is quite thick.

One player starts the game by rolling the *wela*. As it rolls along each player runs after it and throws his dart at the rim. The player whose dart sticks wins the game. This is a Hopi Tribe game.

Whipping Tops

Ages: 9–12
Players: 4 or more; individual; informal
Place: out-of-doors

Supplies: lashes, tops
Activity—pastime: striking, throwing
Appeal: skill

The American Indian boys often play with tops in the winter, skillfully spinning them on ice. The tops are made of various materials, such as wood, stone, acorns, nuts, horn, bone, and sometimes ice. Often the tops are colorfully decorated. The whip is made of long buckskin lashes fastened to an unbarked stick. The top is grasped with the index finger and thumb and twirled so that it spins when it strikes the ice. By means of the whip the top is kept spinning. Some players even set their tops in motion by using the whip as we use a top string.

Whirling Circles

Ages: 9–12
Players: any number; groups of four; file
Place: gymnasium; out-of-doors

Supplies: not any
Activity—relay: running, whirling
Appeal: competition, rhythm, skill

This is a relay in which four players from each side run as one unit. An obstacle is established about 40 feet in front of each team. The players are grouped in fours. Each group froms a circle. At a signal, the first four of each team run forward, encircle the obstacle, and run back to the starting point to touch off the next four, always twirling as they run. The object is to see which team finishes its whirling circles first.

ALASKA

Eskimo Football

Ages: 9–12
Players: 20 or more; two-group; line
Place: out-of-doors
Supplies: football

Activity—athletic: kicking, running, throwing
Appeal: competition, problem solving, skill

The playing area for the game is the space between two long parallel lines. The distance between the lines depends upon the number and the ability of the players. The Eskimo players scratch the lines on the ice or hard dry snow. The players divide into two teams. Each team stands on a line and faces the center of the field. The umpire stands midway and at one end of the space between the lines. He starts the ball rolling slowly between the teams. As the ball stops rolling, the umpire calls, "Ai," which is the signal for the teams to rush forward and kick the ball across the opponents' line. The winner is the successful team.

A variation of the game is that the two teams stand 10 feet apart within the playing area instead of on the lines. The players form a compact wall by standing very close together. The umpire throws the ball down between the teams. As a unit the teams rush forward to kick the ball. If the ball is kicked through the wall of players, the teams quickly break ranks. The defensive team tries to keep the ball from crossing the line in the rear. The offensive team tries to score by kicking the ball over the line.

Gegoudge

Ages: 9–12
Players: 6 or more; group-and-one; line
Place: out-of-doors

Supplies: walnuts
Activity—pastime: pitching
Appeal: skill

A hole is dug in the ground to represent the *bank*. An equal number of walnuts is given to each player. One player, the *banker*, stands near the hole. The other players stand about six feet away from the *bank* and each takes his turn at pitching walnuts into the *bank*. If a player succeeds in pitching an even number of walnuts in the *bank*, he receives that many walnuts from the banker; otherwise he loses all of his walnuts to the *banker*.

Guessing Game

Ages: 9–12
Players: 10 or more; group-and-one; informal
Place: gymnasium; out-of-doors; schoolroom

Supplies: 20 or more small sticks
Activity—pastime: guessing
Appeal: problem solving

One player is selected to be *It* and holds twenty or more small sticks. He arranges the sticks in several groups. The other players close their eyes until *It* calls, "Ready." Each player then quickly guesses the number of groups. The first one calling the correct number becomes *It* for the next game. This, like "Ha-Goo," is a *Thlinget* (KLIN-ket) Tribe game.

Ha-Goo

Ages: 9–12
Players: 20 or more; two-group; line
Place: gymnasium; out-of-doors

Supplies: a brightly colored banner
Activity—hunting: not smiling
Appeal: competition

This game is popular with the Thlinget (Klin-ket) children in Southeastern Alaska.

Two parallel lines 30 feet apart are drawn on the ground. The players are grouped in two sides and stand on the lines facing their opponents. A *captain* is appointed for each side. The *captain* of one side signals with his banner (a rag fastened to a stick) and cries "Ha-goo" or "Come on." One player from the opposite side advances while his opponents try to make him smile by saying funny things or making funny faces. If the player smiles the least bit, he is out of the game and another player is sent out from his side. If he crosses to the opposite side without smiling, he has captured the banner and returns with it to his side. The play continues until all players except one have been eliminated. The object of the game is to hold the banner last.

Hands and Feet Race

Ages: 9–12
Players: 10–30; single-group; line
Place: gymnasium; out-of-doors
Supplies: not any

Activity—contest: running on hands and feet
Appeal: competition, skill

The players lean forward touching their hands to the ground. The arms and legs are held very stiff. The object of the game is to hitch or jump forward. The race is very strenuous and should be short.

Jumping Forward Race

Ages: 9–12
Players: 10–30; single-group; line
Place: gymnasium; out-of-doors

Supplies: not any
Activity—contest: jumping
Appeal: competition, skill

The players stand with arms folded across the chest and jump forward to a goal line about 15 feet away. The feet are held close together and the knees are rigid. This may be used in relay formation also.

Musk-Oxen

Ages: 9–12 (boys)
Players: 12 or more; two-group; circle
Place: gymnasium; playground

Supplies: cloth or paper bags
Activity—hunting: dodging, throwing
Appeal: competition, skill

The players are divided into two sides. The members of one side encircle the other players who have pulled the skins of musk-oxen (heavy paper bags may be substituted) over their heads. The circle players try to hit the others with blunt arrows. A time limit may be set for the game. The number of players remaining within the circle when time is called constitutes the score. The two sides change places and the game continues.

Noo-Gloo-Took

Ages: 9–12
Players: 4 or more; single-group; informal
Place: gymnasium; home: schoolroom

Supplies: pierced ivory, pins, string
Activity—pastime: striking
Appeal: competition, skill, problem solving

Each player has a piece of ivory that is pierced through and through with holes and is connected to a pin by means of a long string. He holds the pin in his hands and whirls the ivory through the air. He tries to catch it on the point of the pin. If he fails, the ivory hits his hands. If he succeeds, he wins. Even if he does not catch it, he only says "Yi! Yi!" and tries again. This game is sometimes called the "stick and pin" game.

Over the Hill Shinny

Ages: 9–12
Players: 6 or more; individual; informal
Place: out-of-doors

Supplies: balls, clubs
Activity—athletic: running, striking
Appeal: competition, skill

This game is much like shinny and something like golf. The ball is a bone from the flipper of a seal. The club is a rib bone from a walrus. Each player has his own ball and club and in turn tries to score one point by knocking the ball over a hill of snow. The player first scoring 10 wins.

Reindeer Hunt

Ages: 9–12
Players: 2–10; single-group; informal
Place: out-of-doors

Supplies: antlers, arrows, bows
Activity—pastime: shooting
Appeal: competition, skill

Reindeer antlers are stuck in the snow on the hillside. The players slide down the hill on their ice sleds and as they dash by the antlers they shoot their arrows at them.

If a player is successful in knocking down an antler, he takes it as his own. The boys continue to shoot until all antlers are down. The game is over when all antlers have been knocked down. The player who has claimed the greatest number of antlers wins the game.

Rolling down the Hill

Ages: 9–12
Players: 4 or more; individual; informal
Place: hillside

Supplies: not any
Activity—athletic: forward roll
Appeal: repetition, rhythm, skill

The head is placed on the knees and the hands grasp the ankles. The players roll forward over and over until they reach the bottom of the hill. Then they race up the hill and start over again.

Sandbag Ball

Ages: 9–12
Players: 6–16; single-group; compact circle
Place: gymnasium; out-of-doors

Supplies: playground ball
Activity—athletic: batting, kneeling
Appeal: competition, skill

A ball about the size of our baseball is made of seal skin partially filled with sand. The players usually kneel in a circle or stand in a small area. The ball is batted in the air. The players strike it with the palm of the hand and try to keep it from falling to the ground. If a player strikes and misses the ball, he is out of the game. The last player in the circle wins.

Variation: If the ball falls to the ground, the game ends and a few minutes' rest is allowed before beginning anew. There may be two groups in competition.

Shinny

Ages: 9–12
Players: any number; single-group; informal
Place: out-of-doors

Supplies: balls, clubs
Activity—athletic: running, striking
Appeal: skill

This game is played on the ice. Each carries a long stick made of a walrus bone. There is a ball made of the walrus tusk that is driven back and forth across the ice. The object of the game is to drive the ball a great distance and then recover it.

Spinning Tops

Ages: 9–12
Players: 2 or 4; individual; informal
Place: gymnasium; out-of-doors

Supplies: tops
Activity—stunt: running, throwing
Appeal: skill

This is a combination of an indoor and outdoor activity. The Eskimo children usually spin the top by twirling the long stem between their hands. The top is set in motion and then the owner immediately dashes out of the igloo and runs around it, trying to get inside again before the top ceases to spin.

Alaska—Shinny.

Tack-Whang! Tack-Whang!

Ages: teen   Supplies: arrows, bows
Players: 6 to 10; single-group; in-   Activity—pastime: shooting
  formal   Appeal: competition, skill
Place: out-of-doors

Each player has a bow and a number of marked arrows. He shoots
arrows straight up into the air and continues to shoot until the first
has fallen. Then he does not shoot another one until all the players
have had to stop shooting. When each player has stopped, the arrows are counted. The player having the greatest number of arrows
wins. They are ready to shoot again. Sometimes only those are
counted that stand upright or fall in a drawn circle.

HAWAII

Bowling the Maika Stone

Ages: teen
Players: 2–6; individual; informal
Place: out-of-doors

Supplies: flat, round stones
Activity—pastime: bowling
Appeal: competition, skill

Two sticks are driven in the ground a few inches apart. Heavy, flat, round stones like big, thick mud cakes are bowled from a distance so they will roll between the two sticks.

During the *Makahiki*, a festival of games, bowling the *Maika* stone was a popular professional sport. A skilled player often rolled the stones 30 or 40 yards; however, players have been known to roll them 100 yards with accuracy. Some of the stones or disks were

Hawaii—Bowling the Maika Stone.

made of compact lava and these were highly prized by the players. The owners of the stones usually oiled them and wrapped them in cloth after using them.

A counterpart of this age-old activity from Hawaii's past is the game of bowling so popular in the States today. Much may be said of the relative economy of such play in Hawaii (also of the popular Italian game, *bocci*), in contrast to the tremendous outlay of bowling theaters, playing equipment, and costuming all of which are considered essential to bowling in the United States today.

Appendix A

DEFINITION OF TERMS

ATHLETIC ACTIVITY. An athletic activity is the more highly organized, competitive type of game or sport in which an organized group scores as a unit. Participation in an athletic activity calls for skillful use of the body in handling materials such as balls, bats, sticks, and other objects.

CONTEST. A contest signifies a type of activity in which two or more persons compete to test their strength and skill. It differs from a stunt in that it always contains the element of competition.

HUNTING ACTIVITY. A hunting activity is a play situation in which there is the chase or tag element. The skills used in play of this type are the fundamental motor movements, such as running, hopping, leaping, jumping, and dodging.

PASTIME ACTIVITY. A pastime activity is one in which appeal is chiefly for the entertainment of the participants, usually few in number. A game of this type may call for competition, problem solving, and the use of motor skills.

RELAY. A relay is an activity in which two or more teams are matched. The first player from each team starts from "scratch." He passes his advantage or handicap to his successor as do all other players who, in succession, carry through an enterprise too long and too strenuous for an individual to complete at maximum efficiency.

STUNT. A stunt is a self-testing activity. It may be executed on the basis of competition, but its chief appeal lies in the opportunity it affords the individual to test his own skill in the use of his body.

Appendix B

SUGGESTIONS FOR USING THE BOOK

SUGGESTIONS FOR TEACHING

The following general suggestions are offered with the hope that they will aid the leader in play in planning and executing his work:

Prepare: Have a thorough knowledge of the organization, skills, techniques, and rules of the game, stunt, relay, or contest. Know that the activity is suitable to the ability and experience of the players. Have the supplies and equipment ready for use.

Motivate: Create the atmosphere of the activity. State the name of the activity and if possible, give its origin and the traditions connected with it.

Organize: Organize the children into groups, sides, leaders, and "It" players. (Some mark of distinction for each group facilitates the playing.) Assign the players to their positions on the playing area.

Explain: State the object of the activity. Describe in a few well-chosen words the steps by which the object is reached. State a few simple rules. Give the players the opportunity to ask questions.

Play: Start the activity at a given signal. Allow play to continue for a while. Clear up doubtful points as the situation demands. Interrupt the play when it is necessary to clarify a rule or to adjust a standard of conduct. Discuss ways in which the play may be improved. Demonstrate and practice a skill only when that particular skill seems to be fundamental for the success of the activity at that time. Continue the play. Drill in skills only when the players recognize the need of improved technique.

Stop Play: Stop the activity before it dies or the players become tired. The weather conditions, the attitude of the leader, the disposition of the group, and the nature of the activity itself all have their influence upon the length of time an activity will hold the interest of the players. Allowing an activity to die not only affects the moral of the plays, but also creates a dislike for the activity itself; the experience is disintegrating rather than integrating.

Evaluate: Announce results. Comment upon the good points of the situation. Encourage the players to analyze their weak points and to discuss ways of improving them.

CRITERIA FOR PLAY LEADER

In games and play activities the leader must have clearly in mind certain criteria by which he judges the conduct of the individual and the group. It is well for him to observe the children in play and to ask himself the following questions:

1. Do the players enter into the play with enthusiasm?
2. Do the players accept the object of the game as worthwhile and play to that end?
3. Does each player indicate a feeling of belonging to the group?
4. Is the selfish player adjusting to the needs of the group?
5. Is the timid player entering into the activity?
6. Is the handicapped player given an opportunity to participate as actively as possible?
7. Is the discipline of the group reasonably satisfactory?
8. Do the players show proper respect for leadership?
9. Do the players show conscious effort to keep a balance between companionship and activity?
10. Are the players given the opportunity to discuss their experiences in the game?

The leader of play activities should keep in mind that a worthwhile aim of play is to develop the character and social efficiency of the individual and to lead him to better adjustment in society.

SUGGESTIONS FOR SCHOOL GROUPS

A. Physical Education and Recreation

1. *Point out* the social responsibility of all participants. Set the stage for play. Have participants enact it according to the rules of the game.
2. *Insist* that shared activity played hard and fast by the rules is more fun than when one or two individuals steal the show.
3. *Teach* for the dual role of leadership and followership.
4. *Play* series of games that show similarities in play patterns the world around.
5. *Play* series of games that are unique to specific countries.
6. *Teach* athletic skills common among children and youth of other countires; *use* these skills in their game situations; *emphasize* the ingenious use of natural materials by boys and girls in other countries.
7. *Demonstrate* the adaptability of specific games to varying play areas.
8. *Implement* an international playday on elementary, junior high, and senior high level—separately or combined.
9. *Compare* the clever approach to competition as demonstrated in games of certain societies, namely those of the Eastern peoples.
10. *Execute* international Olympics, using relays, athletic games, individual and couple stunts and contests. *Invite* persons from the community who are from other countries to help in some capacity.
11. *Climax* the year with circus International or a Latin American Carnival. Many games, stunts, and relays lend themselves to the circus idea. Singing games and dances may enhance the affair.

12. *Schedule* a Trip Around the World Spring Festival, combining games, folk dances, and singing games.

B. Social Studies

1. *Motivate* a study of a country by introducing it with games from the country.
2. *Enliven* the study as it progresses with play and games from the country.
3. *Climax* the study of a country or a continent with a Game-bor-ee. Have children, students select and execute the events.
4. *Teach* origins of game, when possible, to show influence of customs and legends on play patterns.
5. *Compare* the games from the countries studied to games of other lands. Point out the influence of climate and geographical area on the type and degree of activity.
6. *Include* games from other countries in an international assembly program.

C. Arts and Crafts

1. *Enliven* figure drawing with sketches of action in game situations.
2. *Study* costumes (color, style, and usage) and dress in other countries.
3. *Design* typical or stylized art patterns of other countries.
4. *Create* basic papier-mâché figures of boys and girls; use them in puppetry games. The play of the children of the Far East lends itself well to dramatization.
5. *Develop* a game map in connection with social studies.
6. *Construct* game boards and other simple equipment.
7. *Make* a game scrapbook (let individuals or groups design the cover); *collect* games from own and other lands; *illustrate* with figure sketches and game diagrams.

D. Language Studies

1. *Write* a description of a favorite game from another country.
2. *Read,* then *explain* an international game to the class.
3. *Play* animal and alphabet games with young children.
4. *Write* the conversation of a game in which two or more characters speak several times.
5. *Expand* interest in folklore through reading game origins.
6. *Write* stories, poems, essays on play, games—their ways of helping to develop better bodies, have fun, make friends, understand boys and girls in other lands.
7. *Create* a story about play in all countries, using game titles as the framework for characters, action, and geographical setting.
8. *Write* an article for the school paper on "Games at Home and Abroad," "Play is Everywhere," "Fun Comes to Our School."

SUGGESTIONS FOR CAMPS, CLUBS, AND RECREATION GROUPS

1. *Plan* an International Games and Sports Day, invite an interested friend.
2. *Assign* a photography and a creative writing group to work with the Sports Day committee.

3. *Schedule* a tournament of table games from many lands on cold and rainy days; include physically handicapped persons.
4. *Dramatize* and play game-charades using games, "Blarney Stone" (Ireland), "Charlie Over the Water" (Scotland), "Going to Jerusalem" (North America, Germany), "Angel and Imp" (Puerto Rico), "Tug-of-War" (Uganda), "Pickle Jar" (Korea), and many others.
5. *Plan* international games party for adults; for shut-ins; for men and boys only; for gals and guys.
6. *Make* game equipment in crafts shop; supply hospital gamerooms with table games—give game background if possible.
7. *Build* campfire program around games, contests, and stunts from many lands.
8. *Plan* an "International Tour," stopping in various countries to *teach* a game to the boys and girls and to *learn* their favorite game.
9. *Establish* a game Trading Post as a weekly exchange of games from other lands.
10. *Conduct* a story hour, drawing folklore from games; let children create a game from a favorite story.

SUGGESTIONS FOR PARENTS

1. *Make* puppets of game characters.
2. *Dramatize* games on rainy days and with shut-ins.
3. *Plan* international party for tots, teens, or tottering adults. The gamut of play can run from the "Horseshoe Pitching" of the pioneer days in North America, "Teeter Totter" in Korea, "Ha-do-do" in India, "Scatter Compass" in Sweden, to a climax with the "Piñata" from Colombia and Guatemala.
4. *Use* a game-legend as a human interest story in a talk to a club, PTA, or church group.

Appendix C

BOOKS OF GAMES AND SPORTS PLAYED IN THE UNITED STATES

American Association for Health, Physical Education, and Recreation. *Physical Education for High School Students*. Washington, D. C.

Armbruster and Irwin. *Basic Skills in Sports*. New York: C. V. Mosby Co.

Borst, Evelyne. *The Book of Games for Boys and Girls: How to Lead and Play Them*. New York: The Ronald Press, 1953.

Donnelly, Richard, Helms, William G., and Mitchell, Elmer D. *Active Games and Contests*. New York: The Ronald Press, 1958.

La Salle, Dorothy. *Guidance of Children Through Physical Education*, 2d ed. New York: The Ronald Press, 1957.

Larson and Hill. *Physical Education in the Elementary School*. New York: Henry Holt and Co., Inc.

Neilson, N. P., and Van Hagen, Winifred. *Physical Education for Elementary School*, rev. ed. New York: The Ronald Press, 1956.

Salt, E. Benton, Fox, Grace I., and Stevens, B. K. *Teaching Physical Education in the Elementary School*, 2d ed. New York: The Ronald Press, 1960.

INDEXES

Games of Many Lands

Age Level

GAMES FOR AGES FIVE THROUGH EIGHT

GAMES FOR AGES NINE THROUGH TWELVE

GAMES FOR TEENAGERS

Degree of Activity

ACTIVE GAMES AND SPORTS

African London Bridge, 17
Alpine Tag, 128
Archery Game, 214
Ataya Patya, 100

Bag Race, 166
Ball Kick Game, 216
Ball Play, 216
Barley Break, 128
Baste the Bear
   Denmark, 138, 139
   Germany, 129
Bathing Game, 27
Ben Hur, 90
Big Snake, 25
Blarney Stone, 183
Blind Cow, 90
Blind Man's Buff, 37, 143, 146
Blindfold Horse Race, 29
Blow the Horn, 163
Boat Race, 30
Bokwele, 14
Bounce the Ball, 54
Brazen Fly, 146

California Relay, 218
California Relay Football, 218
Call the Chickens Home, 38
Carpenteros, Carboneros, Cardinales, 192
Cat and Mouse, 39
Catch Your Tail, 30
Chase and Catch, 60
Chili Chelone, 147
Chinese Wall, 40
Chocolonga, 204
Chueca, 198
Chytrinda, 147
Circle Tackraw, 81
Circle Thread the Needle, 168
Clown Game, 219
Coelho Natoca, 196
Crab Race, 55
Crown the King, 129
Czars, 134

Danish Rounders, 138
Deeb, 90
Dieci Passaggi, 155
Digging Peanuts, 69
Dima, 87
Disco, 169
Dog Collar, 130
Dog and Hare, 140
Donkey Game, 99
Dress Up Relay, 91

Early Ball Game, 193
Eating the Fish's Tail, 41
Ephebike and Epikoinos, 148
Eskimo Football, 229

Fielding Race, 171
Fishing by Hand, 42
Football, 70
Foxes and Cabbages, 43
French Dodgeball, 164
Frog Dance, 75

Gato Doente, 197
Going to Town, 44
Golden Gates, 135
Gorelki, 135
Grab the Husk, 71
Grab It, 25
Greased Pole Contest, 71
Greek Ball Game, 149
Guard the Blind, 140

Ha-Taik-Kyen-Ha-Ki, 61
Hand Tag, 153, 155
Handball, 16
Hands and Feet Race, 231
Hanna Ala Nahar, 84
Hawk Catching Young Chickens, 45
Hawk and Hens, 15
Hen and Wild Cat, 16
Hockey, 95, 207
Hop Tag, 95
Horse, 20

Wela, 228
Whirling Circles, 229
Whom Will You Take?, 98

Xoxo, 16

MODERATE GAMES

QUIET GAMES

Playing Area

GAMES FOR THE GYMNASIUM

African London Bridge, 17
Alpine Tag, 128
Ampe, 24
Angel and Imp
  Cuba, 203
  Puerto Rico, 206
Angel and the Devil, 190
Attention of the Mind, 28
Atya Patya, 100

Bag Race, 166
Ball Kick Game, 216
Bamboo Pole Race, 54
Barley Break, 128
Bas-Quoits, 217
Baste the Bear
  Denmark, 138
  Germany, 129
Battledore and Shuttlecock
  China, 217
  North American Indian, 208, 210
Bimbo, 154
Blarney Stone, 127, 183
Blind Cow, 90
Blind Man-Bee, 100
Blind Man's Buff, 37
Blinzlis, 132
Bokwele, 14
Borkem Topa, 86
Bounce the Ball, 54
Brazen Fly, 146
Buying a Lock, 38

Call the Chickens Home, 38
Carpenteros, Carboneros, Cardinales, 192
Cat and Dog, 68
Cat and Mouse, 39
Catching Fishes in the Dark, 39
Centipede, 146
Charlie over the Water, 181
Chase and Catch, 60
Chicken Market, 155
Chili Chelone, 147
Chinese Chicken, 40
Chinese Wall, 40

Chinnabeer, 86
Chytrinda, 147
Circle Tackraw, 81
Circle Thread the Needle, 168
Coconut Shell Hitting, 68
Coelho Na Toca, 196
Cops and Robbers, 96
Cow's Eye, 40
Crab Race, 55
Crown the King, 129
Czars, 134

Danish Rounders, 138
Deeb, 90
Digging Peanuts, 69
Dima, 87
Disco, 169
Dodge Ball, 217
Dodge Tag, 170
Dog Collar, 130
Dog and Hare, 140
Dove and Hawk, 41
Dress Up Relay, 91

Eating the Fish's Tail, 41
Egg Game, 184
Ephebike and Epikoinos, 148
Exchange, 164
Exchange Race, 170

Fiber Game, 77
Fielding Race, 171
Figures of Clay, 193
Finding the Leader, 79
Fire on the Mountains, 183
Fishing by Hand, 42
Five and Ten, 171
Flower Pot, 42
Follow Chase, 155
Forcing the City Gates, 42
Fox and Geese, 43
French Dodgeball, 164
Fruit Sale, 44
Fuul Ei, 133

GAMES FOR HOME AND SCHOOLROOM

GAMES FOR OUT-OF-DOORS

Type of Activity

ATHLETIC

Alam, 89

Ball Kick Game, 216
Ball Play, 216
Bat and Stick Game, 93

Circle Tackraw, 81
Chueca, 198
Clown Game, 219

Danish Rounders, 138
Dieci Passaggi, 155
Dima, 87
Dodge Ball, 217
Donkey Game, 99

Early Ball Game, 193
Ephebike and Epikoinos, 148
Epkedrisnos, 149
Eskimo Football, 229

Fist Ball, 100
French Dodgeball, 164

Grab It, 25
Greek Ball Game, 149
Guli Danda, 101

Hockey, 97, 209
Human Skittles, 172

Jumping the Beanbag, 30
Jumping Fox, 46
Jumping Game, 99

Kick Basket, 80
Kinxe, 221
Kittuppullu, 104
Kukla, 96

Masters and Slaves, 82
Melon Dance, 17
Mount Ball, 150

Olympic, 150
Over the Hill Shinny, 232

Peggity, 62
Peteca, 198
Pilma, 194, 195

Saddlebags, 210, 224
Sandbag Ball, 233
Schlagball, 132
Seashore Football, 225
Shinny
  Circle, 226
  Wood, 226
Striking the Stick, 50
Surprise Ball, 152

Tabaat, 94
Three Court Dodgeball, 165
Three Sticks, 78, 79
Throwing to the Stars, 105
Tip Cat, 180
Tok-Ki Chi-Ki, 65
Tutush, 99

CONTESTS

Abumbutan, 27

Bag Race, 166

Carnival Game, 129, 191

Dog Collar, 130

Foot Game, 77
Frog Dance, 75

Ghosts, 159
Greased Pole Contest, 71

Hands and Feet Race, 231

HUNTING

PASTIME

RELAYS

STUNTS